THE CASE
FOR
CHRISTIAN
HUMANISM

The Case
for
Christian Humanism

by
R. William Franklin
and
Joseph M. Shaw

WILLIAM B. EERDMANS PUBLISHING COMPANY
GRAND RAPIDS, MICHIGAN

Library of Congress Cataloging-in-Publication Data

Franklin, R. W., 1947-
   The case for Christian humanism / by R. William Franklin and
Joseph M. Shaw.
      p.   cm.
   Includes bibliographical references.
   ISBN 0-8028-0606-6 (pbk.)
   1. Christianity and religious humanism.   I. Shaw, Joseph M.   II. Title.
BR128.H8F73   1991
230'.046 — dc20   91-26337
                                                           CIP

To
the Memory of
Harris Kaasa
(1926–1983)

Contents

CONTENTS

Introduction

The Case for Christian Humanism is the second of two books issuing from a four-college project called "Humanism in an Age of Limits: A Christian Perspective," supported by grants from the National Endowment for the Humanities. The earlier book, *Readings in Christian Humanism,* was a selection of texts by Christian writers ranging from Augustine and Benedict to Dorothy Sayers and Martin Luther King, Jr. It has been used at a number of colleges as a textbook.

The present volume discusses the essential themes of the tradition of Christian humanism for a wider audience of church members, clergy, students, and professors. Our basic premise is that the classical faith confessed by Christians in every generation implies a strong and caring interest in human beings as such. The entire redemptive work of God both in Israel and the church is to be perceived as enhancing and enriching human life on this earth.

Christian humanism is an aspect of the gospel showing new signs of life. Long neglected and often misunderstood, Christian humanism is nothing other than the traditional message of Christianity with the accent on how the coming of Christ into the world implies God's loving care for human creatures and all that affects our well-being. The fact of the Incarnation, God's sending of Jesus Christ to be part of the human world, is the foundation of Christian humanism. No clearer sign is needed to show that God is actively engaged in leading humanity toward its intended fulfillment.

I

The idea of "Christian humanism" goes back at least to the period of the Renaissance. It emerges today as a newly recovered resource for the individual believer, for the Christian community as a whole, and for a world filled with new possibilities that Christian people are called to explore. Our purpose in again presenting the classic understanding of Christian humanism, especially at this turning-point in our history, is to display the power of the gospel for addressing anew the critical task of making life on this planet more human in the face of the rising forces of dehumanization.

The triumph of movements for human liberation in recent history has demonstrated again the power of faith to lift human beings from oppression and despair. We need only to think of Martin Luther King, Lech Walesa, and Desmond Tutu to be reminded of the revolutionary power of Christian lives marked by steadfastness, patience, and endurance.

Too often in the past Christianity has allowed itself to be identified with the forces that act against human concerns, whether through misinterpretation of the gospel, the bad behavior of Christians, or the polemic of uninformed, anti-Christian opinion — an opinion increasingly voiced on college campuses. Today as we approach a new millennium there is a great opportunity for the church to recover and proclaim a full-bodied gospel that underscores how passionately God cares for every human being and for humanity as a whole. In its preaching the church has often not succeeded in making clear to its members that the gospel as "the power of God for salvation" is at the same time a humanizing power. The work of Christ not only leads people to heaven; it also points the way to a truly human life on earth. Now is the time for this message to be articulated clearly by the churches.

Christian humanism is a voice raised in behalf of human life and values, but the general public — not to mention churchgoers — has not been hearing this voice. The loving affirmation of humanity that is expressed in a quiet hour of worship, a passage of Scripture, the words of a hymn, the thought of a theologian, the greeting of a friend, or in "the lives of faithful and godly people" is not the stuff of newspaper headlines and television talk shows. To attract public notice, it seems, religion must be bizarre, controversial, entertaining, or tinged with scandal. The humanism born of faith is not likely to command that sort of public attention since it concentrates on quite ordinary matters: faith in God related to the day-to-day concerns of living.

Of course the word *humanism* itself is a stumbling block and has in recent years been an object of controversy. Nothing is basically wrong with the term *humanism,* but it is the victim of an erratic history of connotation. Despite its wholesome associations with the Renaissance scholarship of five centuries ago, with the humanities, with human nature, and with the character and quality of being human, this controversial word suffers from having been tarred with the brush of being an anti-God philosophy.

The first three chapters of this book will address the problematic history of the term and the questions usually asked about placing the words *Christian* and *humanism* together. A brief "dictionary exercise" in Chapter 1 will show that "humanism" has a range of meanings far beyond what many secularists have in mind when they try to claim the term as their exclusive property. Christians have no need to fear the concept of humanism. The gospel of Christ has always urged people in no uncertain terms to love, honor, and help their neighbors, their fellow human beings.

In fairness to those who affirm Christianity but are uncomfortable with the word *humanism,* we recognize that there are indeed anti-God versions of humanism that stand in opposition to the Christian faith. One cause even claims the name "religious humanism," but it is in fact a naturalistic, secularistic humanism with a vengeance. It is unacceptable to Christians because it rejects the existence of any power superior to humans, transcending human life. What is also disturbing about "religious humanism" is that while it purports to honor humans by lauding their dignity, worth, and unlimited capabilities, it actually does them a disservice by treating them as natural objects. They are simply a part of nature, nothing more.

Over against this reduction of humans to objects in nature, Christian humanism insists on the dignity of the human creature based on the work and call of the Creator and the incarnation of the Word of God in human form. Judaism and Christianity affirm the full dignity of human nature, while certain secularistic philosophies, such as Nazism and some forms of behaviorism, have defined humans as nothing but animals.

At the same time and in the light of the biblical view of creation, Christian thought affirms the unique relationship of the human species to the rest of the natural environment. In the current struggle to save the environment the Christian community can insist that human beings, while indeed part of nature, are called by the Creator to live in harmony with creation, to be responsible stewards of its riches and not exploiters. When human beings claim to be free from any responsibility toward transcendent authority they are tempted to arrogate for themselves the right to plunder the earth; the disastrous results of that attitude are plain for all to see. Underscoring human accountability for the planet is a remarkable sentence in the book of Psalms that declares: "The heavens are the Lord's heavens, but the earth he has given to human beings" (Psalm 115:16).

II

Thanks to the agitations of the Holy Spirit who continually renews the community of faith, we see in these last years of the twentieth century some healthy stirrings that point to a new day for Christian humanism. The first chapters describe some of those developments. As the case for Christian humanism unfolds in the rest of the book, we will make it clear that the themes of Christian humanism are not theories for abstract speculation but living instances of the gospel at work.

Christian humanism is found where the gospel is found; in the Bible as it is read, studied, and interpreted; in the worship life of the churches where the liturgy builds the congregation into a community that prays and gives thanks; in varied practical ministries that extend help to humans; in theology as it speaks about God in ways that assist human comprehension. These experiences at the heart of Christian life define Christian humanism.

If Christian humanism is a resource that will contribute to the renewal of Christianity during the rest of this century and into the next, it cannot be a marginal notion cultivated by a few enthusiasts, but must be appreciated as a force found at the center of what the Christian community does. Fads and fancies come and go, but as long as Christian faith is alive on this earth, there will be communities of people reading the Bible, worshipping God around word and sacrament, serving their neighbors, and developing a theological understanding regarding the content of their faith.

The four parts of the book, in alphabetical sequence, take the reader to these concrete places where Christian humanism can be seen and touched. Part I, "Affirming Christian Humanism," begins the journey with the basic question, "What is Christian humanism?" and with some necessary pieces of history. Part II, "Beginning with the Bible," shows that long before Christianity the Hebrew Scriptures were a veritable storehouse of humanistic insight. Both Jesus and Paul were informed by Hebrew humanism that, combined with their distinctive additions to the humanistic heritage, became the foundation of Christian humanism.

Part III, "Coming Together in Worship," might prove to be the most valuable part of the book, because the present generation of Christians could be on the threshold of rediscovering an ancient, priceless treasure: the mystery of the meaning of humanity found in the praise of God. Breezes in diverse quarters seem to be blowing in that direction. Movements of renewal in the Roman Catholic Church, for example, are essentially not new doctrines, but rather new experiences of the liturgy for laity as well as clergy. Similar things are happening in Protestant churches: the people of God realizing anew how the praise of God in worship is intimately related to their daily lives and the needs of their neighbors.

Part IV, "Doing Theology for Humans," properly comes at the end because Bible and worship are more accessible to laity than theology. Nevertheless, theology has always had its own particular value within the life of the church. Theology should not be thought of as a realm dominated by learned experts and limited to divinity schools. Are we aware that by virtue of their instruction in Bible and catechism, children and young people receive — or ought to receive — most of the theological training that goes on in local churches? Moreover, the interest of lay people in theological study in the parishes has been a striking if largely unpublicized sign of the stirrings of Christian humanism in this century, and there is every reason to expect that lay study of theology will continue and flourish in the coming century.

The emphasis in Part IV is that the classical doctrines of God, Christ, and Holy Spirit are being considered today in a way that sheds light on the human meaning of divine actions. It is not that God's redemptive work has changed or that God's sovereignty is challenged, but theologians are now asking how the understanding of humanity can be enlarged through fresh approaches to the God-human dialogue. For example, in the Preface to his book *The Theological Imagination,* Gordon D. Kaufman writes, "The theological imagination devotes itself to the continuing critical reconstruction of the symbol 'God,' so that it can with greater effectiveness orient contemporary and future human life" (p. 12). Even the great Karl Barth, famous for his insistence on the otherness of God, toward the end of his career wrote an essay entitled "The Humanity of God." Barth too felt the pull toward a theology more responsive to human longings. For all his rigorous theocentrism, Barth acknowledged the profundity of the fact that the eternal Word of God chose to assume human nature.

III

This book is dedicated to the memory of Harris Eugene Kaasa who died of leukemia in December 1983. Professor of religion at Luther College, Decorah, Iowa, Harris was co-editor with Charles Buzicky and ourselves of *Readings in Christian Humanism.* From 1978 he had been a director of the four-college project "Humanism in an Age of Limits: A Christian Perspective," from which that book emerged.

Harris Kaasa perceived Christian humanism to be a suitable description of what church-related colleges could contribute to higher education. In his view it was also a promising way to restate the relationship between the Christian message and society as a whole.

During the summer of 1983 Dr. Kaasa devoted his waning energies to an essay that surveyed developments in theology related to the tradition of Christian humanism. The following sentences are the final paragraph of that essay:

> Christian humanism is a venerable tradition. It is firmly rooted in divine revelation, especially that self-revelation of God which we have received in the Bible. It has inspired worship and devotion down through the centuries in a community of those called by God into the faith-relationship. It has given rise to profound theological thought of considerable variety. It has led countless numbers of dedicated men and women to grapple with complex moral issues and to live sacrificially, sometimes at the cost of their very lives. It is a way of believing, thinking, and living which remains profoundly Christian — and humanistic. Indeed, it offers the most solid ground for the upholding of that reverence for human life which is the essence of all humanism.

It is of particular interest that what Harris wrote about the tradition of Christian humanism anticipated the outline of this book with its emphasis on Bible, worship, and theology. We also note that Harris understood Christian humanism in terms of living, not just believing and thinking.

Harris Kaasa was a Christian humanist who had learned to live within limits. Long years of illness made him candid but never gloomy or self-pitying about his mortality. As a theologian whose thought was shaped by the Bible, the heritage of Martin Luther, and the realism of Reinhold Niebuhr, Harris trod the earthly path of faith as a humble, forgiven sinner. As a canny observer of the society he shared with other noble but flawed human beings, Harris respected the limits of human culture even as he enjoyed those aspects of it available to him: family, church, college, theology, history, music, and the life of the mind shared with friends and colleagues.

Knowing his graying beard and salty observations, his friends compared Harris to an experienced sea captain who harbored no illusions about the difficulties human beings might face during the voyage through life. His physical sufferings and the ailings of those dear to him formed a character acquainted with grief and dependent on grace. As the years and increasing illness took their toll, Harris grew in stature in the eyes of friends, students, and colleagues who marveled at his patience and fortitude.

The product of a small town on the Iowa prairie and heir to a deep Lutheran piety, Harris was without question the typical shy person. He was convinced that others were more learned, more sophisticated, and better versed in the ways of the world than he. Yet, as his friends firmly attest, he was a man of pronounced intellectual gifts, very well educated in this country, in Norway, and in England, a clear thinker, an avid reader, a skilled teacher, and a powerful preacher of the gospel.

Harris was also the acknowledged master of the humorous anecdote, sometimes outrageous, sometimes too subtle for all hearers. His special penchant was for jokes having to do with his own ancestral people, the Norwegians. He could always be counted on to come up with still another droll tale about befuddled immigrants, crafty peasants, pompous pastors, or hapless husbands and wives floundering helplessly in unbelievable and hilarious tangles of comic confusion.

Though descended from Norwegian Lutherans, Harris Kaasa was an ecumenical Christian humanist. At his memorial service the church was filled with people, with the sounds of the glorious music of J. S. Bach, and with the voices of worshippers singing the great hymns of faith: "O Day Full of Grace," "When I Survey the Wondrous Cross," and "O God Our Help in Ages Past." One of the tributes was given by a veteran Roman Catholic priest, Harris's partner in an early ecumenical exchange between

St. John's University and Luther College, the school where Harris had taught for twenty-five years. For Harris, ecumenical fellowship was a natural and essential ingredient in Christian humanism. It belonged to his appreciation of the church, of theology, and of the human sojourn.

The ultimate source of Christian humanism is the gospel. In the words of Harris Kaasa in the essay cited above, the heart of the gospel is this: "That God, our creator and sovereign Lord, against whom we have all rebelled, has, because of what Jesus Christ has done, forgiven our rebellion and reconciled us to God, setting us free from the fear of death and condemnation and giving us eternal life. This is where all Christian theology must begin and end. It is the very foundation of a Christian humanistic view of life."

These are plain but weighty words. They speak of God, Christ, human sin and divine forgiveness, freedom, and eternal life. These are basic elements of the theology that informs Christian humanism and provides its foundation.

IV

In conclusion, we might well anticipate two questions the alert reader may already be asking. First, does this book, *The Case for* Christian *Humanism,* argue that only those who believe in Christ can know what it means to be human? Is Christian humanism an exclusive point of view, rejecting all other interpretations of the meaning of being human?

In response let us say that our avowed purpose in the book is to bear witness to Christian humanism as a vital and long-standing aspect of the Christian faith. Our desire is to give the humanistic aspect of Christianity the fuller public consideration it deserves. In making the "case" for Christian humanism we are presenting and recommending insights into human life and culture that have their origin in the Christian faith. We invite the reader to consider whether or not these insights are in harmony with the message of the gospel and also whether or not they point in the direction of a full and valid human existence.

Both to us and to most Christians the meaning of being human is most amply embodied in Jesus of Nazareth, the definitive human being. Christians do not expect to find some other key to the meaning of humanity that will move them to abandon their faith in Jesus Christ. In fact, many

Christians would contend that since so many other humanisms have failed, it is the duty of the church to make Christian humanism as widely known as possible and thereby to recommend it to everyone.

At the same time, many believers in Jesus are ready to grant that here and there in human history we find persons, ideas, and impulses, not bearing the label "Christian," that reflect in a profitable way the gracious intention of God toward the human cause. The existence of such glimpses of authentic humanity serves to restrain many Christians from adopting a rigidly exclusivistic position regarding Christ and human fulfillment. Rather, it moves them to humility and to gratitude to God for bestowing humanistic wisdom on a variety of persons and forces striving for human authenticity.

A second question on the mind of the reader might be this: Does the appearance of a book about Christian humanism imply that the authors are peddling a liberal or even radical interpretation of Christianity? To this we would respond with a quiet and courteous "No." The interpretation of the Christian faith found in this book is a traditional one, biblical, confessional, ecumenical. The most explicitly theological section of the book, Chapters 10, 11, and 12, is constructed according to the traditional Trinitarian scheme of God, Christ, and Spirit. The book does not issue anything new in the area of formal theology; it simply aims to show that Christian humanism is and must be informed by the familiar theology of the church. The touchstone of this theology is Christ. As Christ is central to the classical creeds, so he is central to the explication of Christian humanism. Moreover, the Christ in question is not the watered-down, "good example" Christ of old-style liberalism, but the crucified, risen, and reigning One, the Son of God and Son of man, the man from Nazareth who preached, taught, healed, and died for the sins of the world, the risen Lord now present in the church and destined to be honored by all humankind as King and Lord.

The Case for Christian Humanism will have fulfilled its purpose if readers discover that the mainstream of traditional Christianity offers magnificent resources to anyone desiring a fully human life. In the past, the gospel's strong affirmations of humanity have been obscured both by conservatives who have denied the humanistic elements of the faith and by secularists who have contended that a healthy humanism must renounce transcendent religion. In the 1990s, more and more humanists in the universities see in the Western Christian tradition only its association with the oppression of much of humanity throughout its history on the basis of race, gender, or class. In the meantime, searching and suffering human beings have remained uninformed about the humanizing power of God's love in Christ. Our hope is that this book will enable its readers to experience a fuller measure of human joy, strength, and peace as a result of examining the case for Christian humanism.

PART I

AFFIRMING CHRISTIAN HUMANISM

Chapter 1

What Is Christian Humanism?

The time has come to speak a clear word for Christian humanism. It is time to remind Christians and non-Christians alike that a rich and deep humanism has characterized Christian faith and life from biblical times to the present. But for more than a decade loud voices claiming to represent biblical faith have been making indiscriminate attacks on any and all forms of Western humanism. From another side, voices of secular wisdom have been saying for two centuries that humanism belongs exclusively to those who interpret human existence with no reference to God. In a form of ideological tyranny on American college and university campuses today, strident secularists claim that they alone represent the humanistic tradition.

The aim of this book is to present the case for Christian humanism as a power for good in the world of today and into the next millennium. "What does it mean to be human?" is an urgent, universal question, not a point for leisurely, detached debate. Christian responsibility for the welfare of human persons demands that the community which claims Jesus Christ as its sovereign should make clear to all who will listen that the good news of Christ offers enrichment and fulfillment to humankind.

Christian humanism affirms the teaching of Genesis 1:27 that human beings are created in the image of God, but its crowning belief is the gospel statement "And the Word became flesh and dwelt among us" (John 1:14). In the words of an old hymn:

> Tell abroad God's goodness proudly
> Who our race hath honored thus
> That he deigns to dwell with us.[1]

"True Christian humanism is the full flowering of the theology of the Incarnation," wrote Thomas Merton.[2] By sending the Son into the world in Jesus of Nazareth, God honored the human race by choosing to dwell in its midst. The incarnate one is also the crucified one. The mystery of the Incarnation indeed flowers to produce the tree of the cross. "It is said of him who dies on the cross, deserted by God and by men, 'Ecce Homo! Behold the man!' "[3]

In the humanism created by the gospel of Christ, men and women and children discover a God who affirms their full humanity in the midst of weakness and suffering, not one who makes divine love conditional upon human success. Most worldly humanisms, on the other hand, extend most of their wares to the elite achievers, the rich and capable, with relatively little to offer those who struggle and fail. Christian humanism rests on God taking human form, the doctrine of the Incarnation, and God's Son being rejected and killed, the doctrine of the Atonement. This is good news for *all* humanity.

The business of this chapter is to clarify the meaning of Christian humanism in relation to other forms of humanistic thinking. We will take up the questions that naturally arise in any discussion of humanism and Christianity, conduct a little dictionary exercise, and note the benefits and themes of Christian humanism. Implicit in what follows is the reminder that *Christian* humanism was once the mainstream of Western thought. Other types of humanism arrived later on the cultural scene.

---

1. Martin E. Marty, "Simul: A Lutheran Reclamation Project in the Humanities," *The Cresset,* 45 (December 1981), 10. The hymn is by Christian Keimann, 1646, translated by Catherine Winkworth.

2. Thomas Merton, "Virginity and Humanism in the Western Fathers," in *Mystics and Zen Masters* (New York: Farrar, Straus & Giroux, 1967), 114. Merton's major essays on Christian humanism can be found in Part III of *Love and Living* (New York: Farrar, Straus & Giroux, 1979).

3. Jürgen Moltmann, *Man: Christian Anthropology in the Conflicts of the Present,* trans. John Sturdy (Philadelphia: Fortress Press, 1974), 19.

Clarifying Christian Humanism

Just what *is* Christian humanism? To begin modestly and simply, Christian humanism points to the deep interest in human beings, their life, well-being, culture, and eternal significance, that belongs to the Christian faith. Central to that faith is Jesus Christ, the divine Son of God and brother to every human being. Christian humanism shares with other humanistic philosophies the desire to protect and enhance human existence, but it is unique in finding the source and goal of human powers in God the Creator, Redeemer, and Spirit.

In today's world Christian humanism occupies a place between two opposing interpretations of life. On one side are Christians adamantly opposed to "secular humanism" — really to humanism of any sort. They equate humanism with atheism and therefore regard Christian humanism as an impossible contradiction. For instance, some of these Christians in 1981 objected to a textbook referring to Desiderius Erasmus (1469-1536) as a Christian humanist, which of course he was. "How can a Christian be a humanist?" they asked. "It is impossible to be a Christian humanist. Humanists do not believe in God."

The answer to such people is to point out that many humanists *do* believe in God, that it *is* possible to be a Christian humanist, and that Christians who are humanists have not added some kind of liberal twist to the Christian faith, but have listened to what the biblical message has to say about human concerns.

On the other side is what is often called "secular humanism," an interpretation of humanity that limits itself to "merely" human interests, regarding human persons as complete masters of their own affairs and destinies and deliberately excluding the transcendent from its philosophy. Some extreme, antireligious humanists have declared, "Humans are responsible for what we are or will become. No deity will save us; we must save ourselves."[4] But not all secular humanists are self-conscious atheists; some simply ignore religion or reduce it to a purely private set of opinions and feelings. Among such people the assumption prevails that the decisive powers at work in the world are economics, science, reason, and military strength. It is ideologically "correct" in many academic circles today to regard Christianity as a dehumanizing force.

4. *Humanist Manifestos I and II* (Buffalo: Prometheus Books, 1973), 16. See also Paul Kurtz, *Forbidden Fruit: The Ethics of Humanism* (Buffalo: Prometheus Books, 1988).

Secular humanists should consider that Christian humanism was on the scene long before the rise of the modern secularistic worldview and that most of the finer values now confidently claimed by nontheists and secularists — values such as the sacredness of human life, freedom of conscience, compassion for the poor, and devotion to peace — are intrinsic to the Christian worldview. Indeed, these familiar values have flourished in a climate long framed by Christian thought and practice.

Both secular humanists and Christian antihumanists have certain fixed ideas about just what humanism is and stands for, while Christian humanists see it differently. Although a dictionary definition will not establish once and for all what humanism is, it is at least a useful starting point.

A Dictionary Exercise

Dictionary definitions of humanism range from generally accepted factual statements to controversial, debatable views. No one quarrels with the definition of humanism as "the study of the humanities."[5] Nor can anyone dispute the historical fact that devotion to the humanities is commonly traced to the Renaissance and its revival of interest in the Greek and Roman classics. It should be noted, however, that the first Renaissance humanists were devout Christians who had no intention of abandoning the church and its faith. Moreover, such reformers as Luther and Calvin were able to produce in the sixteenth century a profound, creative reinterpretation of the Bible, in part because the Renaissance made possible the careful study of Greek and Hebrew, the biblical languages.

Another unobjectionable way of talking about humanism is to use such phrases as "devotion to human interests" or "the character or quality of being human."[6] Would any Christian want to say, "I'm sorry, but it is contrary to my faith to be devoted to human interests" or to insist that there is something evil in discussing "the character or quality of being human"?

5. *Funk & Wagnalls Standard College Dictionary* (New York: Harper and Row, 1977), s.v. "humanism"; *Webster's New Collegiate Dictionary* (Springfield, Mass.: G. & C. Merriam, 1949), s.v. "humanism."

6. *Funk & Wagnalls; The Oxford English Dictionary* (Oxford: Clarendon Press, 1961), s.v. "humanism." For a new look at Renaissance humanism see William Kerrigan and Gordon Braden, *The Idea of the Renaissance* (Baltimore: Johns Hopkins University Press, 1989).

But when a dictionary offers "human nature"[7] as a concise definition of humanism, the casual reader may not realize that an important issue is at stake. For most people, "human nature" is an expression so familiar that it seems to require no further comment. According to a general way of thinking, humans are unique, possessing a distinctly *human* nature, and for good theological reasons Christians would agree. But some atheistic existentialists and a good many behaviorists are prepared to defend just the opposite view. Humans are not unique, they maintain, and there is no such thing as human nature.

In his novel *Lost in the Cosmos,* Walker Percy points up the irony of the modern objective consciousness which "will go to any length to prove that it is not unique in the Cosmos, and by this very effort establishes its own uniqueness." "Name another entity in the Cosmos," he asks, "which tries to prove it is not unique."[8] Christian humanism bears witness to the crucial importance of insisting on the uniqueness of human nature. It claims that the human capacity for a relationship with God sets the human creature apart as possessing a special dignity not given to other beings within the created order.[9]

The dictionaries can also offer definitions of humanism about which Christians should be wary. *Webster's Third New International Dictionary,* for instance, offers this:

> a philosophy that rejects supernaturalism, regards man as a natural object, and asserts the essential dignity and worth of man and his capacity to achieve self-realization through the use of reason and scientific method — called also *naturalistic humanism, scientific humanism.*[10]

If these words were the *only* definition of humanism, and if the dictionary possessed absolute authority, then Christians would have to dissociate themselves from humanism once and for all. That part of the Christian community sometimes referred to as the New or Christian Right seems to accept this definition as the only way to understand "humanism." As one spokesman for that group has written, humanists "have totally rejected

7. *Webster's New Collegiate Dictionary.*

8. Walker Percy, *Lost in the Cosmos* (New York: Farrar, Straus & Giroux, 1983), 254.

9. Emil Brunner, "Man in the Universe," in *Christianity and Civilization* (New York: Charles Scribner's Sons, 1949), 78.

10. *Webster's Third New International Dictionary* (Springfield, Mass.: G. & C. Merriam, 1976), s.v. "humanism."

God, creation, morality, the fallen state of man, and the free-enterprise system."[11]

The humanism described in *Webster's Third* is clearly inconsistent with the Christian faith in its rejection of supernaturalism and in its treatment of the human as a natural object. On the other hand, there is nothing un-Christian in affirming "the essential dignity and worth of man." Similarly, Christian thought does not reject reason and scientific method, although it understands them to be limited and partial in their capacity to aid humans in achieving self-realization.

But *Webster's Third,* which many regard as the final authority among dictionaries, has more to say on humanism. To the consternation of many Christians, it adds a further definition of humanism as "a religion subscribing to these beliefs: RELIGIOUS HUMANISM."[12] In recent public discussions, Christian antihumanists have expressed outrage at the efforts of secularists to raise humanism to the level of a religion. They have a point, to be sure, but it must be added that *Christian* humanism is not the same as *religious* humanism. Religious humanism as a movement is so small as to be insignificant. According to church historian Martin Marty their numbers are few, their average age is somewhere in the seventies, and their influence is very slight.[13]

It may be surprising to learn that *Webster's Third New International Dictionary* also mentions *Christian* humanism among its definitions: "A philosophy advocating the self-fulfillment of man within the framework of Christian principles — called also *Christian humanism.*" Does such a statement settle the matter in favor of a *Christian* definition of humanism? Hardly, but it does show that Christian humanism is a recognized form of humanism and that the secularistic, antitheistic view is not the only one.

Two other ideas appear in the dictionary definitions. One is that humanism can be described as an ethic, a positive, caring interest in human beings, suggested by such terms as "devotion to human welfare," or "interest or concern for man," or "humanitarianism."[14] It seems obvious that

---

11. Tim LaHaye, *The Battle for the Mind* (Old Tappan, N.J.: Fleming H. Revell, 1980), 187. For more analysis of Christian antihumanism see Robert Clouse, "The New Christian Right, America, and the Kingdom of God," *Christian Scholar's Review,* 12 (1983), 3-16.

12. *Webster's Third.*

13. Cf. Martin E. Marty, "Dear Republicans: A Letter on Humanism," *The Christian Century* (January 7-14, 1981), 16. See also Martin E. Marty, "Secular Humanism: The Religion of," *The University of Chicago Magazine,* 79 (Summer 1987), 2-6.

14. *Webster's Third.*

these aspects of humanism can be correlated with traditional Christian values.

Another archaic idea associated with the term, offered in the historically oriented *Oxford English Dictionary,* is that humanism once meant the "belief in the mere humanity of Christ."[15] The history behind this definition is that when the word *humanism* first appeared in the English language in Great Britain it denoted a specific doctrine, that is, a view that departed from the orthodox belief that Christ is both true God and truly man. Unfortunately, conservative Christians who distrust humanism are prone to seize upon the incriminating word "mere" as further proof that humanism is destructive of orthodox Christian faith. For its part, Christian humanism affirms not the "mere humanity of Christ" but the full humanity, even as it affirms the divinity of Christ.

What are the findings from the dictionaries? From the standpoint of an informed Christian view, four forms of humanism are unacceptable. Christian humanism must clash with a humanism that rejects supernaturalism, that regards human beings as natural objects, that claims to be a religion, or that fosters a doctrine of the "mere" humanity of Christ. On the other side, Christian humanism is consistent with a humanism understood as the study of the humanities, devotion to human interests, a humanitarian ethic, and as "self-fulfillment . . . within the framework of Christian principles," though Christian humanism is much more than that.

Further, Christian humanism is fully mindful of the Renaissance but notes with special interest how already well-established Christian themes formed part of Renaissance thought. Moreover, in accepting "human nature" as a meaning of humanism, a Christian thinker will insist that a unique capacity for a relationship to God is the ultimate hallmark of human nature.

The dictionary exercise is helpful but neither conclusive nor complete. Various historical factors have played their roles in producing the definitions published in dictionaries.[16] In the next two chapters we

---

15. *The Oxford English Dictionary.*

16. Five other recent definitions of Christian humanism can be found in the following sources: Walter Kasper, "Christian Humanism," *Proceedings of the Catholic Theological Society of America,* 17 (1972), 1-17; Konrad Hecker, "Humanism," *Sacramentum Mundi* (Basle: Herder, 1969), 74-78; Nicola Abbagnan, "Humanism," *The Encyclopedia of Philosophy* (New York: Macmillan, 1985); D. J. Forbes, "Christian Humanism," *New Catholic Encyclopedia* (Washington, D.C.: The Catholic University of America, 1967); Pope John Paul II, "Affirm Values of Christian Humanism in Your Service," English *L'Osservatore Romano* (March 25, 1988), 12. Christian humanism in the Orthodox tradition is defined in Nicholas

will examine some of the key historical changes that account for the present status of Christian humanism.

Themes of Christian Humanism

To conclude our clarification of the meaning of Christian humanism, we need to add a brief description of the benefits humankind reaps from the fact that God in Christ has visited the habitation of the human race. These benefits constitute the chief *themes* of Christian humanism.

The first theme is that in Christ the individual person is rescued from lonely isolation and made a member of a historic community. A strictly secular worldview has little comprehension of this benefit. It clings to the notion that individual and community are rival concepts, that the winning of individual selfhood means standing apart from others, and that living in community is a diminishing experience, requiring the surrender of one's individual integrity.

The community not only supports genuine personhood but also constitutes a powerful instrument for winning human freedom in the public arena. The recent changes in eastern Europe have been due to the communal power of the people, not to the alleged genius of individualism, as some have claimed, naively equating democracy and individualism. Democracy, we must remember, is the rule of the people.

We grant that one of the benefits of democracy is that the individual person is respected and given the franchise, but the force that has brought about recent changes in the political landscape has been the powerful witness of a community. In Poland that force was the workers' union, *Solidarity,* which in turn had the support of the Roman Catholic Church in that country. In Leipzig in East Germany people gathered outside a Lutheran church every Monday night for weeks prior to the dismantling of the Berlin wall in 1989 to express their longings for political change and to pray for peace. Within an oppressive society, the church offered a forum where the hunger for freedom could find articulation and gather support, where the longings of the individual could be forged into the power of a community.

Berdyaev, *The Divine and the Human* (London: G. Bles, 1949), and in his *The Fate of Man in the Modern World* (New York: Charles Scribner's Sons, 1935). See also Sergius Bulgakov, *Social Teaching in Modern Russian Orthodox Theology* (Evanston: Seabury-Western Theological Seminary, 1934).

Christian humanism points to a new reality: a human community that enhances personal selfhood and engages in the struggle for peace and justice. Not every community promotes the welfare of humanity. History knows of all too many collectivistic perversions of community wherein genuine human life is stifled by tyranny. The fact that the present century has experienced the antihuman collectivism of communism and fascism has caused many in the Western democracies to be suspicious of the concept of community and to cling ever more closely to its supposed opposite, individualism.

The Christian humanism and the forms of service described in this book are unabashedly related to the life of a specific community, the gathering of believing persons known as the church. The church finds ample claim to legitimacy in Scripture, history, and the cumulative experience of untold numbers of believers who have lived and died in its fellowship. It is also the case that modern social science reinforces through its findings what ordinary religious believers have known for centuries, that genuine selfhood and personhood develop through interaction with other human beings. Such interaction has been going on for centuries in the church, and yet it is one of the special marks of the Christianity of recent years to have grasped anew the reality of the church as community. A new note has been sounded in many denominations: mission and worship are carried out in the context of a "fellowship of believers." The God whose desire is that all persons should be saved (1 Tim. 2:4) also invites all to share in the fellowship and worship of the church.

The corporate fellowship of believing persons is one of God's highest and most humanizing gifts. Many who have been searching for a truly human existence have been deceived by a culture that promises satisfaction of human longings through a highly privatized pursuit of profit and pleasure. Secular wisdom declares, "Look out for Number One!" but the gospel of Jesus Christ says, "We are one in the Spirit." In short, we discover our true humanity as we enter the life of God's family.

A second theme of Christian humanism is the discovery that in Christ the world of material reality — the earth, the human body and its senses, the humble objects of daily use — can be a vehicle of the Holy Spirit to bless humanity. In its most transcendent moments, the church handles water, bread, and wine. Here is a paradox typical of biblical faith. Both matter and spirit, the earthly and the divine, the body and the mind, are instruments of God in the service of human purposes. Divine life comes to humankind in earthly dress. How do we know this? Through the biblical doctrine of creation, to be sure, but more dramatically through the central paradigm of the Incarnation of the Word in Christ: "The Word became flesh and dwelt among us."

Another paradoxical theme of Christian humanism is that full human freedom is realized under the authority of Christ. "So if the Son makes you free, you will be free indeed," says the Gospel of John. This principle has been confirmed time after time in our century; Christians imprisoned for advocating freedom were more free than their captors. Dietrich Bonhoeffer, Martin Luther King, and Nelson Mandela are prominent names that come to mind, but countless others have experienced freedom by giving their ultimate allegiance to the lordship of Jesus Christ. Another aspect of the freedom paradox is that the proper use of freedom, as St. Paul taught, is in serving one another in love. The servant is a persistent image for the biblical humanist.

Still another paradox stemming from the Incarnation is that human history is touched by eternity. Because of Christ, human life and human history are within, not alien to, God's purposes. Christian humanism rejects the fallacy that time, because it is marked by corruption and decay, has nothing to do with eternity. On the contrary, the coming of Christ tells the human race that earthly time and history are permeated by divine energy and are therefore significant for God's purposes. Thus an ordinary action like giving a cup of water or lighting a candle may have an importance reaching far beyond the limits of time. It is within time that we hear the gospel that promises eternal life to all who believe.

All these important themes of Christian humanism can be expressed in the form of dialectical pairs of ideas. From ancient to modern times, Christian humanism is always concerned with the relationship of the individual to the community. It expresses in a variety of ways the unique Christian insight that both matter and spirit are in the service of God and of human purposes. It acknowledges that faith implies both freedom and authority. And finally, Christian humanism holds that the incarnation of Christ gives significance to both time and eternity.

Such themes suggest the rich embrace of Christian humanism, reminding the Christian community of humanistic dimensions of the gospel that it has lost sight of, partly by yielding to the pressure of secular influences. In too many instances, the secular realm's claim to have a corner on everything that carries the "human" label has gone uncontested by Christian men and women. The church, pictured by Dietrich Bonhoeffer during Nazi times as being at the center of the human village, seems to have accepted the peripheral role its critics decry, humbly muttering that it must be busy with divine things while yielding ground to a brash secularism that claims complete dominion over the human enterprise. In the academic community, where Christian humanism should find a natural home, the Christian voice has been intimidated into silence by the regnant secular ideologies.

The recovery of Christian humanism can be part of a total renewal that will fire the church in this new age boldly to claim the human realm for the illumination and healing of Jesus Christ. People of faith know that renewal does not take place through slogans or cosmetic artifices but through the working of the Holy Spirit, and the central function of God's Spirit is to give honor to Christ, the incarnate and crucified Son of God. Therefore the Spirit, the agent of creation and renewal for all living things, is also the agent of humanization because Jesus Christ is the definitive human being.

We think of the Spirit's work in the continuing order and beauty of the world and in the harmony of natural life, but we should also train ourselves to think of the Spirit as that power which raises human life to new levels of insight and service. One thinks, for example, of such exemplary humans touched by the Spirit as Mary the mother of Jesus, Saints Benedict and Francis, Dante Alighieri, Johann Sebastian Bach, John and Charles Wesley, John Henry Newman, Susan B. Anthony, Frederick Douglass, Mother Theresa, and others.

But the notion of Christian humanism invites us to have in mind another important constellation of persons who have taught and inspired millions with their lives and their witness to Christ. It is the communion of saints in all ages. This vast company includes persons whose lives have reflected the humanness of Christ in loving, thoughtful actions. It also embraces many who reported their experiences for the benefit of others: writers of letters, composers of hymns, obscure poets, unheralded preachers or teachers who spoke or wrote a timely word that helped someone move a step closer to true humanness.

The themes of Christian humanism suggested above do not exhaust the possibilities. In every generation men, women, and children will discover new regions of experience from which to draw further on the benefits of humanism. The reflections of thoughtful persons weighing the needs and opportunities of their age will always be an important resource for all who examine the human story from the perspective of Christian faith.

Chapter 2

Christian and Secular Humanism

This chapter, an exercise in history, answers the questions often asked when humanism and the Christian faith are juxtaposed. Isn't "humanism" the same as *secular* humanism? If not, then why do we tend automatically to regard humanism as a secular thing? Is there a humanism that is not secular? Can one actually speak of a *Christian* humanism? If there is such a thing, and if it has been around a long time, how did secular humanism come to occupy such a prominent place in modern popular thought? Why do we hear so much about secular humanism and practically nothing about Christian humanism?

A rapid survey of the key historical developments that can answer such questions would yield three stages in the intellectual history of humanism: at its beginning, two traditions share one stream of development; then the stream begins to divide; and eventually a secular humanism distinctly separate from Christian humanism emerges. The story is a complicated one if we were to explore it in great detail, but this survey only points out the principal stages at which humanism has acquired different meanings at different points in history.

Two Traditions in One Mainstream

In the first centuries of the Christian era two major forms of humanism merged to form a single powerful stream that lasted for over a thousand years. First there was the humanism of early Christianity, based on God's revelation attested to in the Bible. In time this early Christian humanism met and merged with the humanism of classical learning based on pre-Christian Greek philosophy and culture.

The two traditions coexisted in relative harmony because both understood human beings as having a preeminent place in the universe distinct from and above the nonhuman natural world. Both regarded humans as receiving their significance from outside themselves, whether from the Creator of Jewish and Christian faith or from the eternal world of Greek idealism. Though the Greeks singled out reason as the distinctive feature of the human, they understood reason as putting human beings in touch with the divine world.

Christian thinkers also considered human beings to be rational, but they credited the gift of reason to the creative work of God. Of supreme importance for Christian humanism, however, was the biblical concept of *imago dei,* the belief that humans were created in the image of God. This doctrine meant that the highest, noblest human quality was our capacity to respond to the call of God and to enter into personal relationship with the Eternal One. In the Christian view it is not the innate gift of reason that distinguishes the human from the rest of creation but the human's relation to God.

The fourth-century church father Augustine, well-versed in Greek thought, recognized the limits of reason and the need for faith. Reason was important in helping the Christian understand his or her faith, but full self-knowledge could not be attained by reason alone. In his *Confessions* Augustine used a new genre of introspective literature, illustrating through his spiritual autobiography how God had led him from a life of wantonness and spectacular depravity to a new level of self-understanding far beyond the capacity of unaided human reason. Ultimately, as Augustine saw it, human beings have to do with a God who is "the source from which the light of reason itself is kindled."[1]

---

1. Augustine, *De Vera Religione,* xxxix, 72, quoted by J. V. Langmead Casserley, *The Christian in Philosophy* (London: Faber and Faber, 1949), 72. For more on this theme see T. A. Lacey, *Nature, Miracle and Sin: A Study of St. Augustine's Conception of the Natural Order* (London: Longmans, Green, 1916).

Although he possessed one of the greatest intellects of the classical world, Augustine knew that reason alone was insufficient to provide all the guidance needed for a full life. He was beset by anxiety and torn by doubt before his conversion to Christ. He came to see that the authority of God is the source of human fulfillment, a fact that reason subsequently understands.

But what about the Christian doctrine of sin, which was a central concern for Augustine as he reflected on his early life? Did it not make Christian humanism radically different from non-Christian classical humanism? Theologically yes, but there was some common ground in that both traditions held the view that human beings had a moral obligation to strive for fuller realization of their humanness. The ancient Greeks urged the exercise of temperance, courage, and wisdom to attain the highest good. Socrates taught that "the unexamined life is not worth living" and Plato pictured people as prisoners in a cave where they regarded shadows as reality.

The Christian analysis articulated clearly by Augustine was indeed more radical: the human problem is not simply ignorance but sin, the proud tendency to rebel against the Creator. Yet Christian thought could still be positive about human existence because of God's redeeming work in Jesus Christ. Despite the fall into sin a new quality of life was open to sinners who received God's forgiveness in Christ.

The great Christian thinkers like Augustine, and later Thomas Aquinas in the thirteenth century, rejoiced in the glory of human beings and the value of reason, but they knew from Scripture that humans were finite and limited, separated from God and thereby from the truth because of their fall into sin. Augustine stressed the need for faith if reason is to be restored, while Aquinas taught that what reason could disclose had to be supplemented by divine revelation. "In divine matters the natural reason has its failings," he wrote.[2]

Both Greek and Christian humanism sensed that the human being cannot be understood apart from basic relationships, including the relation of human beings to nature. The human is not alone in the universe. Among the Greeks it was Aristotle in particular who stimulated his successors to ponder the order and rationality of the universe. Later the Stoics used the concept of logos (reason, mind) as the principle by which humans under-

2. Thomas Aquinas, *Summa Contra Gentiles,* bk. 1, chap. 2 (4), quoted in *Readings in Christian Humanism,* ed. Joseph M. Shaw, R. W. Franklin, Harris Kaasa, and Charles W. Buzicky (Minneapolis: Augsburg, 1982), 198. On Augustine and humanism, see also Eugene TeSelle, *Augustine the Theologian* (New York: Herder & Herder, 1970), and Henry Chadwick, *The Early Church* (New York: Penguin Books, 1987).

stood themselves as both above nature and at the same time in harmony with the orderly cosmos. The creation stories in Genesis show that the human's unique relation to God implies at the same time a unique place within the created order as God's steward. Rebellion against God's word results in alienation from other humans and from the world of nature.

By the time of the Middle Ages, however, nature seemed chaotic and forbidding, a source of fear and anxiety, even as God seemed remote and austere. In that atmosphere medieval monasticism performed an important service for Christian humanism by meditating on human experience as a means of knowing God. The result was to dignify the human, to underscore the friendship between God and humanity, and to reinterpret the universe as friendly and familiar rather than threatening. The monks even pondered the humanity of God, as the title of a famous treatise — *Cur Deus Homo* (Why God became man) — written in 1100 by the father of scholasticism, Anselm of Canterbury, indicates.

Anselm awakened a remarkable Christian optimism, for *Cur Deus Homo* put the human at the center of a creation adapted to our intelligence. In the midst of his mischievous pupils, who posed insoluble theological questions in order to keep their kindly abbot in his study, Anselm taught that by refining our human faculties through learning we give glory to God and draw closer to a benevolent and intelligible Creator. It was no accident that the university would appear in the generation after Anselm as the new instrument of Christian humanism.[3]

In the high Middle Ages Thomas Aquinas (1224-1274) combined these fresh scholastic impulses from monastic life with his fondness for the ideas of Aristotle into a synthesis that still stands as one of the landmarks of Western humanism. Aquinas made the human the point of the universe, relating God's whole creative act to the human struggle for salvation, and placing the Incarnation once again at the heart of Christianity. In intellectual creatures alone, Aquinas taught, is found the image of God. Because it only is capable of supreme good and it alone is the image of God, the human provides the link between the universe and the divine mind, understands what nature is like and what God is like, and unique among all creatures is capable of receiving grace.

---

3. On *Cur Deus Homo* see G. H. Williams, *Anselm: Communion and Atonement* (St. Louis: Concordia, 1960), and J. McIntyre, *St. Anselm and his Critics: A Re-interpretation of the Cur Deus Homo* (Edinburgh: Oliver and Boyd, 1954). For an overview on monasticism and humanism see David Knowles, *Christian Monasticism* (New York: McGraw-Hill, 1969).

By this grace and the liberty of free will, Aquinas maintained, the human person transcends all the world of nature. Even the natural knowledge of the angels does not extend to the secrets of the heart. And far from discouraging human knowledge and the knowledge of science, Aquinas made the knowledge of sensible things a prerequisite for Christian theology. He saw science as a way to God. For this reason, Christian scientific interest in the Middle Ages focused on "final" not "secondary" causes, on *why* rather than *how* nature functions. This attitude explains why the Middle Ages made only slow progress in the direction of the modern scientific method.[4]

The renewal of Christian humanism in the monasteries, with the preservation of learning and art in rich variety, and the scholastic synthesis of revelation and reason as represented by Thomas Aquinas flowered into an impressive humanism in the young European universities. It paved the way for the appearance, around 1300, of Renaissance humanism, and of the scientific revolution that would come two centuries later.

The Stream Begins to Divide

The people of the early Christian and medieval periods of western Europe did not distinguish moment by moment between what was Christian and what was classical in their day-to-day lives. Daily life tends to be all of one piece. It is the person as a whole who thinks, makes decisions, and acts. Yet it is one of the admirable qualities of human beings that they are able to reflect on their lives and, in retrospect, analyze the source of those attitudes or influences that have been of special importance to them.

Looking back on the development of humanism, as modern observers we see that the mainstream, a flowing mixture of Christian and classical elements, began to divide as Western culture felt the impact of the Renaissance and Reformation between about 1300 and 1600. For a thousand years, the accepted understanding of human life had taken for granted both divine sovereignty and human accountability. With the advent of the Renaissance the stream did not divide abruptly into secular and Christian

4. On Aquinas and medieval humanism see Etienne Gilson, *The Christian Philosophy of St. Thomas Aquinas* (Austin: Octagon, 1956); R. W. Southern, *The Making of the Middle Ages* (New Haven: Yale University Press, 1953); and Frederick C. Copleston, *A History of Medieval Philosophy* (New York: Harper & Row, 1972).

rivulets, which is the popular understanding of the period.[5] Nevertheless, the revival of classical humanism was indeed significant in opening the way toward an eventual secular humanism.

At the outset, Italian humanism showed no disposition to attack or undermine the medieval Christian view of humans as responsible creatures of God. Francesco Petrarch (1304-1374), the father of Renaissance humanism, added a zeal for the classical Roman writers Virgil and Cicero to a conventional but sincere Christian faith. His love for the form and content of ancient Latin and Greek writers did not lessen his devotion to his saintly model, Augustine. Once while climbing a mountain Petrarch pulled from his pocket an edition of Augustine's *Confessions* and read a passage that redirected his mind from the beauties of nature to the greatness of the soul. He wrote that he was stunned when he read the following words, which capture something of the spirit of Christian humanism:

> Men go to admire the high mountains and the great flood of the seas and the wide-rolling rivers and the ring of ocean and the movements of the stars; and they abandon themselves![6]

The humanism of the Renaissance advocated an education in the liberal arts and classical literature with the aim of attaining the good life. That meant diversity and individuality, but also the practical expression of right living. How one lived was more important than how much doctrine one had mastered. A century after Petrarch, Marsilio Ficino (1433-1499) used the works of Plato to provide a philosophical foundation for the renewal of Christian life. As a Christian humanist, he wrote the *Theologia Platonica,* combining Christian theology and Platonic thought. He believed that the Platonic notion of the highest good was to be found in the knowledge of God, and he accorded humans great dignity as the beings who served as the link between the material and the spiritual realms.

5. In his book *Jesus Through The Centuries* (New Haven: Yale University Press, 1985), 146, historian Jaroslav Pelikan cites the view of Konrad Burdach that the Renaissance arises "not in opposition to the Christian religion . . . but out of the full vitality of a religious revival."

6. Francesco Petrarch, *Letter Describing the Ascent of Mont Ventoux,* quoted in *Readings in Christian Humanism,* 238. A classical treatment of Renaissance humanism is J. A. Symonds, *The Renaissance in Italy* (New York: G. P. Putnams, 1970); and more recently Ernst Cassirer et al., *The Renaissance Philosophy of Man* (Chicago: University of Chicago Press, 1971); and Myron P. Gilmore, *The World of Humanism 1453-1517* (New York: Harper & Row, 1962).

Ficino's belief in education as an instrument for the reform of church and society exerted a strong influence on the most famous of the northern Christian humanists, Erasmus of Rotterdam (1466-1536).

Ficino's pupil and friend Pico della Mirandola (1463-1494) made his mark on the history of humanism with his *Oration on the Dignity of Man*. What Pico wrote in youthful exuberance about humans' capacity to choose their own nature has been translated by some modern thinkers into a denial of the uniqueness of human nature, the opposite of what Pico intended. Happily and liberally blending elements of Christian teaching with Hebrew, Greek, Arabic, and other streams of learning, Pico set out to describe the special place of humans in the universal chain of being. At one point he imagined the Creator addressing Adam in these words: "Thou, constrained by no limits, in accordance with thine own free will, in whose hand We have placed thee, shalt ordain for thyself the limits of thy nature."[7] Secularists would applaud the idea of humans defining their own nature but Pico, although carried to excess by the notion of human self-determination, still maintained that it was God who bestowed the gift of freedom.

Where the Italian humanists made much of the ancient classics of Greece and Rome in praising the dignity of both the human and the natural creation, the northern humanists of the sixteenth century concentrated their enthusiasm on biblical antiquity, the Hebrew Scripture and the Greek New Testament. Petrarch, to be sure, had shown an interest in church reform in that he wished to see the papacy return from Avignon to Rome, but he and other Italian humanists accepted the status of Christianity for what it was, hoping only to resuscitate the faith by extolling the freedom and potentiality of the human.

The northern humanists, on the other hand, soon recognized the prospect of effecting a serious reform of the church with the aid of the original biblical languages. Erasmus of Rotterdam, uniting the Christian and classical as Ficino had done, undertook a penetrating criticism of both society and church in such works as *The Praise of Folly* (1511) and *The Handbook of the Militant Christian* (1503).

The Christian humanism of Erasmus centered on *humanitas* and *pietas*, words that became so familiar in American higher education that

7. Pico della Mirandola, *Oration on the Dignity of Man,* cited in *Readings in Christian Humanism,* 245-46. See also W. J. Bouwsma, *The Interpretation of Renaissance Humanism* (New York: Macmillan, 1959); and two books by Paul Kristeller, *Renaissance Thought: The Classic, Scholastic, and Humanist Strains* (New York: Harper & Row, 1961), and *Renaissance Thought II: Papers on Humanism and the Arts* (New York: Harper & Row, 1965).

they are often found carved over college buildings and gates, as over the facade of Harvard's Memorial Hall. For Erasmus the first concept, *humanitas,* was classical, and the second, *pietas,* was Christian. *Humanitas* meant the love of humankind; the dignity of the human was basic, because the human alone of God's creatures is endowed with speech and reason. Accordingly, human behavior should correspond to the seemly and the rational, for that is the nature intended for us by the Creator. *Pietas* meant reverence, devotion, and the enrichment of humanity through the Christian virtues of compassion, patience, forgiveness, and humility. With such values in mind, Erasmus sought a widespread reform of Europe in the sixteenth century by means of persuasion rather than through compulsion or revolution.

Yet how would men and women be won to *humanitas* and *pietas?* Erasmus found his answer in study, study of the humanities and Scripture. For genuine reform to take place Erasmus urged that the classics and above all the Bible be placed in the hands of *all* people: "Would that, as a result, the farmer sing some portion of them at the plow, the weaver hum some parts of them to the movement of his shuttle, the traveller lighten the weariness of the journey with stories of this kind!"[8]

The new edition of the Greek text of the New Testament, published by Erasmus in 1516, was a shining instance of how Renaissance humanist scholarship directly influenced the coming Reformation. At the heart of the reforming labors of Luther, Calvin, and others was the exegesis of the Bible, now made more accurate with the aid of the revived knowledge of Hebrew and Greek.

The dividing of the Christian-classical mainstream of humanism began as the Renaissance vigorously brought forward the classical conception of humans as rational beings, related to the divine through reason (logos) and distinguished from the nonhuman creation by that same logos principle. The Reformation for its part restated the biblical interpretation of humanity that included not only the "image of God" idea and the story of the fall (Genesis 1–3), but also the possibility of the new creation of human persons through the redemptive work of Christ. The classical-Renaissance line would lead to a secularistic view of humans as free and autonomous while the biblical-Reformation line understood human freedom to be relative, stressing dependence upon God as basic to the human condition.

8. Desiderius Erasmus, *Paraclesis,* quoted in *Readings in Christian Humanism,* 293-94; see also Roland H. Bainton, *Erasmus of Rotterdam* (New York: Crossroad, 1982).

Erasmus was both Renaissance man and mild reformer, whereas Luther and Calvin were more thoroughgoing reformers who benefited from the Renaissance recovery of biblical languages. With irony and high literary skill, Erasmus had sincerely addressed himself to the improvement of Christian living, but Luther went a significant step further and attacked medieval scholastic theology at its very center. What does the Word of God tell human beings about God's nature, about human nature, and about sin and salvation?

Luther and Erasmus clashed on the fundamental issue of the human will. Erasmus contended that the will had *some* freedom in responding to the grace of God, but Luther heatedly countered that while humans had free will in the ordinary conduct of their daily affairs, they had none when they stood before God. Precisely "with regard to God, and in all things pertaining to salvation or damnation, man has no free will, but is a captive, servant and bondslave, either to the will of God, or to the will of Satan," wrote Luther.[9] Erasmus's conviction that men and women cooperate freely and fully with God in the gift of salvation was to be a foundation of the Catholic humanism that flowed from the Council of Trent into the seventeenth and eighteenth centuries.

Just as the Renaissance was not a sudden leap into secularism, neither was the Reformation a crass repudiation of humanism, as some have concluded from Luther's forbidding position on the bondage of the human will. Though it is true that Luther is almost never called a humanist, yet there are important humanistic implications in his three great reforming principles: the authority of Scripture, the doctrine of justification by faith, and the priesthood of all believers.

First, the authority of Scripture clearly frees the human person from all other authorities except the Word of God, and the Word bestows its own profound freedom. Second, justification by faith humanizes people by releasing them from the need to please God by their virtue and works, thus liberating human energy for the service of God and the neighbor. Third, the priesthood of all believers underscores the responsibility Christians have to bring the Word of God to those around them, to be priests to their neighbors. All three of these principles bespeak an extremely high view of what it means to be human when the good news of Christ delivers

---

9. Martin Luther, *The Bondage of the Will*, 638, cited in *Readings in Christian Humanism*, 330. See also E. H. Harbison, *The Christian Scholar in the Age of the Reformation* (New York: Charles Scribner's Sons, 1956; repr. Grand Rapids: Wm. B. Eerdmans, 1983).

people from sin and guilt and frees them to address the noblest human tasks.

There was also a Catholic reformation, expressing itself in the Council of Trent which met from 1545 to 1563. The central affirmation of the council — human cooperation with God in the work of salvation — responded to the new Protestant principles with a clearly formulated doctrinal system that sought to preserve the incarnational focus of the previous thousand years of Christian teaching, with implications for Christian humanism in the future.

First, alongside the Bible, the Council of Trent valued tradition: the experience, concern, and intercession of the great Catholic saints were made available for the spiritual strengthening of the contemporary faithful. Trent reinstated the practice that each day in the Catholic calendar should honor the memory of some human imitator of God, while statues and stained glass were welcomed as aids for remembering those heroic and pious believers and their deeds which, taken together, make up Catholic tradition.

Second, this proximity of heaven to earth and of God to the human was vividly portrayed in Tridentine prescriptions for worship. After the sixteenth century, Catholic liturgy conveyed in a variety of ways the belief that the entire church militant on earth is united closely with the church triumphant in heaven.

Finally, Trent was willing to speak of human authority in the church and the necessity of a universal primate who could symbolize and strengthen the fundamental unity of the human family, locating this authority and this "personal focus" of Christian affection in the Bishop of Rome.[10]

The image of a mainstream starting to divide might obscure the fact that both Protestant and Catholic currents made up the Christian branch of the stream. Both the Protestant Reformation and the Council of Trent together would continue to exert Christian influence on the whole of Western culture. The primary historical fact is the division of the stream into Christian and secular humanism. The two branches are to be distinguished, but as they developed they were never totally separated. The Christian part of the stream was exposed constantly to emerging secular forces, while the secular branch continued to interact with Christian influence.

10. The humanism of Trent is surveyed in J. A. Froude, *Lectures on the Council of Trent, delivered at Oxford 1892-1893* (London: Longmans, Green, 1896).

Secular Humanism Emerges

No one remains completely untouched by the secular in our world. The word itself is from the Latin *saeculum,* which means "age" or "world." The secular is the time and place that surrounds us. The thoroughgoing secularist believes that this age or this world is all that belongs to reality. The Christian disputes this view, but concedes that until he or she is ushered into eternity, there is no other place to be than here in this world, in the midst of the assorted hopes and fears of this age. In the 1960s, in fact, some theologians were so eager to embrace and virtually baptize the secular order that they seemed close to losing all touch with the specific substance of the Christian tradition.

Here our task is to sketch the rise of secular humanism in the period following the Reformation of the sixteenth century. Secular humanism took from the Renaissance its emphasis on human dignity, individuality, freedom, and potential. Unlike Renaissance humanism it may, in some cases, reject faith in a God who transcends the human dimension and provides its deepest meaning. This dictionary definition offers a succinct description of secular humanism for our purposes: "A philosophy that asserts the dignity and worth of man and his capacity for self-realization through reason and that often rejects supernaturalism."[11]

In actuality, most secular humanists are nonmilitant people who simply choose not to go on record as rejecting God or the supernatural. Instead of actively opposing religious faith they prefer to keep their thoughts about God to themselves. They nevertheless remain uncritical of a culture that places full confidence in human judgment alone and full value on what this world in itself has to offer.

To put it simply, the emergence of secular humanism was the result of two movements. The first was the exaltation of human reason following the spirit of Renaissance humanism. The second was the reduction of the human to the level of the natural world following the spirit of a positivistic interpretation of the physical sciences. In both cases, the uniqueness of the human person is lost, becoming identical with rationality on the one hand or reduced to a phenomenon within the physical world on the other.

Such is the persistence and popularity of the notion that human dignity is found in reason that few people today, least of all intellectuals, even think to question it. When religious disputes and, worse, religious

11. *Webster's New Collegiate Dictionary,* 1977, s.v. "humanism."

wars left Europe in turmoil during the seventeenth century, many believed that reason held out the best hope for humankind. In their own way, orthodox Christians also joined in the praise of reason, hoping to demonstrate that their theological formulations were more reasonable than those of their rivals. In 1695 John Locke wrote a book called *The Reasonableness of Christianity,* claiming that religion cannot be contradictory to reason.

The perennial appeal of reason, since the time of the ancient Greeks, is the idea that reason brings the human person into contact with the divine. The popular version of this idea is that in every person there is a divine spark, the mind or spirit, which is part of the eternal, divine fire. The other part of the human being, the body, the lower element, regrettably links humans with animal nature and with evil, but this aspect is not the essential one, according to this line of thought. In essence, the human person is the reason or mind or spirit by which one shares in the divine world.

The serious flaw in this kind of anthropology (or doctrine of human nature) is that the person in his or her concreteness has no real, individual existence. The actual person, a totality of body, mind, spirit, and affections, disappears into the mist of the vast, universal, but impersonal divine reason.[12] The classical-Renaissance attempt to magnify the greatness of the human being by elevating reason to the level of the divine actually produced, not a vigorous humanism, but an abstract, elitist conception of the human person in which the supposedly essential part of the person, the reason, was merged with the abstract, universal mind. The nonessential part, the body, was regarded as unworthy, having its place on the lower level of base physical appetites.

But at the very time that human reason was being elevated in this fashion, a new set of challenging ideas appeared in the wake of exciting discoveries in science. Shortly after the discovery of the new world, the old European world was shaken by the claim of the Polish astronomer Copernicus (1473-1543) that the sun, not the earth, was the center of the heavenly system and that the earth moved in orbit around the sun. During the next century, evidence for the truth of the Copernican view was provided by Galileo with his telescope, Kepler with his laws of planetary motion, and Newton with his law of gravitation. Sir Francis Bacon (1561-1626) lent theoretical support to the advances in physical science by

12. Emil Brunner, "Man in the Universe," *Christianity and Civilization* (New York: Charles Scribner's Sons, 1949), 1:87. See C. W. Kegley, ed., *The Theology of Emil Brunner* (New York: Macmillan, 1962).

expounding the inductive method, which enabled one to move from observed facts to wider and deeper generalizations.

How was humanism affected by these developments? In the first place, once the Copernican revolution was assimilated, scientists, clergymen, and ordinary people together had to adjust their thinking to a new perception of the universe in the seventeenth century. No longer could people assume a cozy world where the earth was the center of everything and the human family was comfortably installed as the recognized proprietor of every significant reality. That familiar universe was gone, and suddenly human beings felt "exposed to the dread of infinity in spatial terms."[13]

But the adjustment was made. With the help of Sir Isaac Newton's mathematical demonstration of the gravitational motions of heavenly bodies in the 1680s, a new view of the universe gained wide currency that lasted until the twentieth century. The Newtonian cosmos is governed by strict mechanical laws, which humans can understand by applying their powers of observation and reason. Moreover, the new cosmology gradually shifted the perception concerning the relation of humans to nature. Before, philosophy and theology had commented on nature from the standpoint of the situation of human beings within history. Now, nature and its mechanical laws seemed to furnish the key for the interpretation of human beings and history.

Seventeenth-century philosophers demonstrated a parallel shift from reliance on ancient authorities to an empirical mode of reasoning. In 1629 Descartes adopted the method of doubting everything until it was proven, and the proof he demanded had to carry the same weight as a mathematical demonstration. Spinoza reduced reality to a single substance, God or nature, while Leibniz discussed an infinite number of substances, "monads," containing innate ideas that human reason alone could draw forth to clarity. Locke denied the existence of innate ideas, arguing that human persons gain knowledge as reason reflects on experience. None of these famous thinkers denied the existence of God, but their influence created an era of rationalism that paved the way for the Enlightenment of the eighteenth century.[14]

As Enlightenment rationalism came to full force, the way was made clear, for the first time in Western history, for the appearance of explicit

13. John Dillenberger, *Protestant Thought and Natural Science* (Garden City, N.Y.: Doubleday, 1960), 26. Cf. also Alan Richardson, *The Bible in the Age of Science* (Philadelphia: Westminster Press, 1961); and J. Bronowski, *Science and Human Values* (New York: Harper & Row, 1965).

14. For examples of these points see Werner Jaeger, *Humanism and Theology* (Milwaukee: Marquette University Press, 1943).

atheism as a legitimate philosophical position. Paul Henri Holbach, a rationalistic philosopher, declared that "supernatural ideas," by which he meant the traditional Christian doctrine of God, had "obscured morality, corrupted politics, hindered the advance of the sciences, and extinguished happiness and peace in the very heart of man."[15] Many philosophers of the eighteenth century advanced their own substitute for revealed religion, Deism, which was an attempt to retain God in a distant, honorary capacity while giving first place to reason and the natural sciences.

The church and its life were by no means disabled by science and rationalism, but Christianity could not avoid being affected by the many changes in the air. The popular assumption that the church always and automatically opposed the development of science is much too sweeping. It is not generally known, for example, that young scholars associated with the early decades of the Reformation encouraged Copernicus to publish his findings. The University of Halle, known as a center of pietism, introduced experimental science in 1694 and led other German universities to follow suit in making the study of the universe an academic discipline. At times the church was mistaken in its reactions to the new scientific discoveries, but at other times it was in the right. In some quarters the church erred in thinking that it had to defend the three-storied universe of biblical and Babylonian antiquity against Copernicanism. On the other hand, the church showed a correct instinct in opposing the use of the Copernican discovery as a weapon against the Christian doctrine of revelation.[16]

In the face of rationalism the church took an ambivalent stance. Many of its theologians heroically argued that Christian doctrines were eminently reasonable. In some controversies, though, it became necessary to affirm the truths of divine revelation over against the decrees of reason. Both lay and learned Christians felt pressured by science and rationalism to take a stand in the eighteenth century in defense of biblical miracles and prophecies which, in effect, became a battle to defend the Bible. The unhappy aspect of this well-intentioned struggle two centuries ago was the tendency to associate Christian faith with the belief that the Bible was a book of information, the repository of true propositions, rather than the record of God's gracious activity in behalf of humankind. A number of devout thinkers tried to do

15. Quoted in *Readings in Christian Humanism,* 362. On Christianity in conflict with secularism in this period see Peter Gay, *The Enlightenment: An Interpretation* (New York: Vintage Books, 1960).

16. See Brunner, "Man in the Universe," in *Christianity and Civilization,* 1:84.

justice to science and religion by speaking of God as the author of two books, the book of nature and the book of Scripture.

The issues were only intensified in the nineteenth century as the world came to terms with the ideas of such figures as Darwin, Nietzsche, Freud, and Marx. Darwin's valid point that the study of origins showed that humans had much in common with the animals was taken by many to justify the view that the human was nothing more than a complicated animal. The church overreacted to Darwinism, thinking that the theory of evolution necessarily destroyed the doctrine that human beings had been created in the image of God. As in the case of Copernicanism, however, there was some validity in the church's opposition to the antihumanistic implications drawn from Darwin's teaching. The church rightly sensed that humanism itself was in danger if Darwin's theory was used to support the claim that a human being was nothing but an animal, however complex and sophisticated that animal was. "The problem was," writes a modern historian, "that a biological description of man had become a statement concerning the nature of man . . . as if man's *descent* determined his *nature*."[17]

The drift toward a secularistic humanism was furthered by the influence of positivism in the nineteenth and twentieth centuries. Positivism, a philosophy espoused by Auguste Comte (1798-1857), held that the only things one can know are those for which *positive* evidence can be gathered from natural phenomena. This philosophy negated all metaphysics and proclaimed a natural religion of humanity. Positivists argued that the method of empirical observation, which had disclosed so many marvels in the physical universe, should be applied to all other realms of knowledge, including philosophy and the social sciences.[18] Comte went so far as to construct an entirely new kind of religion with humanity, "the great being," in the place of God. He introduced an elaborate "cult of humanity," with its own priesthood, sacraments, and "positivist calendar" in which the names of scientists and scholars replaced those of the saints.

17. Dillenberger, *Protestant Thought,* 221. Two overviews of the rise of this era of secularism are Owen Chadwick, *The Secularization of the European Mind in the Nineteenth Century* (Cambridge: Cambridge University Press, 1975), and Jacques Barzun, *Darwin, Marx, and Wagner* (New York: Doubleday, 1958); on Marxism see Alasdair MacIntyre, *Marxism and Christianity* (Notre Dame: University of Notre Dame Press, 1984), and N. V. Baneyee, *Buddhism and Marxism: A Study in Humanism* (New Delhi: Orient Longman, 1978); and on Nietzsche see Walter Kaufmann, *Nietzsche: Philosopher, Psychologist, AntiChrist* (New York: Vintage Books, 1960).

18. See F. S. Marvin, *Comte: The Founder of Sociology* (London: Chapman and Hall, 1936).

Nietzsche interpreted Darwinism as supporting a "struggle for power" in which Christian "slave morality" must give way to the glorification of the superman. Freud located the clue to human nature in the sex impulse, and Marx found it in economic forces. For all of these thinkers, humans were simply part of nature, the products of natural forces, and in no way related to any transcendent reality or metaphysical realm. Christian humanism does not deny that humans are subject to struggles for power, sex drives, and economic needs, but it rejects the underlying assumption in all of these theories that humans are totally immersed in nature as helpless victims of irrational forces within and without.[19]

All humanism, not just Christian humanism, is threatened by a positivistic naturalism that regards humans as irrational creatures, enslaved by their environment and heredity, and deprived of purpose and unity. It should be noted how a naturalistic philosophy of human nature actually runs counter to the Enlightenment's enthusiasm for the powers of human reason. Christian humanism is properly critical of secular views that make exaggerated claims for the ability of reason to solve all human problems, but over against the irrationalism of Nietzsche, Freud, and Marx it must defend the gift of reason as a valued quality of human nature.

Similarly, Christian humanism is on the side of the free exercise of the scientific method, but in behalf of the human race it protests against the distortion whereby science is hailed as an all-encompassing philosophy of life. A naive confidence that science eventually will create a perfect society is often part of the secular humanist's creed. By contrast, Christian humanism acknowledges that imperfection and relative attainments will continue to characterize human life in this world.

To summarize, secular humanism emerged in Western history as the result of two powerful movements, the elevation of *reason* as the dominant qualifier of what it means to be human, and an interpretation of the *scientific method* that entirely limited human beings to the natural realm. These two movements were not always in harmony with one another, but in the popular mind "reason and science" were perceived as twin designations for the conception of the human as autonomous and unlimited in potential on the one hand, and, paradoxically, as subject to the forces of

19. On the response of the churches to this context in the nineteenth century see Hugh McLeod, *Religion and the People of Western Europe, 1789-1970* (Oxford: Oxford University Press, 1981); and Ninian Smart et al., *Nineteenth Century Religious Thought in the West*, vol. 1 (Cambridge: Cambridge University Press, 1985).

the natural world on the other hand. This inconsistency was reconciled by the secularistic belief that the more objective facts we gathered about the human organism the more effectively reason could use those facts to control human behavior.

The central characteristic of secular humanism is the abandonment of metaphysics and revealed religion. Metaphysics means that there is a reality beyond *(meta)* the physical realm. Religion means the service and adoration of God or a god. Secular humanism interprets human life exclusively in terms of a one-dimensional universe and calls upon persons to rely upon themselves rather than upon God. Christian humanism interprets human existence in light of the conviction that everything in the universe, and especially the human family, receives its very life and significance from the divine reality beyond this visible world, from God who is Creator, Redeemer, and animating Spirit.[20]

20. See Quirinus Breen, *Christianity and Humanism* (Grand Rapids: Wm. B. Eerdmans, 1968).

Chapter 3

Christian Humanism Revives

During the four centuries between the end of the Reformation and the present era, Christian humanism survived, though it was severely tested and its voice muted. The current revival of Christian humanism is a reassertion of the humanistic claims that have always been part of the Christian tradition. The revival is spurred by a widely felt need in both church and world to reclaim the value the Christian faith places on the human person.

Part of the need for a new defense of Christian humanism is that the wholesale condemnation of all humanism by some Christians during the past decades demands a response. An additional stimulus comes from the creative energies unleashed by recent changes in world politics, above all the restoring of a voice to believers in Jesus Christ in countries once dominated by communism. But the roots of the present recovery of Christian humanism lie farther back in history. Our purpose in this chapter is to identify those historical roots and underline their significance.

In later chapters we will relate Christian humanism to the Bible, to the church in its worship, and to theological developments. In this chapter we look at significant historical moments in each of these areas that have cleared the way for Christian humanism now to reassume its rightful place as an important component of Christian faith and practice.

The Reformation

The Reformation of the sixteenth century was an important turning point for the continued assertion of Christian humanism. The reformers reestablished the priority of the gospel in every aspect of the Christian tradition. Starting with the Gospel accounts and Paul's letters, the Reformers stated in fresh and powerful terms that God is essentially a gracious God who is unconditionally *for* humanity and the world. The sign of God's favorable disposition toward the human race is Jesus Christ, the Son of God and definitive human being, who lived, served, died, and rose again for the purpose of bringing human beings into their rightful, loving relationship to God. This reconciliation between God and human beings was made possible by the forgiveness of sins and the bestowal of new life, a life in union with Christ, upon all who believe.

Christian humanism is impossible apart from the divine-human transaction in which ordinary people, not just monks and nuns and clergy, humbly confess their wrongs, believe God's promise that there is forgiveness in Christ, and personally discover the overwhelming fact that God is a gracious God. For people who know what it is to believe in Christ and confess his name, Christian humanism comes as no innovation, but simply the acknowledgment of the fact that God in Christ makes everything new. The entire range of human experience, they find, is illumined by the cross and resurrection of Christ.

Luther and Calvin did not have the last word on how the grace of God permeates all of life, but they had a realistic vision of the Christian's responsibility in a world marred by sin. Luther taught that the kingdom on the right hand was ruled by God through the gospel and the kingdom on the left was ruled by God through the law. Both kingdoms belonged to God. Calvin wrote volumes on the sovereign rule of God over all things. Both stressed that faith was the key that provided access to a life of human fulfillment in joyful service to God and loving service to the neighbor. Both were mindful of the greatness of human possibilities for good even as both were keenly aware of how destructive sin can be in perverting human endeavors.[1]

---

1. The most recent treatments of Luther and Calvin on these themes are Heiko O. Oberman, *Luther: Man between God and the Devil* (New Haven: Yale University Press, 1990); and William J. Bouwsma, *John Calvin: A Sixteenth-Century Portrait* (Oxford: Oxford University Press, 1988), particularly chap. 7, "Humanism."

Adjusting to Science

A second turning point for Christian humanism came with the church's gradual adjustment to the rise of science. This complicated story may be summarized in the observation that in the long run the biblical message of God's grace and human freedom encouraged rather than opposed the search for new knowledge about the world and human existence. The notoriety of the Roman Catholic Church's condemnation of the work of Galileo in 1633 should not obscure the fact, now more fully recognized, that Western science developed on Christian soil. Centuries of Christian emphasis on the distinction between God and God's creation, and on human persons as the highest creatures of God with delegated authority over the world, provided the theological and psychological warrant for human investigation of the universe.[2]

We should not, on the other hand, minimize the seriousness of the many science-religion controversies over the years. Certainly there has been fault on both sides. It is fair to say, however, that a popular *perception* that religion and science are at odds persists even after many of the issues have been resolved. One factor leading to improved discussion between faith and science is a better informed view of the nature of the Bible. When Christians have treated the Bible as the believing community's witness to the loving actions of God in history, and not as a collection of authoritative statements on scientific matters, they have had much less difficulty in appreciating the role of science in a changing world.[3]

2. A classical account of this conflict from the perspective of secular humanism is Bertrand Russell, *Religion and Science* (New York: Oxford University Press, 1961). More recent global, environmental concerns are discussed in John M. Mangum, ed., *The New Faith-Science Debate: Probing Cosmology, Technology, and Theology* (Minneapolis: Augsburg Fortress, 1989).

3. For a broadly based and judicious treatment of science and religion see Ian G. Barbour, *Issues in Science and Religion* (Englewood Cliffs, N.J: Prentice-Hall, 1966). Barbour discusses the contribution of religion to the rise of science on pp. 44-50. Further books on this topic to consider are Stanley D. Beck, *Modern Science and Christian Life* (Minneapolis: Augsburg, 1970), J. Bronowski, *Science and Human Values* (New York: Harper & Row, 1975), and Don Cupitt, *The Worlds of Science & Religion* (New York: Hawthorn Books, 1976).

Studying the Bible

How the Christian community has gained a better understanding of the Bible is a third turning point for Christian humanism. The shift happened when scholars combined the Reformers' insights concerning Scripture with the historical-critical method of studying the Bible. Luther and Calvin and their coworkers were careful scholars sensitive to the religious character of the biblical message. They allowed the redemptive *message* of the Bible to take precedence over problems related to the ancient *forms* in which that message was cast. Luther used the vivid image of the Scriptures as the "cradle" in which Christ was laid. Christ at the center of Scripture becomes the criterion by which other features are evaluated.

Where the Reformers found the authority of the Bible in its message of God's redeeming love, later generations allowed the question of authority to center narrowly on the book itself. Now the Bible was declared to be authoritative because God had guaranteed its absolute inerrancy in every detail of history and science. Human participation in the writing and transmittal of the biblical materials was given scant attention. Had such language been available in that era, the proponents of the Bible as a book of correct information could have expressed their claim by saying that it was a "printout from a heavenly computer."

This rigid conception of the Bible altered as the historical-critical method of investigating the Bible gradually gained acceptance. The aim of historical-critical study, which began in the eighteenth century, was to apply to the Bible the same careful methods of examination as scholars applied to other ancient literature, such as the Greek epics. In its early days, biblical criticism was sometimes employed by unbelieving skeptics who hoped to discredit Christianity by explaining the miracles in naturalistic terms or by trying to prove that the "real" Jesus was simply a Jewish prophet raised to divine status by gullible or deceitful followers. But the Bible survived all such critical scrutiny. In the past century or so leadership in historical-critical Bible study has been in the hands of devout, well-trained scholars whose ranks include conservatives and liberals, Jews and Christians, Roman Catholics, Protestants, and the Orthodox.

Common to all of them is the conviction that the divine character of Scripture makes its meticulous study important and the human aspect makes it possible. For Christian humanism, as for Christian theology generally, the nature of the Bible is inferred from the fact of the Incarnation. Just as God appeared among human beings in the form of a man, so the divine Word of God also presents itself in the human form of a book to be read, studied, and proclaimed. The more people hear and learn about the love of God for humankind from the Bible, the more they also learn about the meaning of being human.[4]

Catholic Revivals and Christian Humanism

A fourth factor in the widespread, modern resurgence of Christian humanism is found in a cluster of "Catholic" revivals in the nineteenth century among Roman Catholic monks and theologians in France and Germany. The term "Catholic revival" may even be extended to the witness of such Lutheran figures as Wilhelm Loehe in Bavaria and N. F. S. Grundtvig in Denmark. The Oxford Movement (1833-1845), with its emphasis on tradition, ritual, and dogma, was another parallel attempt to return the church to a character consistent with its Catholic past.

In 1833 in France, some Roman Catholics came to the conclusion that in the advanced secularism of a democratic and industrial society, a revival of Christianity could be achieved only through a restoration of the church as an institution with a marked emphasis on the liturgy, the official cycle of Catholic worship. As the claims of revolutionary secular humanism seemed to prove empty, Benedictine monks lifted before France the church and its liturgy as a source and model of human endeavor. In a nineteenth-century society in which worship had been cut off from daily affairs and relegated to the strictly spiritual plane, the Benedictines dramatized the bond between the eucharist and social justice and found in Catholic worship an act that held up a pattern of more dignified human relationships that actually could be realized in the temporal order.

At the same time, the Danish Lutheran Grundtvig came to appreciate anew that the eucharist is both the praise of God and the means for being incorporated into a human community, the local church, in whose life of worship the parish comes to understand the full humanity God intended for it. And similarly, against a one-sided Puritan spirituality that had deprecated the human body and its senses and portrayed material

4. An account of the relationship between biblical criticism and humanism may be found in Rudolf Bultmann, "Humanism and Christianity," *The Journal of Religion*, 32 (1952), 77.

externals as signs of hypocrisy in religion, the Oxford Movement within the Church of England valued liturgical worship once again as the noble heritage of the church of Christ and also rediscovered the ancient truth that the eucharist gives new significance to earth as well as to eternity, to matter as well as to spirit.

The rediscovery of the social dimension of the Catholic Church and the renewal of its social mission were also joined with a revival of liturgical worship in German Catholicism by Johann Adam Möhler (1796-1838). Möhler fostered in the laity a love of the church and its worship services; he reasserted the strongly humanistic potential of Christian worship as a basis for Catholics to deal with a hostile secular order in Germany. Building on the central affirmation of the Council of Trent, Möhler asserted that humans are, in a deeply mysterious way, the instruments of God's gift of salvation of which they are also the beneficiaries. Liturgical acts are the chief signs of human participation in the redemptive process, and it is for this reason that all members of the community should actively perform their proper role in a church service.

Möhler's theology, born in the fire of controversy with the German state of Württemberg, closely identified Christ with the institutional Catholic Church. Only in an international religious community, with a marked transcendent dimension, could a full humanism be guaranteed for nineteenth-century Europeans. This transposition allowed Möhler to fuse his theology of worship and his theology of church into one whole based upon the Incarnation, the doctrine of God becoming human in the life of Jesus Christ.

His teaching that the mystery of the Incarnation is reflected both in a human act, the eucharist, and in a human institution, the church, became one of the fundamental theological contributions of the nineteenth century to modern Catholic thought. The church is a visible, divinely constituted society which is the sacramental manifestation of God's saving mercy. The celebration of the eucharist is the supreme action by which each Christian comes into her or his own as a member of Christ's body and experiences union with the community. This linking of corporate worship to the concrete institutions of the church and Möhler's favorite biblical phrase, "the church as the mystical body of Christ," came to stand behind the thinking of almost all modern German and French Catholic theologians.[5]

---

5. On the humanism of the nineteenth-century "Catholic" revivals see R. W. Franklin, *Nineteenth-Century Churches: The History of a New Catholicism in Württemberg, England, and France* (New York: Garland, 1987); Cuthbert Johnson, *Prosper Guéranger: A*

Interpretation of Human Nature in the Twentieth Century

Protestantism introduced a fifth turning point in the modern revival of Christian humanism: the development of a new Christian anthropology, or doctrine of human nature. Protestant thought preserved the insights of Reformation theology and restated them powerfully in the twentieth century. It gradually made its peace with science without surrendering to superficial scientific claims, it turned historical-critical study of the Bible to positive advantage, and it outlined a Christian view of human nature, which is one of the central concerns of Christian humanism.

The chaos of the twentieth century forced responsible people to give serious thought to what it is that constitutes genuine humanity. The optimistic assumption that "people are basically good" has been found wanting and the pessimistic assumption that people are nothing but animals has seemed to be dangerously self-fulfilling. Evidence for human brutality and human nobility in baffling mixture abounds in public and private spheres.

The genius of the Christian interpretation of the human person is that it is both realistic and hopeful. The realism stems from the classical Christian teaching that "all have sinned and fall short of the glory of God" (Romans 3:23). Perhaps few Christian teachings are so firmly corroborated by the actual experiences of persons and societies. The facts of human depravity, both on the individual and on the social level, are there for everyone to see.

Reinhold Niebuhr taught many in his generation to realize that sin is more than an individual's misdeed; sin is a condition that produces distortion and injustice in the entire social fabric. Niebuhr began his ministry as an urban parish pastor, witnessing firsthand the bruising social results of the mindless confidence that a liberal culture, laissez-faire economics, and intrinsic human goodness would make the kingdom of God a reality on earth. He went on to become the prophetic voice of a chastened Christian conscience, addressing a nation and a world caught in the degradation of two world wars and the alienation of an advanced industrial society. Since Niebuhr's day, thoughtful Christians of the later

---

Liturgical Theologian (Rome: Analecta Liturgica, 1984); Louis Weil, *Sacraments and Liturgy: The Outward Signs* (Oxford: Basil Blackwell, 1983); and Christian Thodberg and Anders Thyssen, *N. F. S. Grundtvig: Tradition and Renewal* (Copenhagen: The Danish Institute, 1983).

twentieth century have sought to claim and preach a redemption that not only rescues the solitary sinner but also delivers the social order from the power of evil.[6]

Despite the penetrating witness of Niebuhr and those who listened to him, and despite massive evidence of destructive human pride and greed and hate, many secularists and sentimental religious believers continue to cling to the fragile axiom that "deep down" people are basically good "at heart." To give them the benefit of the doubt, perhaps they are trying to say that human beings were created good originally and that *something* of that goodness remains, despite the gross antisocial behavior of some people. Indeed, the Christian tradition has endorsed a similar way of viewing the human situation: the "fall" of the first couple impaired human nature, but did not destroy it. Sin must indeed be taken seriously, but God has not given up on humanity.

But Christian thought has more to offer than a sentimental belief in a deeply buried residue of goodness in the human soul. It offers, from Scripture and ultimately from God's own heart, the announcement that God forgives sin and re-creates the sinner, making him or her a new creation in Christ (2 Corinthians 5:17). The secular mind needs to hold on to a confidence in some shred of virtue hidden somewhere within the human personality because it has no resources for coping with the brutal fact of sin.

Christian faith, on the other hand, can afford to be candid about human weakness, even human defiance of God, because it teaches that God graciously makes provision for the return of rebellious human creatures to their proper relationship to their Source and Savior. The "good news" of the entire Bible is that what God asks of human beings is not perfection but the willingness to come back to the Father's house. Human hope is built on knowledge of God's power to forgive and renew, giving the person a new start.

The potential of Christian faith and hope for human fulfillment has too often been held in check, however, by a kind of Christian pessimism that makes the doctrine of sin the sum total of the doctrine of human nature. When asked, "What is the Christian view of the human being?" many orthodox Christians have been taught to answer by rote, "The human being is a sinner." The theological validity of this statement has cut off discussion in some circles of what the rest of the Christian tradition has

6. The most recent comprehensive study of Niebuhr is Richard Fox, *Reinhold Niebuhr: A Biography* (New York: Pantheon Books, 1985).

to say about humans, their special status under God and their potential as well as their sin.

Thus some Christian thinkers in the past few decades have recognized that a fresh interpretation of human nature is needed, both for the Christian community itself and also for the larger society. Their aim has been to show that biblical and Christian teaching about human nature does not end with the doctrine of "original sin" but goes on to a closer look at the positive aspect of what it means to be human in the light of the total Christian tradition. Theologian Wolfhart Pannenberg writes that "the unity with God that the Christian community confesses about Jesus cannot be opposed to man's nature as such. In his personal unity with God, Jesus is then the fulfillment of the human destiny, the true man."[7]

Aided by the social sciences to realize the depth and complexity of the human psyche and to value anew the importance of human interrelationships, theologians are seeking a more dynamic view of human nature than people have come to expect from Christianity. Monika Hellwig, for example, wants to move away from static views of human nature to a definition of the human that speaks of freedom and the ongoing creative process wherein women and men find their true humanity in response to the liberating call of God.[8] Liberation and humanization go hand in hand in what contemporary theology is saying about human nature.

At the same time, hope for human fulfillment has been kept realistic by the tragic lessons of recent history. The way human beings have abused one another over the past decades reminds all thoughtful persons that the old doctrine of original sin is anything but obsolete. Nevertheless, the Christian proclamation of the redemptive power of God's "good news" still shows itself to be effective, often in those places in the world where brutality and oppression are most severe.

To sum up, human nature is sinful, true enough, but God forgives sin when humans repent and return to their creator. The Christian tradition offers a unique kind of hope in the claim that humans can be renewed by being attached to Jesus Christ, the one human being who embodies the fullness of human nature under God. To be fully human, according to

7. Wolfhart Pannenberg, *Jesus — God and Man,* trans. Lewis L. Wilkins and Duane A. Priebe (Philadelphia: Westminster Press, 1968), 345.

8. Monika Hellwig, "Hope and Liberation: The Task of Sexual Complementarity," *Liturgy* (October 1970), quoted in *Readings in Christian Humanism,* ed. Joseph M. Shaw, R. W. Franklin, Harris Kaasa, and Charles W. Buzicky (Minneapolis: Augsburg, 1982), 649.

Christian teaching, involves coming to terms with oneself in relation to God and at the same time expressing one's humanity in relation to other human beings. Human existence is not simply animal existence nor is it solely a spiritual existence, detached from history and society. The human person is a whole being, body, mind, and spirit, whose wholeness is threatened by isolation and oppression. The Christian doctrine of human nature, therefore, seeks to do justice to the human phenomenon in all of its vital relationships, with God, with other humans, with nature, and with history.[9]

The Twentieth-century Liturgical Movement

Unique to the Christian view of human wholeness is the weight it gives to the worship of God. As we described earlier, some forces for the renewal of the humanistic dimensions of worship were already at work in the nineteenth century. In the twentieth century, the clear lines of a single liturgical movement could be detected slowly touching all of the major Christian churches and underlining the centrality of the eucharist as the great meeting place where the believer enters into vital relationships with God, neighbor, nature, and history. The liturgical movement has been marked by its effort to teach women and men to find in prayer a meaningful activity with social implications in the midst of economic hardship. The eucharistic humanism of our century has been a humanism of community in an era when secular humanism revels in individualism and is attracted to the image of the solitary, autonomous hero. In such a civilization, where social bonds have deteriorated, corporate worship is a sign showing how to rebuild a Christian common life in four ways.

The first is a renewed sense of the corporate nature of the church itself, the idea that the parish is the body that can most effectively carry the gospel to the world. A second insight of the liturgical movement is that the local church in its worship must lay hold of human life and form it not only in the abstract realms of theology but also in the concrete realities of marriage, work, sickness, health, leisure, and rest.

A third conviction involves concern for those alienated from the economic order. One thing the church should be able to give is a sense of

9. These developments are summarized in Helmut Thielicke, *Being Human . . . Becoming Human: An Essay in Christian Anthropology*, trans. Geoffrey W. Bromiley (Garden City, N.Y.: Doubleday, 1984).

belonging to a human community; without community there is no Christian hope for the ragged and the naked, the oppressed and the weary. And so a fourth emphasis of the liturgical movement has been that the foundation of Christian community must be the renewal of the full and active participation of the laity in public worship everywhere. A liturgy in which all participate can become a witness to a new Christian humanism that could safeguard the dignity of the individual within the context of a larger community. Against the gray landscape of twentieth-century dehumanization, the breaking of bread can teach in powerfuly symbolic language an end to selfishness and narcissism and the emptiness and frustration that result in withdrawal from others.

By the 1970s the face of Christendom had been transformed by the liturgical movement, suggested by the shift of altars from dark sanctuaries into the midst of actively participating congregations. The voice of Roman Catholicism had changed too, for within its churches mass was being celebrated in the language of the people for the first time in a thousand years. Catholicism has been renewed from the wellspring of the vernacular liturgy. Lutheran churches have found their way back to well-trodden sixteenth-century ground: to give proper standing to sacrament as well as word. Throughout the world the eucharist has supplanted morning prayer and evensong as the chief form of Anglican worship. To the Reformed Churches and the Methodists the liturgical movement has communicated the newfound sense of the corporate nature of the church, demonstrating that by frequent and even weekly celebration of the Lord's Supper, congregations could be built up into active communities of service and love.[10]

The Ecumenical Movement

The aspiration for Christian unity can be traced from New Testament times and has found various expressions at different periods, but it has never been

10. On the humanism of the twentieth-century liturgical movement see R. W. Franklin and Robert L. Spaeth, *Virgil Michel: American Catholic* (Collegeville, Minn.: The Liturgical Press, 1988); Robert L. Spaeth, *The Social Question: Essays on Capitalism and Christianity by Fr. Virgil Michel* (Collegeville, Minn.: St. John's University, 1987); Donald Gray, *Earth and Altar: The Evolution of the Parish Communion in the Church of England to 1945* (Norwick: Alcuin Club, 1986); and J. M. Barkley, "The Liturgical Movement and Reformed Worship," *Church Service Society Annual,* 31 (1961), 13-22.

so potent as in the last half of the twentieth century. Growing doctrinal agreement among the major Christian bodies has been reinforced by liturgical reforms derived from the wider knowledge of early Christian worship, the fruit of the liturgical movement in many churches. The ecumenical network of relationships now established among the world families of churches has the potential for a significant advancement of Christian humanism in our own time.

Perhaps the most prominent example of this is *Baptism, Eucharist and Ministry (BEM),* the ecumenical convergence statement published in 1982 by the Faith and Order Commission of the World Council of Churches. This document is the work of one hundred theologians representing not only the WCC churches but also the Roman Catholic Church; some nonmember evangelicals were also among the authors.

BEM details how Christians are called to convey to the world the image of a new humanity grounded in Jesus Christ; it provides a comprehensive theological defense for understanding the church as a sharing and healing community whose ministry is an extension of the actual power of Christ himself. In this exemplar of the new ecumenical theology, the whole of the church's life is presented as an enlargement and prolongation of what God has done in Christ, and *BEM* links this broadening of the doctrine of the Incarnation in the direction of the whole of humanity to the opening of the borders of the church to embrace all who confess Jesus as Lord. At the societal level the presence of the "Lord of Life" means that all barriers, whether of sex or race — or of Christian denomination — must be transcended.

One of the significant gains for humanism in the churches of the future can be this recognition that Christianity comprises a family of persons from many nations, diverse backgrounds, and all races. The drive for unity has underscored the humanistic insight that God's creative and redemptive work in the world is intended to bring the children of Adam and Eve into one community. How to realize this wider unity of the human family must be one of the church's immediate tasks into the next century.[11]

---

11. *Baptism, Eucharist and Ministry,* Faith and Order Paper No. 111 (Geneva: World Council of Churches, 1982); for analysis of this paper see *The Journal of Ecumenical Studies,* 21 (1984), entire issue devoted to "Baptism, Eucharist and Ministry: Its Reception in the U.S. Churches." See also *And So Set Up Signs . . . : The World Council of Churches' First 40 Years* (Geneva: WCC Publications, 1988) and Ernest W. Lefever, *Nairobi to Vancouver: The World Council of Churches and the World, 1975-1987* (Washington, D.C.: Ethics and Public Policy Center, 1987).

Christian Humanism for a New Day

We have cited a number of signs that Christian humanism may have a fresh opportunity to present its understanding of the human story to receptive minds. The world of the 1990s is a very different one from that of the preceding decades since World War II. And without exaggerating the prospects, we detect a new readiness to consider a Christian interpretation of human life and destiny in the world at large, and a new openness to the tradition of humanism in the churches.

This is certainly the case in the mind of Pope John Paul II, who called for a special synod of the Roman Catholic Church in 1990 to reflect on what the demise of communism, the most militant modern form of secular humanism, means for the future witness of Christianity in Europe and even in the entire world. Will Europe on the eve of the twenty-first century regain its old centrality as the homeland of Christian humanism, master its own inner resources and tensions, and extend a fraternal hand to less privileged parts of the world? Reflecting on building a new order, the pope envisions the church as leading an ideologically divided Europe in the recovery of its common roots in Christian verities and in the *philosophia perennis,* a Europe that will not succumb to what he regards as the West's material excesses and spiritual vacuum as it throws off communism and turns to the task of building a common culture from Ireland to the Urals.[12]

A second opportunity to reassert Christian humanism is in the hands of the Protestant churches in the United States. Politicized antihumanism has been on the attack since 1959 when a Reformed Presbyterian theologian, Rousas J. Rushdoony, published his conclusion that the cause of society's ills was a "humanist conspiracy." The popular conservative apologist Francis Schaeffer helped spread this idea in the 1960s. Following his lead, fundamentalist Baptists such as Jerry Falwell, Tim LaHaye, and others continued the antihumanist harangue into the 1970s. They were joined by charismatics such as Pat Robertson in the 1980s, and the New Christian Right and the Moral Majority were born. The peak of the antihumanist

12. John Paul II's vision of a renewed Christian humanism for a united Europe is outlined in these publications by George H. Williams, *The Law of Nations and the Book of Nature* (Collegeville, Minn.: St. John's University, 1984), *The Contours of Church and State in the Thought of John Paul II* (Waco: Baylor University Press, 1983), and "The Ecumenism of John Paul II," *Journal of Ecumenical Studies,* 19 (1982), 693-96. For an Orthodox view, see Anthony Ugolnik, *The Illuminating Icon* (Grand Rapids: Wm. B. Eerdmans, 1988), and John Meyendorff, *Living Tradition: Orthodox Witness in the Contemporary World* (Crestwood, N.Y.: St. Vladimir's Seminary Press, 1978).

influence of this movement was reached in the mid-1980s, a time when the Moral Majority raised eleven million dollars annually and counted the president of the United States as its man, when a series of court cases in the South singled out humanism as the enemy of such cherished institutions as the home, the public school, and the nation itself.

Through a variety of misfortunes, however, by 1990 the political Christian Right had seen its revenues cut by two-thirds, its political candidate Pat Robertson stopped in the South, and the one threat which had fused the many subsects of the Religious Right into one whole — the fear of the Soviet Union — diminished, leaving the movement without a focus.

Today there could be significant benefits for American society if the chastened leaders of the Christian Right would come to appreciate anew the humanistic dimensions of Protestant Christianity. In the local churches are potent but neglected resources, starting with the people themselves, gathering as a community to worship. There is power for human good in the songs and prayers of the faithful, in the sharing of the bread and the wine. And there is untapped power in the Bible when one rediscovers the humanizing benefit that the old gospel story has for all who will carefully study and attend to its message. It lifts human beings from isolation and despair; it gives them purpose in this life and hope for the life to come. Conservatives have nothing to fear in opening themselves to the humanism based on Christ and the gospel.

The tradition of Christian humanism will not be a set of specific answers for the political, economic, and moral problems that confront Europe and the United States in new circumstances, but it holds before the world a perspective on God, the universe, history, and the human spirit that can guide our contemporaries in their search for meaning amidst a changed world order. At the heart of Christian humanism, now as yesterday, is the conviction, supported by centuries of experience in the lives of men and women of all cultures and races, that the fullest realization of what it means to be human can be known through personal communion with Jesus Christ, the Word of God who entered the arena of human life to bring wholeness and freedom to every human being.[13]

13. These developments are detailed and these possibilities are analyzed further in Frederick Edwards and Stephen McCabe, "Getting out God's Vote: Pat Robertson and the Evangelicals," *The Humanist* (May-June 1987), 5-10; Leo P. Ribuffo, *The Old Christian Right* (Philadelphia: Temple University Press, 1983); Carol Flake, *Redemptorama: Culture, Politics, and the New Evangelicalism* (Garden City, N.Y.: Doubleday, 1984); "Judgment in the United States District Court for the Southern District of Alabama, Southern Division" (March 4, 1987), 1-103; Sherryl Kleinman, *Equals Before God: Seminarians as Humanistic Professionals* (Chicago: University of Chicago Press, 1984).

PART II

BEGINNING WITH THE BIBLE

Chapter 4

Humanism in the Hebrew Bible

The primary source of Christian humanism is the gospel, or good news, about Jesus Christ: his life, sufferings, death, resurrection, and lordship. The Christians of the first century instinctively turned to the Hebrew Bible, or to its Greek translation, the Septuagint, in order to understand the full significance of Jesus in continuity with God's redemptive activity in the life of Israel. The coming of Jesus, they believed, was the climactic event in the long history of God's plan to save the world. Now God had visited Israel and the rest of humanity in the form of a man, Jesus of Nazareth, whom they confessed as Son of God.

By searching the Scriptures for light on the figure of Jesus, the first-century Christians, most of whom were Jews by birth, also reinforced their knowledge of what their Bible taught them about human beings in relation to God. The purpose of this chapter is to identify and discuss several humanistic motifs that Christian thought absorbed from the Hebrew Scriptures. First are some observations on what Christian use of the Hebrew Bible implies for Christian humanism and on the human side of the Bible.

Christian and Jewish Humanism

The fact that the first Christians adopted an already existing Hebrew Scripture, later called the "Old Testament," has five important implications for Christian humanism. In the first place, Christians thereby inherited a vigorous Jewish humanism which they could apply, without much alteration, to their own understanding of the human situation under God. For example, the key idea that human beings are created in the image of God was intrinsic to Christian teaching from the outset. Similarly, Jesus' command to love God above all things and the neighbor as oneself are teachings directly traced to passages in Deuteronomy 6:5 and Leviticus 19:18.

A second implication of Christian use of the Old Testament is that Christians and Jews became partners in offering the world a noble humanism made luminous by the power of divine *grace*. The special mark of Jewish-Christian biblical humanism is the revelation that human beings have to do with a *merciful* God. In the words of the Psalmist, "the LORD is merciful and gracious, slow to anger and abounding in steadfast love" (Psalm 103:8). Too often people assume that the Hebrew Bible is ignorant of grace and that the God of the Old Testament is so stern that human beings can only shrink away in guilt and terror. To both Jews and Christians there is only one God; this God is gracious, eagerly disposed to forgive and restore God's children when they go astray.

The third implication is that Christians have learned from the Jewish Scriptures that the Bible's message is about God, God's thoughts, words, and deeds, all of which point to human salvation. The great Protestant theologian Karl Barth stated this basic idea as follows:

> It is not the right human thoughts about God which form the content of the Bible, but the right divine thoughts about men. The Bible tells us not how we should talk with God but what he says to us; not how we find the way to him, but how he has sought and found the way to us.[1]

Although Christians developed a theology that diverged from Judaism on many points, by adopting the Jewish Bible as part of their authoritative Scripture they joined the Jews in making the living God and divine activity *the starting point* of all thinking about humanity. Biblical humanism, Jewish and Christian, insists that the clue to the meaning of human existence is not

---

1. Karl Barth, *The Word of God and the Word of Man* (New York: Harper & Row, 1957), 43.

the human phenomenon itself, as an object for detached scrutiny, but the living God, the Creator and Redeemer of the human race.

Christian inclusion of the Jewish Scripture as sacred and authoritative literature has a fourth implication for Christian humanism, namely, that ancient Israel understood God as one whose will is revealed to humanity *through particular events in history.* Through such events as the exodus, the giving of the covenant, the settling of the people of Israel in Canaan, and the founding of the Davidic kingdom, Bible readers see God at work revealing the saving power and redemptive purposes intended for all of humankind.

A fifth implication of Christian use of the Old Testament is the prominence of *the idea of a special, holy community* in both Judaism and Christianity. The Christian concept of the church has its roots in the Hebrew Bible's concentration on the chosen people of God. Christianity reinterpreted the venerable concept of "the people of God" by putting Jesus Christ at its center, but it continues to share with Judaism the fundamental idea that God's saving work in this world centers in the creation of a people and the leading and sustaining of that people through the challenges and changes of history.[2] Christian humanism affirms this biblical emphasis on the community of faith as one of the uniquely important insights into what it means to be human.

The Human Side of the Bible

The Bible is the Word of God, a divine message announcing God's love for humankind. As Barth said, the content of the Bible is not human thoughts about God but divine thoughts about humans, not how we find the way to God but about how God finds the way to us. Yet there is a human side to the biblical revelation, not in any way opposed to the priority of God's activity, but simply the responding participation on the part of humans in the saving process God sets in motion. The Christian community has always been aware of this human aspect, but has hesitated to say it too loudly lest the divine nature of the Bible seem to be put in jeopardy.

We can see this human side from at least three angles. First, the very purpose of God's self-revelation is *to benefit humanity.* The God of heaven and earth is at work in this world to liberate humanity from

2. See Joseph M. Shaw, *The Pilgrim People of God* (Minneapolis: Augsburg, 1990), 1-10.

everything that stands in the way of the fulfillment God intended. God is indeed the prime actor, but the human community is the prime recipient of divine revelation.

Second, the human community is asked to serve God by *communicating the revelation of God's love.* When God speaks to an individual such as Abraham, Moses, or Jeremiah, these persons are expected and even ordered to tell others what God has said. "Go and tell" is the believer's commission in both Old and New Testaments. Eventually the Bible as a book came into being, the direct result of human beings telling the good news of God and redemption.

A third angle from which one sees the human side of the Bible is the active *human participation in the very formation and interpretation* of the divinely given message. Human persons are not only recipients and trans-mitters of God's Word; they also play a role, in response to the inspiration of the Holy Spirit, in giving shape to the Word. They are not merely passive conduits through which the divine Word passes on its way to eventual printed form. Rather, they are active, conscious participants in fashioning the message God is sending out to the whole world. The traditional view that the Holy Spirit inspired the writing of the Bible substantiates the notion of human involvement, for the Holy Spirit is uniquely God interacting creatively with the human spirit.

Isaiah and Jeremiah used all the human wit and courage they could muster in order to understand and announce the will of God in times of national turmoil and impending invasion. Anonymous poets and singers applied their own talents, with God's help, in composing the beautiful songs in the Psalter. The apostle Paul, using his intelligence and assisted by the Spirit, thought through and explained to others the profound significance of the coming of Christ. At every stage, human persons are directly and responsibly involved in formulating and interpreting the essential message of the Bible.

Humanistic Motifs in the Old Testament

Created in God's Image

Then God said, "Let us make humankind in our image, according to our likeness; and let them have dominion over the fish of the sea, and over the birds of the air, and over the cattle. . . ." So God created humankind in his image, in the image of God he created them; male and female he created them. (Genesis 1:26-27)

The word once translated "man" in this famous text means "human being" or "humankind." God creates humans in God's image, after God's likeness. In the ancient world the image of the king was on display out in the provinces to remind the people who their ruler was. Similarly, the human species reflects and displays the reality of God to the rest of the created order. The human person is like God yet different from God, possessing the image of God yet not being on God's level.

To be human is to be distinct from God and distinct from the animal world. Humans are set apart by such gifts as self-consciousness, speech, and reason, but the most important distinction is the image of God, which means above all the capacity to enjoy a conscious, responding relationship with God. Humans have a special nature because, bearing God's image, they can respond to God's personal call. Being called they are summoned, in their "vocation," to fulfill their human creaturehood, to be what God created them to be, dependent on God, obedient to God, and free to choose between alternative courses of action.

Their dignity is symbolized by their delegated dominion over the other creatures and over the earth. They are not owners and lords, but stewards over God's creation. An important facet of human dignity is responsibility, carrying with it the risk of making wrong choices, of failing to fulfill their stewardship, and of falling short of their destiny of reaching fulfillment within the bounds of their creaturehood. The commands to be fruitful and multiply and exercise dominion indicate that these human creatures have the capacity to respond to God's Word.

The two creation stories in Genesis 1 and 2 supplement each other in portraying God's creative action and human reactions. Genesis 2 uses the picture of God planting a garden and creating "a living being" to be the gardener. Where God's word in Genesis 1 is the word of creation and command, in Genesis 2 it specifically includes the prohibition against eating of the tree of the knowledge of good and evil. From Genesis 1 it is clear that the full definition of human being must encompass both male and female. In Genesis 2 the man and the woman are given to each other for human companionship, and together they face a moral decision regarding the forbidden tree: "of the tree of the knowledge of good and evil you shall not eat, for in the day that you eat of it you shall die" (2:17).

Human responsibility is thus seen in the creation stories as both restrictive, "you shall not eat" of that particular tree, and positive or creative, "be fruitful, multiply, have dominion." A symbol of the humans' special role as God's stewards and co-creators is the privilege of naming the birds and the beasts. Responsibility involves multiple relationships: with God, with each other (man and woman), and with nature. When the first sin takes place it damages the relationship with God, causes estrangement between man and woman, and upsets the harmony between humanity and nature.

But the overall impact of the creation stories is to impress upon the hearer and reader the goodness of God and the wonder of the creation, with human beings clearly given the highest place of honor. According to the Bible, to be human is to be created in the image of God. The words of Psalm 8 are an appropriate commentary on this fundamental motif:

> What are human beings that you are mindful of them,
>   mortals that you care for them?
> Yet you have made them a little lower than God,
>   and crowned them with glory and honor. (Psalm 8:4)

Liberation

You have seen what I did to the Egyptians, and how I bore you on eagles' wings and brought you to myself. (Exodus 19:4)

Where the opening of Genesis affirms that to be human is to be created in the image of God, the story of the exodus teaches that to be human is to be free. God's deliverance of the children of Israel from bondage in Egypt has outgrown its old Sunday school status as one miracle story among many; rather, it has emerged in modern study as a major theme of the Bible. Guided by how the exodus motif is continually referred to in other parts of the Hebrew Scripture, scholars now regard the exodus as the central redemptive event in the entire history of ancient Israel.

The liberation motif has assumed particular importance in the contemporary world for people living under oppressive governments, as in many Latin American countries. "Liberation theology" leans heavily upon the exodus as biblical evidence that God is working to bring about human liberation in the fullest sense: economically, politically, and spiritually.

Robert McAfee Brown says that Christians in the Third World are freeing the revolutionary biblical message so that once again it can communicate liberation from oppression.[3]

In his important book *A Theology of Liberation,* the Peruvian priest and scholar Gustavo Gutiérrez indicates how liberation theology consciously aims at binding liberation and humanization together.

> The liberation of our continent means more than overcoming economic, social, and political dependence. It means, in a deeper sense, to see the becoming of mankind as a process of the emancipation of man in history. It is to see man in search of a qualitatively different society in which he will be free from all servitude, in which he will be the artisan of his own destiny. It is to seek the building up of *a new man*.[4]

As experienced in Latin American countries, by African Americans in the United States, by the women's movement, and by other human struggles in our time, the drive toward liberation always means that the oppressed themselves must go through a transformation; they must throw off the mentality of the slave and develop a new self-image of free persons.

Recent developments in eastern Europe and South Africa tell us that through long years of oppression there still remained alive spiritual resources of hope that reminded the oppressed that their destiny as human beings was freedom. Today's liberation movements invariably are fueled by a deep sense that servitude and oppression are wrong because they prevent persons from realizing their proper humanity. For liberation to occur there must be a conviction within the hearts of the downtrodden that to be human is to be free.

The motif of liberation embraces both political and spiritual freedom. Liberation theologians are fully aware that sin and selfishness lie at the root of oppression, and therefore they look to the liberating message of the Bible to deal with sin, guilt, and forgiveness as well as the empirical dimensions of freedom. People living in affluent countries where political freedom may seem secure are just as much in need of liberation as the oppressed in the Third World, because affluence and comfort may also hinder the human spirit from realizing its intended freedom.

3. Robert McAfee Brown, *Creative Dislocation: The Movement of Grace, Journeys in Faith,* ed. Robert A. Raines (Nashville: Abingdon, 1980), 129.
4. Gustavo Gutiérrez, *A Theology of Liberation,* trans. and ed. Sister Caridad Inda and John Eagleson (Maryknoll, N.Y.: Orbis Books, 1973), 91.

Community

Now therefore, if you obey my voice and keep my covenant, you shall be my treasured possession out of all peoples. Indeed, the whole earth is mine, but you shall be for me a priestly kingdom and a holy nation. (Exodus 19:5-6)

This motif implies that to be human is to live in community with others. The Bible's earliest model for the human community is the covenant community of ancient Israel. Modern misgivings about the idea of a "chosen people," whether based on overt anti-Semitism or on liberal democratic ideals, fail to recognize the humanistic value of the covenant community. The Jews, and for that matter their Arab neighbors as well, long ago learned from their own religious teachings that human beings are made to enjoy social relationships and that the isolation of an individual from the community is a fate to be avoided. "Loneliness, the lack of community, the Old Testament only knows as something unnatural," writes Johannes Pedersen, "an expression that life is failing." On the contrary, Pedersen continues, "Community is found wherever the blessing is, community being a common participation of blessing."[5] The Psalmist expresses the value of community in these words, "Happy is the nation whose God is the LORD, the people whom he has chosen as his heritage" (Psalm 33:12).

The Bible does not take the community for granted; it takes effort to maintain harmony among the members within the covenant that binds the entire community to its God. Even so, the humanism of the Bible assumes the community as a given, whereas modern culture thinks the individual is the given and thus regards the community as a task to be achieved.[6] One reason that modern Western culture is so individualistic is that the only model of community known to many is that of a totalitarian communistic society, which is obviously undesirable. Sadly and ironically, the synagogue and the church, which ought to provide good models and experiences of human community, often do not play their rightful role because their own membership has not fully understood and entered into the biblical principle of community.

5. Johannes Pedersen, *Israel I-II,* trans. Aslaug Moeller (London: Oxford University Press, 1926), 263.

6. Two contemporary calls for return to community are books by Wendell Berry: *Remembering* (San Francisco: North Point Press, 1989), and *The Hidden Wound* (San Francisco: North Point Press, 1989).

That principle, stated briefly, is that God has so arranged things among human creatures that fullness of life and God's blessing are best realized in a community of persons. In the creation stories, the only thing specified as "not good" is to be alone (Genesis 2:18). In giving the covenant to the chosen people, God has a dual purpose. First God enjoins obedience to the covenant so that the community will realize the strength and blessing of God in its internal life. Second, as the creator of the whole earth, God forms a special people to serve God and all of humanity as "a priestly kingdom and a holy nation." In other words, the community needs inner integrity and health if it is to fulfill its outward mission to the world.

Christian humanism does not claim that everything from the covenant community of the Bible can or should be carried over into modern society, but it promises that people will experience greater wholeness in their lives when they recognize that God works in the world by establishing a special community to praise God's holy name and to serve human needs. From the great prophets of Israel and Judah has come the enduring principle that a nation that practices injustice toward the poor and helpless thereby weakens itself to the point where it cannot fulfill its servant task to the rest of humanity.[7]

The biblical idea of community offers a distinctive treasure to all who are searching for a healthy humanism. All too often the social or communal dimension is left out of consideration in discussions of what it means to be human. The old individualism perpetuates the view that full personhood means complete autonomy and independence from others. The good news of the Bible is that human beings actually gain in selfhood as they participate in community. Paul Hanson finds in Jeremiah and Ezekiel "a clarification of the biblical notion of community as one in which the individual finds full personhood not through self-indulgent personalism, but by becoming an unstinting contributor to the vitality of the whole people."[8] Membership in a body of persons enhances rather than restricts the unfolding of the personality. Moreover, membership in the family of God brings one into a fellowship of mutual love and service, and with it the privilege of communicating the love of God to the whole of humankind.

7. Paul D. Hanson, *The People Called: The Growth of Community in the Bible* (San Francisco: Harper & Row, 1987). For Hanson's discussion of the work of some of the great prophets, see 148-59 (Amos), 158-67 (Hosea), 181-208 (Isaiah and Jeremiah), and 241-49 for the Suffering Servant of Second Isaiah.

8. Hanson, 208.

Prophecy: Judgment and Hope

He has showed you, O mortal, what is good;
and what does the LORD require of you
but to do justice, and to love kindness,
and to walk humbly with your God? (Micah 6:8)

On the surface, the very idea of judgment seems harsh — hardly a positive component of hopeful humanism. Nevertheless, it is actually part of God's compassionate concern for all people. To remain unjudged would be a greater disaster because it would mean being outside the range of God's word. The prophet Amos warned that the days were coming when God would send a famine on the land, not a famine of bread nor thirst for water, "but of hearing the words of the LORD." People would run to and fro across the earth, seeking the word of the Lord but not finding it (Amos 8:11-12).

Hebrew prophecy says much about God's chastisement of a disobedient people, but the underlying premise is God's continuing faithfulness to the covenant. "You only have I known of all the families of the earth; therefore I will punish you for all your iniquities" (Amos 3:2). The prophets exposed the sins of idolatry and injustice and called the people to repentance and renewed faith. If breaches of the covenant went uncorrected, the consequence was judgment meted out in actual history. The northern kingdom of Israel fell to the Assyrians in 721 B.C. and Judah, the southern kingdom, succumbed to the Babylonians in 586 B.C.

It seemed as if the prophetic preaching had failed, and in the outward sense it had, since no significant national repentance occurred to stave off the collapse of the two small kingdoms. On the other hand, the prophets had fostered a hope which, during and following the exile, kept alive faith in God and the sense of community. The fact that the people in exile preserved and collected the prophetic oracles and made them a permanent part of the life of the restored community indicates that the prophets had not spoken in vain. Through Judaism the whole world heard of a God who judges in order to save. The citation from Micah has always been recognized as giving a universal scope to the divine requirements: to practice justice, to love kindness, and to walk humbly in the company of God.

Israel and Judah were judged because they had gone against the covenant by worshipping other gods, relying on political might, and allowing social injustice to go unchecked in their society. Miraculously, however, the implementation of judgment created new flames of hope. Had Israel been simply a "secular" community, it would have given up when its national structures collapsed, but faith in God gave it a tenacious grip on the future. Had it pinned its hopes on a "pro-Israel moral majority" it would not have survived, because the majority was not notably moral. It was a believing minority that discerned the hope embodied in the prophets' message and kept it alive through the dark times of national judgment. In a letter to the exiles in Babylon Jeremiah wrote, "For I know the plans I have for you, says the LORD, plans for welfare and not for evil, to give you a future and a hope" (Jeremiah 29:11).

What the prophetic preaching of judgment and hope contributes to humanism is, first, the realization that being human means being accountable to God, and second, that one lives in the expectation that God can use even disaster to further the redemptive purpose. The history of Israel and Judah reveals that the God of the covenant does not abandon the people, but suffers with them through the turmoils of defeat, enabling them to fulfill their calling in the world. From this history the rest of humankind learns that the God of the Bible is trustworthy; God's care for the chosen people signifies a larger concern for the entire human family.

Affirming the Future

There is hope for your future, says the LORD: your children shall come back to their own country. (Jeremiah 31:17)

See, the former things have come to pass, and new things I now declare. (Isaiah 42:9)

The God of the Bible affirms human beings in their sufferings by giving them courage to claim the future. Everything had pointed to Israel's sure disappearance from history: the end of the royal house, the loss of the temple, the ruin of the capital city, and the scattering of the population. Yet the people survived because hope survived; in exile Israel remembered its election, its covenant with God, its commitment to God's holy law, and the prophetic promises.

Hope born of faith enabled the people to put content into their vision of the future. One striking example of claiming the future was the order given to Jeremiah while he was a prisoner in the king's palace in Jerusalem. At that very moment the Babylonian army was besieging the city. The word of the Lord to Jeremiah was to buy a field belonging to his uncle. He carried out the purchase; the deed was signed and the money paid in the presence of witnesses. Said Jeremiah to his cousin, his scribe, and the other onlookers: "For thus says the LORD of hosts, the God of Israel: Houses and fields and vineyards shall again be bought in this land" (Jeremiah 32:15).

It was Jeremiah who prophesied the new covenant with the house of Israel and the house of Judah. It would be unlike the covenant that had been broken. It provided for writing the law upon the hearts of the people, that is, at the very center of their beings where both will and emotions were concentrated. It reiterated the ancient promise of election: "I will be their God, and they shall be my people" (Jeremiah 31:33). It also pointed to a new depth of personal knowledge of the Lord, a knowledge marked by the closest intimacy. Finally, the new covenant included a fresh promise of forgiveness (Jeremiah 31:31-34).

In the same prophetic milieu one finds Ezekiel's strange but hopeful vision of the dry bones that come to life, a sign that God will raise up the people and bring them home from exile. Ezekiel also promises, in an interesting reflection of the creation story, that God will put the Spirit within the people and they will live (Ezekiel 37:11-14).

The most eloquent prophet of the exile, whose oracles appear in the latter part of the book of Isaiah, produced a number of songs or poems in which the central figure is "The Servant of the Lord." The first of the Servant songs (Isaiah 42:1-4) states: "Behold my servant, whom I uphold, my chosen, in whom my soul delights; I have put my Spirit upon him, and he will bring forth justice to the nations" (42:1). The other songs (49:1-6; 50:4-9; 52:13–53:12) bring out other functions of the Servant. He will restore Israel, but he will also be a light to the nations. He is a teacher who has been taught, obedient to the Lord and steadfast despite persecution and shame. Finally, the Servant is a startling sight to the nations: one who is despised and rejected by men, one who bears the griefs and carries the sorrows of others, a lamb led to slaughter who pours out his soul to death.

Who is the Servant? One text explicitly identifies him as Israel (Isaiah 49:3; cf. 41:8). Later in the same song the Servant is instrumental in the restoration of Israel, but he is told that a further task awaits: "I will

give you as a light to the nations, that my salvation may reach to the end
of the earth" (Isaiah 49:6). Elsewhere the Bible can set forth a single figure
who represents the community, as when Jacob the patriarch becomes Israel
and Esau is Edom. The Servant may be an individual person who in one
role helps Israel to become its true, servant self, and in another role *is* Israel
as God's light to the nations.

In any case, whether individual or community, a particular person
or the restored nation Israel, the Servant of the Lord in the Isaiah texts is
part of the human order and not a divine being. Even when Christian
interpretation sees in certain descriptions of the Servant the foreshadowing
of the sufferings of Jesus, it clearly has in mind Jesus' human experiences.
For any reader of the Hebrew Scriptures it is striking that the culminating
point of the prophetic tradition and the most profound interpretation of
Israel's role in history come to focus on the figure of a humble, suffering
Servant given by God as a light to the nations.

Through the calling of this Servant, God lays claim to the future.
The Servant's various tasks are human activities: establishing justice, teaching, sustaining the weary with a word, accepting shame and being spat
upon, looking to God for vindication, being despised and rejected, bearing
the sin of many, and making intercessions for the transgressors. A strong
element of mystery surrounds the Servant; it does not seem possible to fix
his identity once and for all. Yet everything about him is consistent with
the basic biblical conviction that God works out the divine will in human
history through the faith, obedience, and suffering of chosen servants.
Those who meditate on the Servant of the Lord instinctively understand
that the most authentic road to the future is the way of the servant.

The Quest for Wisdom

The fear of the LORD is the beginning of wisdom,
and the knowledge of the Holy One is insight. (Proverbs 9:10)

Proverbs, Ecclesiastes, the Song of Solomon, and the book of Job make up
the "wisdom literature" of the canonical Hebrew Bible. Other wisdom
books, included in the so-called "Apocrypha," are the Wisdom of Solomon
and Ecclesiasticus, or the Wisdom of Jesus the Son of Sirach. In one sense,
these wisdom books are the most "humanistic" parts of the Bible and its

related literature, for in them the authors address the concrete issues of ordinary human existence. Moreover, much of the wisdom literature is also "humanistic" in a secular sense. That is, there are teachings, especially in the book of Proverbs, that are based primarily on accumulated human experience, not on divine revelation. It requires no divine insight, for example, to advise "Go to the ant, O sluggard; consider her ways, and be wise" (Proverbs 7:6). Wisdom of this sort was the common property of various ancient cultures.

According to the usual definition, wisdom is the quality of being able to make sound judgments about life and conduct. But the wisdom of the Old Testament goes beyond proverbial sayings and aphorisms. Its hallmark is the recognition of God as Lord and the source of all wisdom. If "the fear of the LORD is the beginning of wisdom, and the knowledge of the Holy One is insight" (Proverbs 9:10), the wisdom in question can be known by humans, but its distinctive character is that it rests on the experience of a personal relationship with God. "Knowledge" in the biblical sense is primarily relational and experiential rather than intellectual, the "knowing" of God in the intimacy of trust and friendship.

Besides defining wisdom as the fear of the Lord, ancient Israel developed the concept of wisdom on two further levels. First, it personified wisdom and construed it as being present with God at the dawn of creation. "The LORD created me [Wisdom] at the beginning of his work, the first of his acts of long ago. Ages ago I was set up, at the first, before the beginning of the earth" (Proverbs 8:22-23). In this sense, wisdom is associated with creation and is a connecting link with the human community, "rejoicing in his inhabited world and delighting in the human race" (Proverbs 8:31).

A second and deeper level of wisdom appears in Ecclesiastes and Job. In these books the writers actually call conventional wisdom into question. Ecclesiastes pays its respects to wisdom by including maxims, but the reader learns not to count too heavily on wisdom of this proverbial kind because life is full of ironies and disappointments. A poor wise man delivered a city by his wisdom, reports the author, but no one remembers him (Ecclesiastes 9:15). Wisdom is not a panacea. It is worth pursuing, yet one should know that "in much wisdom is much vexation" (Ecclesiastes 1:18).

The book of Job shows the full profundity of the wisdom tradition in Israel. In one of his speeches Job asks where wisdom can be found, and he answers in totally nontraditional terms. Humans do not know the way to it; it is not in the deep, in the sea; it cannot be had for gold or precious stones. It is hid from the eyes of all living. Only God understands the way to wisdom; it is God's alone (Job 28:12-27).

Through the anguish of personal tragedy, Job adds a unique dimension to religious humanism. He speaks for all sufferers and questioners who are not satisfied with the familiar answers of a confident piety. Job is the man of faith who stoutly asserts his integrity before God, despite the earnest exhorting of friends that he should confess his sins. Job's unwavering concentration on the issue that he has a right to lay his case before God (Job 23:4) eventually gains a response from the Almighty, who addresses Job, significantly, as a man. "Gird up your loins like a man, I will question you, and you shall declare to me" (Job 38:2).

Finally Job acknowledges that he, as a human being, remains on the level of human creature, having experienced in a profound revelation that God is God. At its deepest level, wisdom is the acknowledgment, in the midst of pain and the lack of clear answers to troubling questions, that humans can come to terms with existence by accepting their creaturely status. Israel's wisdom teaching thus completes the circle of the humanism of the Hebrew Bible. To be human is to seek wisdom, and to know wisdom is to learn through personal experience that humans are made in the image of God.

Another part of the Old Testament that is endlessly rich in humanistic teaching need only be mentioned since it is so familiar. The book of Psalms is loved by all Bible readers because its contents pour forth from the deep wells of human experience. Persons who have known sorrow, loneliness, persecution by enemies, despair, and other pains have found comfort and assurance in the Psalter (cf. Psalms 32, 51, 72). Similarly, persons eager to rejoice in God and in the wonder of divine mercy instinctively resort to the language of the Psalms to express themselves (cf. Psalms 145, 148).

In the book of Psalms appears a remarkable "humanistic" passage referred to earlier in these pages, a statement that tells the inhabitants of the earth that God has presented humankind with an exhilarating but sobering sphere of responsibility. "The heavens are the LORD's heavens," says the psalmist, "but the earth he has given to human beings" (Psalm 115:16).

The idea that the Old Testament is rich with humanism will appear strange to those who are not acquainted with that literature. But the first Christians gained much of their sense of how God's grace raised the level of human existence from their reading of the Hebrew Scriptures. In our own day, Christian humanism is informed and enriched by the insights of the Old Testament.

Chapter 5

Jesus, the Man of God's Own Choosing

The aim of this chapter is to examine features of the life and ministry of Jesus insofar as they shed light on the meaning of Christian humanism. At the heart of Christian humanism stands the Incarnation of the divine Word in the living, historical actuality of Jesus. The clear Gospel basis for this statement is John 1:14: "And the Word became flesh and lived among us, and we have seen his glory."

Augustine and other early church fathers returned often to this text because it taught them that the flesh of the man Jesus was the true image of God and the means for the renewal of that image among human beings. Although humankind had fallen, the image of God in which it had been created had not been lost completely. There is a point of contact between human nature and the Logos which became flesh in the human nature of Jesus. Discussing these important matters in his book *Jesus through the Centuries*, Jaroslav Pelikan comments: "Jesus was, then, not only the image of divinity, but the image of humanity as it had originally been intended to be and as through him it could now become; he was in this sense the 'ideal man.' "[1]

---

1. Jaroslav Pelikan, *Jesus through the Centuries: His Place in the History of Culture* (New Haven: Yale University Press, 1985), 74. This popular book can be read with much profit for its erudite description of how Jesus has been understood and portrayed in various ages and cultures. The material cited is from chap. 6, "The Son of Man."

In looking at the figure of Jesus, we need to include his entire earthly ministry, culminating in the cross and resurrection, and not limit the discussion to something like the Sermon on the Mount, which some might regard as presenting humanistic teachings in an obvious way. Modern biblical scholars agree that the suffering, death, and resurrection of Jesus are of a piece with the rest of his life and teachings.[2] His impact on human history as the man of God's own choosing was the result of his complete commitment to the will and purpose of God, and that commitment led finally to his being rejected by human contemporaries and being vindicated by divine power.

The Birth of Jesus

In the Gospel stories of the birth of Jesus, the evangelists Matthew and Luke leave no doubt that the central person is God's chosen one, the Lord, the Christ, the Son of the Most High. They surround the narratives with prophecies and angelic visits. At the same time and in a completely natural way, they point up the full humanness of Jesus' birth.[3]

About two hundred years after the birth of Jesus, Tertullian, a learned convert to Christianity from paganism, took the heretic Marcion to task for teaching a Docetic version of Christ. The Docetists tried to deny the reality of Christ's flesh and sufferings. They claimed that he only "seemed" (the Greek word *dokeo* means to "seem" or "appear to be") to share in such unmistakably earthly experiences as birth, circumcision, sufferings, and crucifixion.

Tertullian, rightly understanding that salvation depends on a Christ who knew human experience firsthand, vigorously chides Marcion by discussing graphically "the generative elements within the womb," the con-

---

2. John Reumann, *Jesus in the Church's Gospels: Modern Scholarship and the Earliest Sources* (Philadelphia: Fortress Press, 1968), 45. See also Günther Bornkamm, *Jesus of Nazareth,* trans. Irene and Fraser McLuskey with James M. Robinson (New York: Harper & Row, 1975).

3. In his book *The Birth of the Messiah: A Commentary on the Infancy Narratives in Matthew and Luke* (Garden City, N.Y.: Doubleday, 1977), 25, Raymond E. Brown writes concerning the infancy narratives: "On the one hand they leave no doubt that Jesus was the Son of God from the moment of his conception; on the other hand the portrayal of physical birth (plus the Lucan reference to the manger) has underlined the true humanity of Jesus' origins."

cretion "of fluid and blood," and the nine long months of growth. He taunts Marcion, inviting him to declaim against the nativity all he wishes, and then asks, "And yet, in what way were you born?"[4]

In another place, Tertullian attacks Marcion's rejection of Christ's human life on earth and crucifixion in these uncompromising words:

> The Son of God was crucified; I am not ashamed because men must needs be ashamed of it. And the Son of God died. . . . And He was buried. . . . I mean this flesh suffused with blood, built up with bones, interwoven with nerves, entwined with veins, a *flesh* which knew how to die, human without doubt, as born of a human being.[5]

The Gospel accounts of Jesus' birth obviously serve the purpose of announcing that this little child has a unique relationship to God and a special saving mission to the human race. "You shall call his name Jesus, for he will save his people from their sins" (Matthew 1:21). They also drive home the truth that Jesus is completely associated with the human race. The ancient world had no shortage of reports of gods appearing on earth, but it was completely novel to announce that one sent from God had appeared among human beings in the form of a little boy born into a certain family circle well known to a particular village.

Jesus and His Family

The Gospels of Matthew, Mark, and Luke all contain features that realistically show Jesus in family relationships.[6] The opening of Matthew's Gospel is a genealogy tracing the lineage of Jesus from Abraham to David and to "Joseph the husband of Mary, of whom Jesus was born" (Matthew 1:16). The fact that women are mentioned in Matthew's genealogy is somewhat surprising since Luke, whose Gospel is noted for the prominence given to women in the story, does not mention any women in his genealogy.

In chapter 13 of Matthew's Gospel the reader is told that Jesus had

4. Tertullian, *Against Praxeas*, chap. 4, quoted in *Readings in Christian Humanism*, ed. Joseph M. Shaw, R. W. Franklin, Harris Kaasa, and Charles W. Buzicky (Minneapolis: Augsburg, 1982), 95.

5. Ibid., chap. 5, quoted in *Readings in Christian Humanism*, 97-98.

6. Bornkamm, *Jesus of Nazareth*, 53-54.

brothers, named James, Joseph, Simon, and Judas, and sisters (Matthew 13:55-56). This is not the place to resolve the difference between Protestants, who see no problem in Mary's having other children after Jesus, and Roman Catholics, who regard the brothers and sisters as relatives, cousins perhaps, but not siblings of Jesus. The point here is that the Gospels place Jesus within a family setting.

On the whole, Mark's Gospel shows little interest in the human relationships of Jesus, but Mark does lend a very realistic touch when he relates that members of Jesus' own family felt constrained to intervene when the crowds sought out Jesus. "He has gone out of his mind," they said, alarmed at what seemed his excessive or even dangerous abandonment to the demands of the people who had followed him to his home.

Later in the chapter Mark records that Jesus' mother and brothers try to get a message to Jesus as he is surrounded by listeners. His response is a statement that sheds new light on family relationships. Looking around on those gathered about him, Jesus declares: "Here are my mother and my brothers! Whoever does the will of God is my brother and sister and mother" (Mark 3:34-35).[7] Obedience to the will of God entitles anyone to claim family kinship with Jesus.

Luke's Gospel in particular savors the close human ties that Jesus enjoyed with his earthly family. The matchless story of Jesus' birth in Bethlehem has captured the hearts of all generations. Following the Christmas story is the account of Jesus' presentation in the temple, where Simeon and Anna bless God for the child. To Luke also the reader is indebted for the report about Jesus coming to the temple with his parents at the age of twelve for the feast of the Passover.

Luke alone mentions Jesus' growth as a young boy. "The child grew and became strong, filled with wisdom; and the favor of God was upon him" (Luke 2:40). A bit later Luke offers this comment: "Then he went down with them and came to Nazareth, and was obedient to them. His mother treasured all these things in her heart. And Jesus increased in wisdom and in years, and in divine and human favor" (Luke 2:51-52).

Such statements speak for themselves in making unmistakable Jesus' close participation in the life of his family. They are also in harmony with the intention of Luke's genealogy, which is not only to show that

7. But Jesus is also misunderstood and even rejected by members of his family, according to Paul J. Achtemeier, *Mark: Proclamation Commentaries,* ed. Gerhard Krodel (Philadelphia: Fortress Press, 1975), 32-33.

Jesus had a Jewish family tree but to go a step further than Matthew in connecting Jesus with the whole of humanity. The genealogy mentions David and Abraham, but continues all the way back to Adam to signify that Jesus is the new Adam, the head of a new humanity.[8] Writes Howard Clark Kee, "It is obvious Luke wants his readers to know that Jesus is the *world's* redeemer, not merely the deliverer of Israel."[9]

The Temptation of Jesus

Those who are charmed by the birth and infancy stories of Jesus often limit their belief in his authentic humanity to the earliest stage of his life on earth. When faced with the accounts of Jesus' temptation, they tend to focus solely on Jesus' divine power in resisting the devil, forgetting that Jesus "learned obedience through what he suffered" (Hebrews 5:8). Another sentence in the Letter to the Hebrews specifically mentions the temptation of Jesus: "For because he himself has suffered and been tempted, he is able to help those who are tempted" (Hebrews 2:18).

Matthew and Luke present the temptation of Jesus in three distinct episodes, while Mark has this rather brief summary: "And he was in the wilderness forty days, tempted by Satan" (Mark 1:13). The forty days, mentioned by all three synoptic writers and recalling the forty years Israel spent in the wilderness after the exodus, suggest that the historical experience of Israel is being recapitulated in the life of Jesus.[10] All three follow the temptation in the wilderness with the beginning of Jesus' public ministry. Through the testing Jesus clarified his personal vocation, setting the direction in which faithfulness to God's call would take him.

In two of the temptation episodes, the enemy introduces his offer with the words "If you are the Son of God," thus putting pressure on Jesus to use his status as Son of God to win bodily sustenance by changing stones to bread, and to win fame as an extraordinary miracle worker by throwing himself from the pinnacle of the temple. But in the third instance, even

8. Foster R. McCurley and John Reumann, *Witness of the Word: A Biblical Theology of the Gospel* (Philadelphia: Fortress Press, 1986), 105.
9. Howard Clark Kee, *Understanding the New Testament,* 4th ed. (Englewood Cliffs, N.J.: Prentice-Hall, 1983), 185.
10. Cf. W. D. Davies, *Invitation to the New Testament* (Garden City, N.Y.: Doubleday, 1966), 170.

the devil could not summon the gall to preface the invitation to fall down and worship him with the same words, "If you are the Son of God."

In any case, the Gospel stories about the temptation of Jesus reveal a most important aspect of his humanity. It is an injustice to the Gospel writers and to Jesus' identification with human trials and sufferings to interpret these accounts in a way that makes Jesus' successful resistance seem easy, automatic, and predictable. For one thing, as Luke wisely points out, the temptations were not over. The devil left him "until an opportune time" (Luke 4:13). For another, there was more to the struggle than adroit Bible quoting by Jesus, though even with regard to his familiarity with and use of Scripture, Jesus as a human being is fittingly placed alongside all others who discover light and strength from God's Word in times of testing.

The full severity of Jesus' temptation cannot be underestimated. He was being tempted to advance his personal cause and public career by seemingly legitimate means: summoning extraordinary divine powers to aid him. "If you are the Son of God," whispered the devil. But paradoxically, Jesus proved himself the Son of God, not by invoking special help from above, but by accepting the lowly path of human faith and obedience. "Reminded of the divine authority with which he has been endowed, he replies by asserting his humanity," writes G. B. Caird.[11] The tempter seems to delight in enticing humans away from their humanity, as when he promised the man and woman in the garden that "you will be like God, knowing good and evil" (Genesis 3:5). In succumbing, they not only broke faith with their Creator but also forfeited the full realization of their humanity.

In refusing to follow the tempter's advice to compromise the human by grasping for the divine, Jesus turned humanity toward wholeness. Divine and human life are kept in their proper relationship when Jesus rejects the tempter's offers. He helps his brothers and sisters in their temptations, not by displays of heavenly miracles, but by testifying that humans are to live by the Word of God. The Word of God sanctifies human faith and obedience. The word of the enemy disparages human responsibility with false offers of divine privilege.

11. G. B. Caird, *Saint Luke: Pelican New Testament Commentaries,* ed. D. E. Nineham (Baltimore: Penguin Books, 1963), 81.

The Proclamation of the Kingdom

Jesus' preaching concerning the kingdom of God is important to Christian humanism because the central claim in his message is that God is acting with the purpose of bringing human life under God's gracious rule. When Christians pray, "Your kingdom come, your will be done on earth as in heaven," they express faith that God does not keep aloof from human affairs in this world but sets divine energy to work in its midst.

Following his temptation Jesus announced: "The time is fulfilled, and the kingdom of God has come near; repent and believe in the good news" (Mark 1:15). Commenting on the news that "the kingdom of God has come near" or "is at hand," biblical scholars McCurley and Reumann write that the phrase means "'God is/was/and will be king.' God reigns. It has to do more with the *fact* of God's reigning, that is, with God's *kingship,* than it has to do with a territorial *kingdom* — his 'reign' rather than his realm."[12] How was the kingdom at hand? In the words and deeds of Jesus; through his teachings, healings, and exorcisms God was wielding kingly power. The kingdom, or kingship, is of God; it is a *divine* rule, the exercise of *transcendent* power, not another human program.

But God's rule is not obvious. Sin and injustice continue. It takes eyes opened by faith to see how and where God is exerting power in human lives.[13] The hiddenness of the kingdom partly accounts for the mixed reception given to Jesus' miracles and teachings. Sometimes people responded with praise and thanksgiving; at other times they showed only perplexity and unbelief.

For modern readers too there has been puzzlement about the reality of God's rule in human life. Perhaps the chief difficulty is the implicit claim that God can and does act in human affairs. From the fact that Matthew's Gospel happens to use the phrase "kingdom of heaven," some may have felt justified in the assumption that the kingdom has nothing to do with life here on earth. The fact is, however, that Matthew's phrase means exactly the same as "kingdom of God." Some have taken the kingdom to be a utopian society brought about by the sincere moral efforts of good people, but against that view is the scriptural reminder that the kingdom is *of God.*

Many have seized upon a single poorly translated verse, Luke 17:21,

12. McCurley and Reumann, *Witness of the Word,* 98.
13. Bornkamm, *Jesus of Nazareth,* 69.

to think of the kingdom as an inward phenomenon, some feeling or sensation within the individual person. Older translations with the misleading "within you" have been corrected by the Revised Standard Version which reads, "in the midst of you" and by the New Revised Standard Version which has the similar "among you." The "you" in this phrase is second person plural. "Among you" is supported by Frederick Danker in a comment on this verse: "The kingdom of God, Luke teaches, is not to be confused with an apocalyptic moment, for the kingdom of God is 'present among you' (17:21), namely in the activity of Jesus (see 10:9)."[14] It is futile to look for special signs or to believe excited rumors because the kingdom of God is even now right in the midst of the community gathered about Jesus.

Certainly God does rule in heaven, and there is a sense in which God rules in and through the hearts and lives of believing people, but the revolutionary claim of Jesus was that a new era had come for humanity wherein God's kingly rule was set in motion. It was to be seen, not in dazzling signs, not in the destruction of Rome nor in the recovery of Jewish independence, but in the casting out of demons, the giving of sight and hearing, the healing of lepers, the raising of cripples, the sharing of bread, the forgiving of sins, and ultimately, the suffering and death which befell Jesus in Jerusalem.

In seeking to understand the possibilities of a full human existence under God, Christian humanism reflects on Jesus' proclamation of the kingship or rule of God. There it learns that God has entered human life decisively in Jesus of Nazareth, and that the rule of God, while powerful and revolutionary, is at the same time hidden in and among the needs and sufferings of human beings. Its full impact will be revealed in the future but its signs are already present in this world.

Jesus the Teacher

A particular humanistic value attaches to Jesus' teaching ministry both because it was the particular role Jesus chose for himself and because what he taught inevitably provokes thought regarding the human condition. For instance, Jesus told his disciples, "Unless you change and become like

14. Frederick W. Danker, *Luke: Proclamation Commentaries,* ed. Gerhard Krodel (Philadelphia: Fortress Press, 1976), 33.

children, you will never enter the kingdom of heaven" (Matthew 18:3). Everything in Jesus' career sheds light on the question of what it means to be human, but the teachings especially reveal the depth and breadth of his understanding of human beings, both in kindly and challenging terms.

The Gospels portray Jesus as a divinely chosen man through whom God reveals unfailing grace and a hopeful purpose for humanity. They do not picture him as a god in disguise who escapes difficult situations by drawing upon a secret reservoir of divine power. Jesus resisted the tempter by refusing to take special advantage of divine status. He proclaimed the coming of God's kingdom by pointing to the rule of God in the midst of human activities. Similarly, as teacher Jesus accepted the limitations of the teaching-learning situation, including the need for repetition and illustration, his hearers' dullness of understanding, and even the discouraging fact that his teachings would not always be grasped.

A few examples from the Sermon on the Mount and from the parables indicate his intimacy with human experience and his ability to see it in the light of divine truth. The Sermon on the Mount opens with a series of Beatitudes, remarkable in their revelation that the very persons whom society would view with pity or disdain are the ones who now have God's blessing. These include the poor in spirit, mourners, the meek, those who hunger and thirst for righteousness, the peacemakers, and the persecuted.

Interpreting the divine law given through Moses, Jesus reveals a profound understanding of human nature. Those who avoid murder and adultery are asked to recognize these very tendencies in their own hearts. Those who know that the law commands them to love their neighbors are asked to love their enemies as well, for that is the standard set by God, who makes the sun rise on the evil and on the good. It is often assumed that Jesus possessed such insights because he was uniquely the Son of God, and indeed his teaching had a unique force, but study of the Judaism of that era has shown that other rabbis of the time had similar elements in their teaching.[15] Just as Jesus knew the prophets, he also must have known the rabbinic traditions, both the older and the more current.

At many points Jesus appeals to the experience of his listeners. "Which one of you," he asks, "having a hundred sheep and losing one of them, does not leave the ninety-nine in the wilderness, and go after the

15. See Jacob Neusner, *Judaism in the Beginning of Christianity* (Philadelphia: Fortress Press, 1984), 50, 60.

one that is lost until he finds it?" (Luke 15:4). Having told a story of three travelers who saw a beaten, robbed man along the roadside, Jesus appeals to his listeners' judgment: "Which of these three, do you think, was a neighbor to the man who fell into the hands of the robbers?" (Luke 10:36).

The style of the parables makes the listener a participant in the process of understanding. Apparently simple observations about a sower or a grain of mustard seed take on meaning when the hearers or readers begin to reflect on Jesus himself and on his ministry in relation to the rule of God. In one case, the parable of the vineyard, the hearers reacted in anger by trying to arrest Jesus, "when they realized that he had told this parable against them" (Mark 12:12).

The Gospel writers say of Jesus that he taught "as one having authority" (Matthew 7:29; Mark 1:22; Luke 4:32). While it might seem orthodox to ascribe that authority entirely to Jesus' divine status as the Son of God, it is important to remember that Jesus made full use of his human capacities as he presented teachings on human nature, responsibility, and destiny that carry the ring of truth. When King Herod Agrippa gave an oration, the people shouted, "The voice of a god, and not of a mortal" (Acts 12:22). But when Jesus taught in his home synagogue, the people said, "Where did this man get all this? . . . Is not this the carpenter?" (Mark 6:2-3). They were duly impressed by his teaching, but they did not set him apart from themselves as superhuman.

Finally, it should be pointed out that while Jesus' teaching activity is another window on his close relationship to the human condition, his teachings are not to be regarded as simple or commonplace. The tendency often shows itself to regard Jesus' teachings as uniformly soft and innocuous, but the fact is that many who heard them were perplexed or even offended by what he had to say. Robert McAfee Brown insists that the so-called "simple teachings of Jesus" cannot be separated from sin and salvation, from belief in God and Jesus' total mission on earth. "If you do not believe in the God of whom Jesus speaks," writes Brown, "there is little point to taking his teachings seriously. . . . You are to forgive, not because this is expedient or clever, but because God forgives you, and you are to mirror the divine compassion in your own life."[16]

Therefore one cannot expect to find enlightenment about humanity from Jesus without receiving his message about divine authority. As

16. Robert McAfee Brown, *The Bible Speaks to You* (Philadelphia: Westminster Press, 1985), 258.

teacher, Jesus was not content simply to offer pointers on living, but to point his hearers to God, the origin of human life. The humanistic value of his teaching cannot be separated from his mission on earth as the select agent of God's rule. Therefore, in order to grasp in Jesus more of what it means to be human, we must consider him in the fullness of his earthly ministry, his deeds as well as his teachings.

The Mighty Works of Jesus

If the Christian humanism described in these pages is to be in harmony with its source, the Gospel of Christ, it cannot agree with the definition of humanism as "belief in the mere humanity of Christ." Rather, Christian humanism accepts the biblical, orthodox view that Jesus is truly divine and at the same time fully human. That means that one does not limit the search for the humanistic implications of Jesus' life to his birth, for example, or to his teachings, as some humanisms have done. Nor does it allow one to conclude, as conservative Christianity tends to do, that the mighty works or "miracles" of Jesus are meant to prove his divinity, having little or nothing to do with his humanity.

Three aspects of the mighty works of Jesus are related to his human nature and are thus of special interest to Christian humanism. First of all, Jesus does not suddenly switch into his "God" role as soon as he performs a miracle. The Jesus of the mighty works is the same fully human man of God's own choosing who grew up in a human family, was tempted by the devil, and set out to preach and teach. The Gospel writers regard the mighty works as of a piece with preaching the kingdom and teaching. Matthew illustrates this point as he summarizes the Galilean ministry: "Jesus went throughout Galilee, teaching in their synagogues and proclaiming the good news of the kingdom and curing every disease and every sickness among the people" (Matthew 4:23). "Without the miracles, Jesus' acts and the message of the evangelists are incomplete in the extreme," writes Otto Betz.[17]

Second, the purpose of the mighty works is to show that God's kingly power is at work in and through Jesus, and also through his

17. Otto Betz, *What Do We Know about Jesus?* trans. Margaret Kohl (Philadelphia: Westminster Press, 1968), 60.

disciples, and not to prove that Jesus was the Son of God. Word and deed go hand in hand in the ministry of Jesus. The "word" is the proclamation that the rule of God is at hand; the "deed" is whatever miracle Jesus performs at a given time to show people the impact of the rule of God on human lives. That Jesus was the Son of God receives attestation in other ways, such as by the voice from heaven at his baptism. The miracles serve to supplement and confirm the word.

Third, the mighty works of Jesus are always on a human scale and for the benefit of persons in need. They are as directly pertinent to the notion of Christian humanism as anything could be: signs that God cares about human welfare and acts to restore wholeness to broken lives. When the disciples "were straining at the oars against an adverse wind" on the stormy sea, "he came to them" (Mark 6:48). When the crowd was hungry, Jesus provided bread. Some other examples: Jesus cures a deaf man who has an impediment in his speech; he restores the sight of two blind men; he cures a woman who has suffered from a hemorrhage for twelve years. In every instance, Jesus acts out of compassion for fearful, suffering people. He performs mighty works as the agent through whom God grants healing and cleansing. His works serve notice that the powers of evil are being contested and that new powers of life are abroad in the world.[18]

The exercise of faith on the part of those who receive help is also part of the humanistic story of the mighty works. Humans have a capacity to respond in faith when God approaches them through Jesus. Of the centurion who had sought healing for his servant Jesus says, "In no one in Israel have I found such faith" (Matthew 8:10). Here and elsewhere in the Gospels it is certainly not a faith that rests upon knowledge of "the two natures of Christ" or some other refinement of theology. Rather, it is an immediate, intuitive confidence on the part of a needy person that this man Jesus can be trusted, and that in his compassionate deeds the mercy of God is present.

The Gospels also record cases where Jesus could do no mighty works because of people's unbelief. In his home town of Nazareth Jesus taught in the synagogue and the people were impressed by his reputation for wisdom and mighty works. Yet, "he could do no deed of power there," reports Mark, adding that Jesus himself "was amazed at their unbelief" (Mark 6:2-6).

In performing his deeds of power, Jesus continued to serve God and

18. Betz, 60.

his fellow humans as the man of God's own choosing. He did not lay aside his humanness when he performed miracles, nor did he use the miracles to impress upon the public that he was the Son of God. Rather, his actions were an integral part of his total earthly ministry which had as its center the proclamation that the gracious and sovereign rule of God was at hand. Some put their trust in Jesus and felt the power of God in their lives; others thwarted his mighty works, and their own chance at wholeness, by their unbelief.

Jesus' Messianic Vocation

Christian faith has access to a valuable humanistic treasure in the concept of vocation, the idea that every human being is called to believe in God, and to offer his or her life in loving service to humanity. In one generation after another, young people in particular have found a sense of purpose in living when they have allowed God to direct them into spheres of service where their particular talents and interests can best be devoted to the needs of society.

Some may be surprised that Jesus too had to discover and accept his particular calling, which was to be God's Messiah. As God's only begotten Son he was not excused from the human experience of working out his personal calling through prayer and obedience. In this respect, as well as in others, his life illumines the course for other human beings and thereby adds a further dimension to the meaning of Christian humanism.

There is scanty Gospel evidence about Jesus' early understanding of his vocation. The Lukan account of the twelve-year-old Jesus in the temple is fascinating in its singularity. It reveals a precocious lad who not only listened but asked questions as he sat among the teachers. He told his parents that he had to be in his Father's house, but he consented to return home to Nazareth with them. The account closes by observing that Jesus "increased in wisdom and in years, and in divine and human favor" (Luke 2:52).

Bible readers rightly sense that Jesus' baptism was a turning point in his life. In Matthew's account a voice from heaven says, "This is my Son, the Beloved, with whom I am well pleased," implying a pronouncement that others in the vicinity would have heard (Matthew 3:17). In Mark and Luke, on the other hand, the voice declares, "You are my Son, the Beloved;

with you I am well pleased" (Mark 1:11; Luke 3:22), suggesting an experience within Jesus' own consciousness rather than a public declaration. After the baptism the synoptic Gospels (Matthew, Mark, and Luke) describe the temptation. In that experience, as seen earlier, Jesus deliberately chose the path of obedience to the Word of God rather than the tempter's proposed dramatic shortcuts to fame. Jesus remained faithful to his human situation.

Exactly the same kind of faithful obedience to the will of God characterized Jesus' attitude toward Messiahship. Throughout most of his public ministry Jesus does not call himself the Messiah.[19] In the famous confession near Caesarea Philippi, recorded in all three synoptic Gospels, it is Peter, not Jesus, who introduces the term "Messiah" or "Christ." Jesus himself never makes any such statement as "I declare to you disciples that I am the Messiah," but it is Peter who states clearly, "You are the Messiah" (Mark 8:29).

Equally important is the fact that once Peter has spoken of Jesus as the Messiah, Jesus himself immediately refers to his coming sufferings. In other words, to be the Messiah is to go to the cross. Moreover, to be a follower of the Messiah is to take up one's cross and follow him (Mark 8:34).

When on trial toward the end of his life, Jesus gives assent to the Messiah title when asked, but only in an indirect manner. The high priest demands, "Are you the Messiah, the Son of the Blessed One?" and Jesus replies, "I am; and 'you will see the Son of man seated at the right hand of the Power,' and 'coming with the clouds of heaven'" (Mark 14:62). At other times Jesus uses his favorite designation, "Son of man," in connection with his role of service and his impending death (see Mark 8:31; 10:45).

Christian readers of the Bible tend to pack the term "Messiah" full of divine associations, but in Judaism the Messiah was always understood to be a human figure, kingly no doubt, but definitely someone on the human level.[20] In the light of Jesus' life, death, and resurrection, the early church developed a Christology, that is, a theology about the Messiah, that embraced both the divinity and the humanity of Jesus Christ. During his life on earth Jesus surely pondered the Scriptures of his people with their

19. See Hans Conzelmann, *Jesus,* trans. J. Raymond Lord, ed. John Reumann (Philadelphia: Fortress Press, 1973), 48. Conzelmann briefly touches on the so-called "Messianic secret," the theory that attempts to explain why Jesus forbade various ones to tell what he had done and who he was. See James M. Efird, *The New Testament Writings: History, Literature, Interpretation* (Atlanta: John Knox Press, 1980), 38.

20. Reumann, *Jesus in the Church's Gospels,* 260-64.

messianic expectations centering on the kingly Davidic line, and combined his reflections with an acute sense of what God was doing in his own life.

Ultimately, it was God who made Jesus the Messiah. So Peter declared in his sermon on Pentecost: "Therefore let the entire house of Israel know with certainty that God has made him both Lord and Messiah, this Jesus whom you crucified" (Acts 2:36). For Jesus, being "the Christ" or "the Messiah" was not simply a matter of claiming or accepting a title, a way of being identified by others. Rather, Messiahship was a vocation, the "calling" that Jesus accepted, a life of devotion to God, a willingness to follow wherever God would lead him, even to the cross.

What Christian humanism finds in Jesus' messianic vocation is the principle that a human life has meaning when the person involved is faithful to his or her human calling under God. God does not require superhuman performances but fidelity to the opportunities implied by one's abilities, by one's place in history, and above all, by one's receptivity to God's direction.

Death and Resurrection

The full significance of Jesus as the man of God's own choosing cannot be appreciated if we stop short of his death on the cross and his resurrection from the dead. These events are at the heart of the gospel; and the gospel, the good news about Christ, is the indispensable source of Christian humanism.

In the past, the quest for the human relevance of Jesus would frequently try to ignore his death and resurrection, finding that part of the gospel story too strange and jarring to correlate with a comfortable humanism. At best, one might allow that Jesus' death was an inspiring example of dying for one's principles, but the prevailing tendency of older views was to avoid the threatening topic of the cross and to concentrate instead on such congenial images of Jesus as friend of children, lover of nature, or kindly teacher.

One of the lessons New Testament scholars learned from Albert Schweitzer's famous book *The Quest of the Historical Jesus*[21] was that one

21. Albert Schweitzer, *The Quest of the Historical Jesus*, trans. W. Montgomery, 3rd ed. (London: Adam & Charles Black, 1954), 400.

cannot construct the kind of Jesus one wants by selecting some features and ignoring others. In Schweitzer's case, he faulted his predecessors for setting aside Jesus' preoccupation with the end of the world. Similarly, modern students of the Gospels have learned that one cannot ignore the cross and resurrection of Jesus if one seeks a full understanding of the man from Nazareth. He is not merely the "gentle Jesus, meek and mild." Rather, he engages in controversy, offends the religious leaders, causes perplexity among his own followers, arouses suspicion in the Romans, and ends his life as a criminal crucified outside the walls of Jerusalem.

It is a paradox, and a difficult one, to consider that this man Jesus represents what humanity is and can and should be. Jesus does not meet the expected standards of what most would regard as a full human existence. The noblest specimen of humankind dies on a cross. The greatest life ever lived takes as his model the form of a servant. The man chosen by God for the task of redeeming humanity seems to die as a complete failure, rejected by his people, forsaken by his closest followers, and executed by the Romans. He who moves the human soul to long for beauty and harmony is disfigured by beatings and mocked as an impostor. To appreciate the full extent of Jesus' humanity one cannot simply visualize spending a day with him strolling sun-bathed fields in Galilee; one must accompany him all the way to Jerusalem and to the hill where he was crucified.

At every point in the passion events Jesus acted as the obedient, trusting son of his heavenly Father. In the garden he asked that the cup be removed, but he yielded his will: "Yet not what I want but what you want" (Matthew 26:39). When betrayed and arrested, Jesus not only repudiated violent action on his behalf, but refused to summon the legions of angels which would come at his signal. This moment typifies Jesus' determination to remain within the human vocation God had given him. It was by his *not* asking for angelic help that the Scriptures would be fulfilled (Matthew 26:53-54).

Even as he was being crucified, Jesus was taunted and tempted. "He saved others; he cannot save himself. Let the Messiah, the King of Israel, come down from the cross now, so that we may see and believe" (Mark 15:31-32). To the very last, Jesus had to suffer the temptations to forsake his vocation, to depart from his chosen role, and to seek acceptance by a sensational display of power.

Jesus died a completely human death. He expressed the agonizing sense of being forsaken when he cried, "My God, my God, why have you forsaken me?" (Mark 15:34). Mark and Matthew report the centurion's awestruck statement: "Truly this man was God's Son!" (Mark 15:39; Matthew 27:54).

The death of Jesus was accepted as a sad, irrefutable fact. The reports of his resurrection were greeted with a mixture of fear and unbelief. There was anything but an instantaneous outpouring of jubilation. Eventually, the risen Christ himself had to interpret to the mystified disciples what had taken place. Even as the risen one, Jesus continued to bear the marks of his humanity, appearing on the Galilean shore to issue a simple invitation, "Come and have breakfast" (John 21:12).

The resurrection of Jesus certifies that God's commitment to the world does not end with the death of God's chosen one. In his life, in his death, and in his resurrection Jesus is the true man, the representative of humanity. Through his action in raising Jesus from the dead, God assures all people that the final word of God to the human race is life. The dwelling of God with humans is not simply a moment to be measured by the span of Jesus' earthly life; it is a continuing, life-giving presence. Christ's presence at the church's eucharistic table is a sign that he is abroad in the world, ready to bring new life to every heart and home. "Come, Lord Jesus, and be our guest."

Chapter 6

Paul, Witness to the New Humanity

As the leading interpreter of the grace of God in Jesus Christ, the apostle Paul is also qualified as an uncommonly important witness to the new humanity implied by the gospel he proclaimed. Unlike those secular humanists who rest their case for the greatness of human persons on real or potential human achievements, Paul bases his case firmly on God's initiative and action. Yet that does not mean, as Paul's critics contend, that the human recipients of divine action become inert and passive, devoid of true selfhood.[1]

In 1 Corinthians 15 Paul summarizes the gospel he preaches, starting with the facts about Christ and concluding with his own experience. Christ died for our sins, was buried, was raised on the third day, and appeared to Cephas and others, writes Paul. Those are the firm facts of the gospel, but Paul is not finished. There is a further, incredible fact of overwhelming personal meaning in Paul's own experience:

> Last of all, as to one untimely born, he appeared also to me. For I am the least of the apostles, unfit to be called an apostle, because I persecuted the church of God. But by the grace of God I am what I am, and his grace toward me has not been in vain. (1 Corinthians 15:8-10)

1. See, for example, Victor Paul Furnish, *Theology and Ethics in Paul* (Nashville: Abingdon Press, 1968), chap. 4.

"By the grace of God I am what I am" might well be adopted as a suitable motto by any Christian humanist. A personal encounter with the risen Christ delivers the persecutor from his past. The grace of God creates an entirely new basis for selfhood and Paul's realization of his personal worth. The concrete, actual self, the "I," can now be affirmed without apology, for God in Christ has intervened in Paul's personal history to place his total being on a new foundation.

As a result, Paul worked harder than any of the others to whom Christ appeared, but there was no ground for boasting because the grace of God was with him. What Paul relates can help others discover the power of a humanism linked to the reality of Christ. Paul's readers cannot duplicate the apostle's encounter with the risen Christ, nor are they likely to match Paul's pioneer missionary labors, but they can apply Paul's insight to their own experiences.

The key elements in Paul's Christian humanism are universal. The resurrection of Jesus Christ is good news for all people; it can mean a new start for anyone who believes the message. The sense of unworthiness due to one's past actions is not limited to persecutors of the church; everyone can experience release from the shadows of the past. The grace of God, which makes all the difference, is available to everyone. It corresponds to the universal, human need to affirm the self, the personal "I."

The Gospel of Christ

The purpose of this section is to underscore the humanistic relevance of the great New Testament word "gospel," especially as the apostle Paul perceives it.[2] A good place to begin is the oft-quoted statement in the first chapter of Romans: "For I am not ashamed of the gospel: it is the power of God for salvation to everyone who has faith, to the Jew first and also to the Greek" (Romans 1:16).

Gospel means "good news," and good news is pointless if it fails to bring benefit and good cheer to actual human beings. Good news is meant to be published. When Paul uses the word *power* in this verse he means a force that can effect significant change in human lives. The gospel actually

2. For a discussion of the term *gospel* in Paul see J. Christiaan Beker, *Paul the Apostle: The Triumph of God in Life and Thought* (Philadelphia: Fortress Press, 1980), 122.

brings salvation to the person who has faith. *Salvation* means healing and wholeness. It is related to the word *salutary,* "promoting health, curative." Salvation is the process through which the Creator's original intention for human welfare is realized. It can be thought of as the entrance into an authentic human existence. Where sin brought brokenness and sickness, the gospel brings restoration.[3] The healing process is not completed in this life, but it begins within the concrete terms of present historical existence, in the real world where one rubs shoulders with both Jews and Greeks. In referring to *Jew* and *Greek,* Paul clearly indicates that salvation is for all people.

The word *faith* in Romans 1:16 also points to human reality. Faith is the human response to God's beneficent deeds.[4] It is the extending of one's hand to accept a gift, the trust that regards God's word as reliable. Faith is decidedly a human experience, even though, as the letter to the Ephesians points out, "it is the gift of God" (Ephesians 2:8). Through acts of kindness toward human beings, God evokes from them the confidence to trust in God's generosity. Significantly, however, the act of placing one's confidence in God is a human act because it engages the human will at the deepest level. When one decides to trust God, it is on the basis of the good news that God, out of love for humanity, has sent Jesus Christ into the world.

However the gospel is stated, by Paul or anyone else, it always includes both the cross and resurrection of Christ.[5] That God in Christ conquered death for all people is obviously good news, but the message of Christ's resurrection is never separated from the message of the cross. At one point Paul virtually identifies "the gospel" with "the word of the cross," so determined is he to impress upon his readers that the Gospel runs counter to worldly wisdom (see 1 Corinthians 1:17-18). Jews want signs and Greeks seek wisdom, "but we preach Christ crucified . . . the power of God and the wisdom of God" (1 Corinthians 1:22-24).

In building its case on the gospel, Christian humanism has no

3. See Robin Scroggs, *Paul for a New Day* (Philadelphia: Fortress Press, 1977), 19. Many NT references to salvation "denote deliverance from specific ills, such as captivity, disease and devil possession, eschatological terrors, or physical death," writes F. J. Taylor in the article "Save, Salvation," in *A Theological Word Book of the Bible,* ed. Alan Richardson (London: SCM Press, 1950), 220.

4. For further comments on Paul's understanding of faith, see Robin Scroggs, *Paul for a New Day,* 25-28.

5. Beker, *Paul the Apostle,* 207; Furnish, *Theology and Ethics in Paul,* 122.

authority to promise that if one believes in Christ one will have thriving success in every human venture. What it does promise, however, is that all who discover disappointment, pain, and bitterness in their lives can be sure that the Christ of the cross will be there to uphold them and to help them affirm their humanity.

The gospel of Christ is at the same time good news concerning the risen one, the Lord now present in human history to enable all people to know the power of life in a world beset by the forces of death. With other Christians, Paul regarded Christ's resurrection as the guarantee of life after death for believers (1 Corinthians 15:20-23). But the Pauline teaching on resurrection also makes clear that the risen Lord gives his people power for living in their present earthly experience (Romans 8:11; Colossians 3:1).[6]

The Human Benefit of the Gospel

The previous paragraphs showed that the important Pauline term *gospel* is relevant for the human situation because it proclaims the crucified and risen Jesus Christ as bringer of wholeness or salvation to all who trust God. The task of this section is to examine the nature of the salvation offered in the gospel by discussing the humanistic implications of another Pauline term, *justification*.[7]

Paul gives a highly condensed but instructive statement on justification in Romans 3: "For there is no distinction; since all have sinned and fall short of the glory of God, they are now justified by his grace as a gift, through the redemption that is in Christ Jesus, whom God put forward as a sacrifice of atonement by his blood, effective through faith" (Romans 3:22-25). Who needs to be justified? Everyone. Why? Because they have sinned. How are they justified? By God's grace, as a gift. How is grace manifested? Through the redemption in Christ. How was redemption effected? Through Christ's death on the cross. How does a person appropriate it? By faith.

The initiative for justification rests with God; human beings are

6. See Scroggs, *Paul for a New Day*, 29-38.

7. Fresh insights on Paul's understanding of justification are found in Krister Stendahl, *Paul Among Jews and Gentiles* (Philadelphia: Fortress Press, 1976), 23ff. and in Furnish, *Theology and Ethics in Paul*, 143-52. See also N. H. Snaith, "Just, Justify, Justification," in *Word Book of the Bible*, 118-19, and Scroggs, *Paul for a New Day*, 14-20.

"justified by his grace as a gift," writes Paul. "Grace," a unique New Testament term central to Paul's theology, carries the meaning of God's specific saving activity in and through Jesus Christ.[8] Grace always points to what God does for the human race. Justification is impossible apart from its basis in God's grace, that is, in God's redemptive action.

The actual experience of being justified calls for a human response. Both Protestants and Catholics agree on this point. Paul's language sometimes yields the phrase, "justified by faith," and faith, it was noted, is a human act even though it is a gift. In Galatians Paul draws a contrast between faith and works; human beings are "justified by faith in Christ, and not by works of the law, because by works of the law shall no one be justified" (Galatians 2:16). It was this crucial insight that opened the family of God to Gentiles and by implication to all people.

What then are the benefits of justification? What does it mean to be justified? Three answers may be given, two of them traditional and one that may seem less familiar. First, being justified means being made right with God or being brought into the right relationship with God. Because of Christ's death in behalf of sinners, human beings may now be received into God's fellowship despite their failure to meet certain standards of goodness. This answer is good news for humanity because it declares that all persons, without exception, can know the friendship of God.

A second traditional understanding of justification is that it is the equivalent of the forgiveness of sin. Paul clearly links justification and forgiveness with a quotation from Psalm 32: "Blessed are those whose iniquities are forgiven, . . . blessed is the one against whom the Lord will not reckon sin" (Romans 4:7-8). The God who "justifies the ungodly" honors their faith as righteousness and forgives their sins.

A third and less traditional meaning of justification, holding particular promise for humanistic consideration, is related to the root idea of justification as "being made just or right." The other two meanings rightly emphasize the fact that because of God's work in Christ, sinners can be brought into the proper, harmonious relationship with God. The third meaning to consider has to do with *the justified person's own sense of worth*. Not only are barriers between God and human beings removed and sins forgiven, but an additional positive factor is gained: God bestows on

8. See the book by Harold H. Ditmanson, *Grace in Experience and Theology* (Minneapolis: Augsburg, 1977), which makes liberal use of Pauline theology in developing the rich theme of grace.

trusting humans the assurance that they now enjoy a new standing as persons.

Paul himself alludes to this new standing in the statement quoted earlier, "By the grace of God I am what I am" (1 Corinthians 15:10). The same liberating sense of acceptance is available to anyone who believes the gospel. One is forgiven, indeed, but one is also "made right," that is, affirmed in one's specific human situation, endorsed by God in the particularity of one's selfhood. The old has passed away and the new has come.

Newness in Christ

Christian humanism is not an ethical system but it acknowledges that human existence seen from a Christian perspective is enriched by the ethical guidance derived from the gospel of Christ. Any humanism will have a keen interest in principles of human behavior. The charge is sometimes made against Paul that by teaching justification by faith apart from the works of the law he encourages ethical laxity.[9] While it is possible to refute the charge from Paul's ethical teachings, it is only fair to admit that individuals and churches have sometimes misinterpreted Paul as endorsing quietism or as playing down human responsibility to act.

Most of Paul's letters show a fairly consistent pattern: first the apostle presents the gospel, the basic facts about God's redemptive activity in Christ; then he turns to the ethical implications of the gospel for Christian living. What this pattern tells us is that the new *status* in Christ precedes the implementing of the new *life* in Christ. In other words, being precedes doing.[10] Jesus taught the same principle: "Every good tree bears good fruit, but the bad tree bears bad fruit" (Matthew 7:17).

A unique ethical theme in Paul's letter to the Galatians is the idea of Christian freedom, concisely expressed in the phrase "faith working through love" (Galatians 5:6). Freedom has two aspects. On the negative side, Christians are free from the law, free from bondage, free from the requirement of circumcision. On the positive side, Christians are set free by Christ to love and

9. In his book *My Brother Paul* (New York: Harper & Row, 1972), 39, Richard L. Rubinstein defends Paul against the charge of being an antinomian.
10. See Scroggs, *Paul for a New Day*, 57-58.

serve their neighbors. The secret of Christian freedom is to walk by the Spirit. The danger is to misuse freedom "as an opportunity for self-indulgence" (Galatians 5:13), while the proper use of freedom is to serve others through love.

In Galatians 5 Paul contrasts the "works of the flesh" with the "fruit of the Spirit." The former include the expected, coarser sins such as immorality and drunkenness, but they also include more subtle transgressions such as jealousy, anger, selfishness, and envy. The fruit of the Spirit is defined as love, joy, peace, patience, kindness, and the like, all activities against which there is no law. These are the very qualities which the Christian humanist Erasmus defined as the *pietas* which coheres with the fundamental Christian contribution to humanism.

Christians have "crucified the flesh with its passions and desires." That is, they have permitted Christ to put those passions to death. To do so requires a conscious decision, just as one must choose to walk by the Spirit. Free persons must claim their freedom by exercising intelligent choices. When they fail, they will need the gentle, restoring help of their fellow Christians. "Bear one another's burdens," writes Paul, "and in this way you will fulfill the law of Christ" (Galatians 6:2).

Here and throughout his ethical teachings Paul reveals a high view of human capabilities when persons are in a living relationship with Christ. At the same time, Paul is realistic about human proclivities toward unloving behavior. What is revolutionary in Paul's ethics is the dynamics of the new life in Christ. It is the new standing, the fact of being "in Christ" or being "justified" that opens the way to lives of love and service. The old way of human wisdom has always been to strive to earn God's favor by proper conduct. The new way of the gospel is to receive God's favor in Christ as a gift, and in the power of that new status before God to love and serve the neighbor.[11]

Paul's ethical principles are a facet of Christian humanism that the contemporary world needs to know. The way of the law, the way of the policeman, the way of ever-intensified competition will not work. When people discover their worth and dignity as human beings, then they will be free to renounce the use of force and to reach out in love and understanding toward their neighbors. Through the good news of Christ, God is in the process of making new human beings.

---

11. In *Theology and Ethics in Paul*, 213, Victor Paul Furnish writes: "The Pauline ethic is first of all radically *theological* because it presupposes that man's whole life and being is dependent upon the sovereign, creative, and redemptive power of God."

The New Community

The sphere in which the first-century Christians heard the gospel, experienced what it meant to be justified by grace, and found strength to live a new life of freedom in Christ was the church, the new community. "When Paul speaks about the nature of Christian life," writes J. Christiaan Beker, "he does so most often in communal categories." Beker then notes that the phrases in Galatians, "works of the flesh" (5:19) and "the fruit of the Spirit" (5:22), "are predominantly social vices and virtues that are primarily addressed to the community as a whole."[12]

For Paul, the church was the body of Christ because the risen Christ projected his own vitality into the community of those who believed in him. "So we, who are many, are one body in Christ, and individually we are members one of another," writes Paul in Romans 12:5. Similar language occurs in 1 Corinthians 12:12: "For just as the body is one and has many members, and all the members of the body, though many, are one body, so it is with Christ."

Many Christians, to say nothing of the larger population of secularists, have yet to discover the enormous power of the church in assisting persons in the process of becoming human. Swayed by an old-fashioned but discredited individualism,[13] such people are apt to say, "Jesus, Yes, but the church, No."

Yet it can be reported that the church has been rediscovered in the twentieth century through several notable developments. Biblical studies have shown convincingly that the entire message of both Old and New Testaments presupposes God's action in history to establish a "people," a community of persons bound together in faith, love, and hope. The ecumenical movement has generated a fresh awareness of the one church of God even as it has brought the various churches closer together. Countless local fellowships have enabled persons to emerge from self-centered isolation into the beneficial give-and-take of mutual concern among brothers and sisters in the faith.

In the church one experiences a basic fact about human nature, long

---

12. Beker, *Paul the Apostle,* 306. See also Scroggs, *Paul for a New Day,* chap. 3, "The Church: Eschatological Community," 39-56.

13. In the introduction to his book *Jesus and Community,* trans. John P. Galvin (Philadelphia: Fortress Press, 1984), 1-5, Gerhard Lohfink comments on "The Heritage of Individualism" both in theology and in our consumer society.

ago discovered by sages, prophets, and ordinary believers: the human being was created to enjoy close fellowship with other human beings. "It is not good that the man should be alone," said the Creator (Genesis 2:18). In his book *Christ and Culture,* H. Richard Niebuhr writes:

> The deep disease of man, the self-contradiction in which he is involved as individual and member of human societies, is his denial of the law of his being. He seeks to possess within or by himself, whether in the form of physical or spiritual goods, what he can have only in the community of receiving and giving.[14]

Paul knew that a central, not a peripheral, part of the work of God in ancient times was to call into being a people, a community of quite ordinary, even sinful men, women, and children, to whom God gave the covenant and from whom God asked trust in the promises and obedience to the commandments. Through this community, the people of God, the Creator and Redeemer intended to bestow unlimited blessings upon the entire human race.

When Paul himself came on the scene and became a follower of Jesus Christ, he recognized that God's purpose with the chosen community was still in force but that membership in the people of God was now opened to all persons. The immediate occasion for this insight was the acceptance of the gospel by many Gentiles. One of the characteristics of the new age inaugurated by the coming of Christ was the widening of the borders of God's family to embrace all who would respond to Jesus.[15]

Of the many features of the church that one might explore, two in particular hold special interest for Christian humanism. The first is the Pauline idea of the various gifts of the Spirit within the one body of Christ. The second is the worship life of the church, but especially the gathering of the community around the bread and the wine. We should be aware of the fact that the earliest account of the institution of the Lord's Supper is the one given to posterity by Paul in 1 Corinthians 11:23-26.

The reason that Christians take the church seriously is that it is nothing less than the creation of God, the body of Christ, and the temple of the Holy Spirit. That is, it is not one more voluntary organization which

14. H. Richard Niebuhr, *Christ and Culture* (New York: Harper & Row, 1951), 222.

15. Paul D. Hanson, *The People Called: The Growth of Community in the Bible* (San Francisco: Harper & Row, 1987), 392, 402, 437, 440.

one may join or not according to one's time and interests. For Christians, the church is indeed their holy mother on whom they depend for life and nourishment. Moreover, the church is a fellowship which the Holy Spirit supplies with a variety of important gifts, and these gifts always have to do with human abilities and actions. While Paul can call them *pneumatika* (spiritual gifts, 1 Corinthians 12:1) and *charismata* (charismatic gifts, 1 Corinthians 12:4; Romans 12:4), it is obvious that these endowments, for example, prophecy, serving, teaching, contributing, are for practical use here and now in the regular life of the community of faith.

The beauty of the Spirit's work is that the variety of individual endowment strengthens rather than subverts the unity of the community. The modern secularist fears community because it seems to foster conformity. The fact is, on the contrary, that individual differences are welcomed in the church because they are perceived as gifts for the enrichment of the fellowship. "If the whole body were an eye, where would the hearing be?" asks Paul (1 Corinthians 12:17). Participation in the life of the community provides channels through which each person can express and develop his or her individuality, at the same time strengthening the body itself.

A unique feature of the Christian community is that it welcomes the contribution of those who might "seem to be weaker" (1 Corinthians 12:22). Actually, the weaker parts of the body are "indispensable," writes Paul. Some people misinterpret the work of the church as an ongoing talent show, where only people of special training and talents can help the common cause. In Paul's "body" image, however, it is quite a different matter. "God has so arranged the body, giving the greater honor to the inferior member, that there may be no dissension within the body, but the members may have the same care for one another" (1 Corinthians 12:24-25).

The gifts of the Spirit in the community of Christ's body are not to be identified with specialized talents as such, although they embrace and put to good use all the talents people may happen to have. The genius of the Spirit, rather, is seen both in the dedication of human abilities to God's service and in the remarkable process whereby persons with little or no obvious talent contribute to the overall health of the body through highly personal though intangible means. It is not talent, but love at work in a fellowship of which Paul can write: "If one member suffers, all suffer together with it; if one member is honored, all rejoice together with it" (1 Corinthians 12:26).

The focal point in the church's life where suffering and rejoicing together are most vividly experienced is the table of the Lord where young and old, men and women, meet together with Christ himself as the host. Because Paul valued the mutual edification of such an occasion so highly, it is painful to him when he must respond to the report that there are factions among the Corinthian Christians. In the paragraph before he recites the tradition about Jesus taking the bread and cup, Paul expresses his dismay that his friends in Corinth are not truly eating the Lord's Supper; some have acted in privatistic fashion; "each one goes ahead with his own meal," while others have nothing.

It is within that sobering reminder of selfishness and insensitivity to the needs of the poorer members of the congregation that Paul delivers the beautiful tradition of the Lord's Supper.

> For I received from the Lord what I also handed on to you, that the Lord Jesus on the night when he was betrayed took a loaf of bread, and when he had given thanks, he broke it and said, "This is my body that is for you. Do this in remembrance of me." In the same way he took the cup also, after supper, saying, "This cup is the new covenant in my blood. Do this, as often as you drink it, in remembrance of me." For as often as you eat this bread and drink the cup, you proclaim the Lord's death until he comes. (1 Corinthians 11:23-26)

Joseph A. Fitzmyer identifies two aspects that reveal the Lord's Supper or the eucharist as the source of Christian unity: the actual presence of Christ with his people, and the proclamation of Christ's sacrificial death. Regarding the first of these, Christ's presence, Fitzmyer writes: "Since the Lord is identified with such food [see 1 Corinthians 11:27], those who partake of it may not violate its sacred character and his presence by abuses of individualism, of disregard of the poor, or of idol-worship."[16]

As to the second aspect pointed out by Fitzmyer, the proclamation of the death of Christ, one has the right to ask whether Christians today realize that their participation in the Lord's Supper *is* in truth a proclamation of the Lord's death. Is it not more often the case that worshippers assume that the proclaiming of the death of Christ is the business of the pastor and the sermon, whereas the coming to the Lord's table is something done for one's individual spiritual benefit? When we take Paul's words about the Lord's Supper to heart, we must believe that the unified action of believers coming together at the Lord's table to receive Christ's body

---

16. Joseph A. Fitzmyer, *Pauline Theology: A Brief Sketch* (Englewoood Cliffs, N.J.: Prentice-Hall, 1967), 74.

and blood is truly a public testimony, a ringing announcement to the world that Christ has died for the human race and that he will come again.

To anticipate subsequent discussion of the Lord's Supper in chapters to come, it should be stated in connection with Paul's view of the eucharist that he regards what moderns somewhat casually call "going to communion" as an actual *participation* in the blood and body of Christ. He plainly says as much in 1 Corinthians 10:16: "The cup of blessing which we bless, is it not a participation in the blood of Christ? The bread which we break, is it not a participation in the body of Christ?"

The key word in this text is the Greek noun *koinonia*, translated "participation" in the Revised Standard Version, and "sharing in" in the New Revised Standard Version. The root of the word *koinonia* is the adjective *koinos*, which means "common." "Koinonia" is fellowship, participation, sharing in, or communion among those who have something vital in common. The cup and the bread, says Paul, join us with Christ; we participate in his blood and in his body. We and those who worship with us and Christ himself all have something in common: the blood of Christ and the body of Christ. "Because there is one bread," continues Paul, "we who are many are one body, for we all partake of the one bread" (1 Corinthians 10:17). Again, the model and means for human unity is the crucified and risen Christ, present in his body the church through the gifts of bread and wine.

The New Humanity

Paul is described in the title of this chapter as "Witness to the New Humanity." The church as such is not the new humanity, but in the life of the church one can see the outline, as it were, of the new humanity. In the words used by J. Christiaan Beker as a chapter title, the church is to be understood as "the Dawning of the New Age." In the course of the chapter Beker says that the church "is the beachhead of the new creation and the sign of the new age in the old world that is 'passing away' (1 Cor. 7:29)."[17] The church is a very specific entity, with its human members, its tradition, its teachings, its sacraments, and more, whereas the new humanity is less specific, less visible, more of a goal toward which God's redemptive purpose is moving than a concrete entity to be observed. But one looks

17. Beker, *Paul the Apostle*, 313.

to the church and to the thought of the apostle Paul for signs of what the new humanity could be.

A well-known text properly associated with the idea of the new humanity is 2 Corinthians 5:17: "So if anyone is in Christ, there is a new creation: everything old has passed away; see, everything has become new!" A study of the context reveals that the word "so" with which the statement begins takes the reader back to an assertion that Christ died for all and was raised. This new fact of the love of Christ "urges us on," Paul writes, giving a totally new perspective on how one views oneself and on how one regards others.

Christ died for all, "so that those who live might live no longer for themselves, but for him who died and was raised for them" (2 Corinthians 5:15). That is the new perspective on one's own life. As to others, Paul writes, "From now on . . . we regard no one *kata sarka*" or literally, "according to the flesh." The New Revised Standard Version translates *kata sarka* with the words "from a human point of view." In short, Christ's death and resurrection change the way Paul and his fellow Christians look at humanity and at all human possibilities. To paraphrase, "Now that Christ has died for all and has been raised, it is possible for a person to enter into the sphere of Christ and thus to participate in a new order of things."

Paul's reference to "a new creation" in 2 Corinthians 5:17 has to do primarily with human beings, not the physical creation. "If anyone is in Christ, [for that person] there is a new creation." Hence the relevance of this text for the idea of a new humanity. Jesus Christ himself is the definitive "new human," and his death and resurrection open the way for others to enter into him, to join him in the new humanity.

Another feature of Paul's witness to the new humanity is his use of the "Adam" image in 1 Corinthians 15, a chapter devoted to the theme of resurrection. Adam represents fallen humanity; Christ, who proved faithful and obedient, represents a new humanity. "For as all die in Adam, so all will be made alive in Christ" (1 Corinthians 15:22). The first Adam became a living being while "the last Adam became a life-giving spirit" (15:45). The first man was of dust; Christ, the second man, is from heaven. Paul writes: "Just as we have borne the image of the man of dust, we will also bear the image of the man of heaven" (15:49). Christ as the last Adam is meant to rule until all things are subjected to him (15:25); therefore it can be said that he "serves as both the medium and the model of a restored humanity."[18]

18. Calvin J. Roetzel, *The Letters of Paul: Conversations in Context* (Atlanta: John Knox Press, 1977), 79.

Christian humanism is more radical than other humanisms in that it recognizes in the crucified and risen Christ the power to transform humanity. In Romans 12 Paul urges his readers not to be conformed to this world but to "be transformed by the renewing of your minds, so that you may discern what is the will of God — what is good and acceptable and perfect" (12:2). While no one claims that the new humanity is fully realized in the community known as the church, we can say confidently that the church, by having access to the gospel, is in touch with the transforming power of the Christ. The church has its obvious flaws, but insofar as it responds to its risen Lord it points the way toward the realization of a new humanity. With Paul, the church is a "witness to the new humanity."

By accepting the significant role of witness, the Christian individual as well as the church as a body goes before the world with something powerful to say but with considerable modesty about who is saying it. A witness states, under oath, what he or she has seen and heard. The witness may not be able to explain many things which a questioner demands to hear, but like the man whom Jesus healed of his blindness the witness can say, "One thing I do know, that though I was blind, now I see" (John 9:25).

Christian discourse concerning a new humanity is in a similar position. Scripture and experience have shown Christian people the vision of a new humanity, and to some extent various Christian persons have themselves known the taste of a humanity permeated by the life-renewing flavor of Christ's power and presence. But these same Christians are cautioned by Scripture not to claim too much too soon, especially about the quality of human actions and their own activity in particular. Christians too must live by the grace of God, constantly asking forgiveness for their sins, thus admitting that their conduct does not always point to a new humanity. That is one obvious ground for modesty.

But there is a second reason to stick to the witness role instead of claiming to have implemented a new humanity. Christians are a minority in the world today and probably will be tomorrow. The prospect of converting all Jews, Muslims, Hindus, Buddhists, Shintoists, Confucianists, and the millions who have other religions or no religion to the Christian faith is not a bright one. Of course, it never has been bright, but Christian missionary activity has continued just the same. Christianity is indeed a missionary religion and should continue to be so, but classical missionary work is done by means of witnessing. Some hearers will be converted, some will not — but the witnessing goes on. The pluralistic religious situation in the world thus constitutes the second reason for avoiding any triumphalism concerning a new humanity based on faith in Christ.

The church bears witness to such a new humanity, teaches it, recommends it, prays for it, but refrains from declaring that it possesses and controls it. And in the same spirit the church cannot say that the new humanity is for Christians only. A good biblical parallel to the idea of a new humanity is Jesus' proclamation of the kingdom or rule of God. Jesus said that it was at hand, something real that people could actually enter into and experience; he revealed some of its features in his parables; he urged his disciples to go out and preach the imminent appearance of the kingdom. Yet Jesus never placed a placard on the door to the kingdom which said, "For Jews only" or "For Christians only." The kingdom of God means God's kingly rule over all people, all nations, all the world.

The new humanity should not be understood as a rare privilege open only to Christians but as a universal possibility open to all. Christians have been granted some clues as to its nature, and are convinced that the creative source and power of the new humanity is Jesus Christ. But those factors simply point up the obligation Christians are under to tell the rest of humankind what they have seen and heard. As they are faithful in giving their witness to Christ, the author of a new humanity, they will be God's instruments in bringing it to realization, and other people will take notice.

PART III

COMING TOGETHER
IN WORSHIP

Chapter 7

The Lord's Supper:
A Source of Christian Humanism

One quiet but potent source for the revival of Christian humanism in the twentieth century has been the liturgical movement and its reintroduction of several important changes in worship. But any mention of worship as relevant to the vast human problems of war, poverty, or disease is still greeted today with skepticism. An influential leader of the liturgical movement admitted as much when he began an essay by asking, "Can worship help to give jobs or raise wages?"[1]

Even though it has at times receded into the background, a venerable tradition in Christianity holds that the worship of God is an act which empowers women and men who are right with God to make things right on earth. At the fall of Rome, at the Reformation, or in the Age of Revolution, Christian worship has articulated human values often at odds with accepted secular standards. For nineteen centuries some believers have shown that by actively participating in worship they can transform their

---

1. Virgil Michel, quoted in "The Liturgy the Basis of Social Regeneration," in Robert L. Spaeth, ed., *The Social Question* (Collegeville, Minn.: St. John's University, 1987), 1. This skepticism about the social value of liturgy has been a persistent feature of both Protestantism and Catholicism.

society, creating a humane social order that reflects not only material concerns but also the transcendent values of integrity, justice, and beauty. Others in the church, however, remain unconvinced that worship is related to human beings as they exist in the temporal order.

At the heart of Christian worship has always been the sharing of a meal of bread and wine, a recognized sign of human community across society. As there has been one family, the church, so there has been the sharing of one bread and one cup. These essential ingredients of Christian worship have taken on a symbolic importance that, generation after generation throughout Western history, has taught important lessons about human existence.

The bread kneaded together out of many grains into a whole, the grapes losing their separate identity to become wine have often served as striking emblems of social union. Simple images borne out of the intimacy of a family — gathering at table, eating food, savoring the fellowship — have reinforced at worship the consciousness of a new human solidarity and the conviction that a people uniquely one in stature and dignity was being gathered throughout the world.

We know that this meal, the Lord's Supper, was at the center of the community of early Christians for two reasons. First, until the third century the "church" was not understood to be a building or an institution but invariably the assembly gathered for the Lord's Supper. No other group assembly could substitute for this weekly celebration.[2] The measure of a Christian was simply "being in communion," partaking in the corporate act of worship and displaying a fitting conduct in daily affairs. To believe in Christ was to be incorporated into the community of faith, the body of Christ, the fellowship of the Spirit, where the more excellent way of love found concrete expression in celebrating the supper. Worship was the bond of the new community established in the Spirit of Jesus.

Second, it was precisely their attendance at worship that constituted the great crime of the early Christians in the eyes of the Roman state. The firmness with which the martyrs held to their common prayer, and this in spite of persecution, is recorded in numerous early accounts. Under torture, the lay-reader Emeritus cried out in the early fourth century, "Without the Lord's Supper, we cannot live!"[3]

2. Gregory Dix, *The Shape of the Liturgy* (London: Dacre Press, 1945), 18-21.
3. A. Hamman, *The Grace to Act Now,* trans. Malachy Carroll (Chicago: Franciscan Herald Press, 1966), 54.

The lives of these early Christians were spent in circumstances somewhat like our own. It was a world of increasing social chaos brought on by the conflict between a dying pagan culture and the pressure of barbarians invading the Roman Empire. Rome itself, with its stadia and gladiators, was a society familiar with public violence. Rome sought security in its arsenals and armies that it spread strategically around the edges of the Empire. The early Christian places of worship were surrounded by the great masses of the Roman cities, where Christians' freedom was threatened as secular powers sought to force them into chains. The prevailing philosophy depicted human beings as powerless creatures, passive before a dark pagan concept of fate.

The church fathers were Christian scholars who preached and wrote against this background during the first six centuries after Christ. For these first Christian teachers, the Lord's Supper portrayed in a visible way the Christian understanding of the true nature of human society. Worship was not for them a detailed, practical outline of life, but it did lift up a model of true human enrichment and fulfillment through its focus on the Incarnation of Jesus and on the church as his abiding incarnation. The Lord's Supper was a "school" in which the fathers learned two unique things about humanity from a Christian perspective: first that God has created human beings as creatures of fellowship; and second that both matter and spirit are in the service of God's purpose to restore all that belongs to human existence.

In acts of worship the fathers experienced for a moment what the reign of God can be like. They saw in picture language an end to selfishness and narcissism and the emptiness and frustration that result from withdrawal from others. They beheld, in signs, mutual and humble love that dispels human incompleteness and fragmentation. They were reminded of a willingness to sacrifice in the service of fellow men and women. The Lord's Supper was a witness to a humanism that safeguarded the dignity of the individual within the context of a larger community and coordinated the material with the spiritual aspects of life in the work of God.

The Human Community at the Lord's Table

As the first Christians repeated the actions of Jesus at his Last Supper they were aware of his real, objective presence in their midst. They felt his presence in their fellowship with one another, and by this eating and drinking, the unity of the many in Christ was strengthened week after week in the sharing of common food. Christian education took place in the setting of the Lord's Supper; members of the congregation read entire books of the Bible before the ritual meal. In these "lessons" the Bible spoke to the community of social oppression, the sufferings of others, the harm of economic injustice, the effects of prejudice and hatred, and the power of healing grace. Sermons — actually commentaries on the Scripture — accompanied these readings, and the singing of a psalm followed each lesson.

Early Christians spoke of "eucharist," "breaking bread," and "liturgy" as well as "Lord's Supper," but they were all referring to this common action of lessons, psalms, sermon, eating, and drinking. The most popular term for the Lord's Supper in the first Christian centuries came to be "eucharist," from a Greek word meaning "thanksgiving." The fathers called many things eucharist: the bread and wine of the offering, the consecration of the bread and wine, and finally the communion of the whole assembled congregation.

So important was the role of the entire group of people present in celebrating the eucharist that another word for ancient worship was "liturgy." The word is a compound of the Greek term for people *(laos)* and the noun for work *(ergon);* it meant simply "the work of the people." The Alexandrian translators who produced the Septuagint, the Old Testament in Greek, had first used the word "liturgy" to describe the Hebrew worship of God in the third century B.C. *Leitourgia* appears 127 times in the Septuagint, and there it designates the public work of the sacred cult performed in homage to God by priests and Levites juridically invested and set above the masses. The prayers of the assembly of the laity gathered in the court of the Israelites or in the women's court in the temple of Jerusalem are not described as "liturgy."

A significant departure from Septuagint usage occurs in the New Testament at Acts 13:1-2: "Now in the church at Antioch . . . they were worshiping the Lord." Here the writer employs *leitourgia* in a manner closer to its original classical Greek sense: an action performed by an entire human community, rather than by a hierarchy. This usage has important implications for social values. The verse points away from a cultic priesthood; characteristic of the early church it implies no special emphasis on persons of rank and privilege. Acts 13:2 glances back five hundred years to the ancient image of the great corporate liturgies of the assembly of free citizens of the *polis* to describe as a "liturgy" the worship of Jesus Christ in which each Christian took an equal share.[4]

The Christian humanist should be attentive to this widespread early Christian use of the word "liturgy." The "people" at worship were not an audience of passive spectators, but a *laos,* a redeemed people drawn together from all races, all classes, of all degrees of morality and spirituality; not an elite, chosen and distinct. Liturgy was the way in which this people was lifted up into a new "we"-form. The early church used still another Greek word to speak in "we"-language. It is *koinonia,* in Latin *communio;* hence our English word "communion" for the Lord's Supper. *Koinonia* describes the fellowship, sharing, and mutual affection the early church experienced in its worship.[5]

The writings of the fathers show an intense awareness of human solidarity in the eucharist. This worship was no private affair between the individual and Jesus. To the fathers, Jesus did not come into the world merely to save individuals. He came to re-create a people, to begin a new era, to establish a commonwealth. Fellowship with Christ was fellowship with his community at worship.

The whole assembled church celebrated the eucharist. Jesus said, "Do this" (*poieite,* a Greek plural command). Bread was broken that it might be shared. One cup signified a collective "partaking" of the blood of Christ. This understanding of the Lord's Supper or eucharist as a joint action performed by all present is clearly expressed in an eyewitness account of the way it was performed in the autumn of A.D. 96, and is characteristic of all descriptions of Christian worship until the fifth century.

4. On the history of the word *liturgy* and its humanistic implications in Judaism and early Christianity see Antonino Romeo, "Il termine *leitourgia* nella grecità biblica," in *Miscellanea liturgica* (Rome, 1949), 467-547; Odo Casel, "Leitourgia-Munus," *Oriens Christianus,* ser. 3, vol. 7 (1932), 289-302; and Arthur Darby Nock, *Early Gentile Christianity and its Hellenistic Background* (New York: Harper & Row, 1964), 68-86, 124-34.

5. Many scholars today emphasize the notion of "communion" as the key to the images of the church in the New Testament. The concept of "communion" embodies the principle of the believer's relationship to God and Christ in the Holy Spirit; it is related to the eucharist and to the unity that Christ wills for his church. On these points see Jérôme Hamer, *The Church is a Communion* (New York: Sheed and Ward, 1964); and Jean-Marie Tillard, *Église d'Églises. L'ecclésiologie de communion* (Paris: Le Cerf, 1987).

The first Christian prayers come down to us in the plural: *We* pray. *We* thank. *We* offer. *We* praise and glorify. Public prayer was often loudly co-executed by the faithful. Jerome, the translator of the Latin Bible, boasted that in the fourth century the Roman basilicas resounded like heavenly thunder with prayer. Bodily gestures also expressed participation. The company of believers raised their hands with the bishop or presider and knelt silently together on the floor. In the first five centuries after Christ it must have presented an impressive picture when the entire congregation joined in the offertory procession to bring bread and wine, as well as foodstuffs and gifts of charity for the poor, to the altar, and when they again formed a procession for communion.

In the whole of ancient Christendom each church possessed but one altar, with space around it for the community and its action. There were no reserved seats or family pews. There was no elaborate choral music, just a complete and intense concentration upon the corporate performance of the eucharistic action: taking, blessing, breaking, and distributing bread and wine. As late as the eighth century the Roman papal masses were still celebrated in an open basilica with the pope at a free-standing altar in the midst of an active congregation. An unobstructed floor was crucial for the solemn rhythms by which the gathered company played out its ritual role through processions and other common gestures of worship. Ample room was necessary for the entire assembly to raise their hands with the presider in the attitude of the *orante,* the posture of the people standing before the altar with arms outstretched, showing forth the new human dignity of the baptized Christian.

For Irenaeus, a significant thinker in the church of Gaul in the century after the apostles, the communal eucharist held up a pattern of dignified human relationships that could actually be achieved in the temporal order. In many ways Christian society was for Irenaeus more egalitarian than the pagan world. Because active participation in the eucharist was the root from which the communal dimension of life could grow, Irenaeus taught that it was more human to have a participating congregation than a passive audience listening to an impressive orator.

The church's concept of community in worship broke down class barriers. While the Roman cities were deeply divided between rich and poor, powerful and weak, slave and master, man and woman, the eucharist was an act that built togetherness; in its celebration there was no discrimination between high and low, Jew and Greek. Where else in the Roman world were food and drink given equally to all? The eucharist made the structure of a human community possible.

Around the year A.D. 185, Irenaeus wrote words that have become cornerstones of Christian humanism:

> The glory of God is a human being alive. . . . He who feeds our bodies with his flesh and blood in the Eucharist is also he who makes provision for the earthly needs of those same bodies in the order of creation.[6]

In this last sentence Irenaeus took a stand against the second-century Gnostics who proclaimed a self-preoccupied spirituality without the sacraments. The Gnostics believed that human civilization was to be despised and Christianity opened only to an intellectual elite. In the face of the Gnostics, Irenaeus made the bold proclamation that Jesus continues to make his dwelling on earth in *all* his faithful people. Irenaeus called the people the "body of Christ." He reminded his hearers that the goal of the Incarnation, the joining of the material with the divine, continued to be carried out on earth in the midst of the assembly gathered for the Lord's Supper.

Worship and the Material Dimensions of Human Life

The worship of the assembly was Irenaeus's guide to the right understanding and use of physical goods. From the eucharistic perspective, human dependence upon material things was not to be repressed but emphasized and met, not by selfish, self-regarding enterprise, but in the light of the needs of the whole society. The relationship of Christian people to the economic order alters from age to age. But there was once a deep sense in which Christians held all things in common. The faithful were not obliged to give their private property to the local church, but they were encouraged to do so and many of them actually followed this practice. Distribution of church goods was made according to individual needs.

A fourth-century mosaic survives at Aquileia in Italy that represents an offertory procession in which women and men are bringing bread and wine, grapes, flowers, and a bird to the altar. It was a general practice that each man and woman should place upon the altar a little loaf of bread and

---

6. Irenaeus, *Adversus haereses*, 4.20.7.

a small bottle of wine, representing the offering of self and the fruit of labor to God and to the community. The corporate presentation of material gifts — oil, olives, wax, cheese, poultry, milk, honey, and money for the sustenance of widows and prisoners — came to occupy the midpoint of the liturgy. A sermon comes down to us from third-century Carthage in which the bishop Cyprian is scolding a rich heiress of the city for lack of participation in the liturgy, for withholding her gift of charity from the offertory procession.

Writing in Rome in the middle of the second century, Justin Martyr recorded that a kiss of peace was shared among the congregation as a sign of friendship and respect, immediately before this offering of the gifts. The kiss of peace was another striking instance of the way in which the liturgy was regarded as the solemn putting into action before God of the bonds of fraternity and sorority that drew the Christian body into one living entity. Not surprisingly, talk of the kiss of brothers and sisters spread through Rome and stimulated dark suspicions of orgies, of promiscuous vice, of Bacchanalian scandal, and even of organized incest within the liturgical gathering.

The liturgy ended with all present consuming the bread and the wine while standing before the altar. A Gospel codex from Rossano in southern Italy, from about A.D. 500, pictures Jesus standing while giving his disciples, also standing, communion in the form of bread. To eat and drink standing before the altar was the final sign of the equality and dignity of all who participated in this worship shaped by anonymous generations of every class out of the common experiences, the culture, and the living language of the people.[7]

This social and egalitarian sense the early Christians expressed in their worship was so strong that it extended to a fellowship of property and to primitive consumers' cooperatives. Mutual assistance was a material reflection of the unity celebrated in the body of Christ. In Rome the church

---

7. On the role of the laity in early Christian worship with its implications for humanism, see as an introduction: Paul Bradshaw, *Liturgical Presidency in the Early Church* (Bramcote: Grove Books, 1983); Colin Buchanan, *The End of the Offertory* (Bramcote: Grove Books, 1978); Hervé-Marie Legrand, "The Presidency of the Eucharist According to the Ancient Tradition," in R. Kevin Seasoltz, *Living Bread, Saving Cup* (Collegeville, Minn.: The Liturgical Press, 1982); David Power, *The Christian Priest: Elder and Prophet* (London: Sheed and Ward, 1973); David Power, *Gifts That Differ: Lay Ministries Established and Unestablished* (New York: Pueblo, 1980); J. M. R. Tillard, *What Priesthood Has the Ministry* (Bramcote: Grove Books, 1973).

was supporting 1,500 poor people and widows by A.D. 250. In A.D. 254 and 256 the churches of Rome and Carthage sent large sums to ransom the captives of Mediterranean pirates.

Within the community of the faithful the "new creation" was taking shape in the form of economic relationships unlike those of the surrounding secular society. Aristides, a non-Christian defending the Christians before the Roman emperor Hadrian, described these ties:

> The Christians don't consider themselves brothers in the usual sense, but brothers instead through the Spirit, in God. And if they hear that one of them is in jail, or persecuted for professing the name of their redeemer, they all give him what he needs. If it is possible, they bail him out. If one of them is poor and there isn't enough food to go around, they fast several days to give him the food he needs. This is really a new kind of person. There is something divine in them.[8]

The eucharist opened the eyes of believers to see the worth of material things, including the human body, as God's gifts. That Christ chose food as the means of effecting his presence with his disciples was highly significant. Irenaeus taught a reverence for things and persons, not just for spiritual advancement; the value of the goods and property of the earth was a serious issue facing the Christian. As long as the church celebrated the Lord's Supper, no one could say that matter and the body were not sacred to her.

In the early eucharist bread and wine — symbols of everyday labor — were brought to the altar to become the instruments of Christ's presence. The breaking of the bread itself was the chief sign of fellowship and communal living. The Didache, an early Christian collection from no later than the second century, beautifully expressed the relation of the bread of human labor to the unity of the church in the following prayer: "Just as this loaf previously was scattered on the mountains, and when it was gathered together it became a unity, so may your church be gathered together from the ends of the earth into your kingdom."[9]

As time passed, architecture, painting, sculpture, music, and other

8. Tissa Balasuriya, *The Eucharist and Human Liberation* (Maryknoll, N.Y.: Orbis Books, 1979), 26.

9. Arthur A. Vogel, *Is the Last Supper Finished?* (New York: Sheed and Ward, 1968), 169; and also Allan Bouley, *From Freedom to Formula: The Evolution of the Eucharistic Prayer from Oral Improvisation to Written Texts* (Washington, D.C.: The Catholic University of America Press, 1981).

material objects began to be used in abundance in Christian worship. Liturgy addressed itself to and made use of each dimension of the human body and all the senses — hearing, seeing, imagination, emotions, and intelligence. Bread and wine, oil and water, gold and silver, stone and wood, the pageantry of color, the harmony of sound, the odor of burnt incense, all of these sensible things came to be united with the human voice, the gestures of the body, and the wisdom of the mind to form a hymn of praise to the Creator.

In worship, the fathers beheld for a moment "creation redeemed and at prayer," and so they believed that they could already see paradise in the landscape around them, even though it was only the arid desert of the Middle East.[10] Called to the service of nature "as into a sacred service," they took the deepest, most spontaneous, most human delight in the material world.[11] Their style of worship did justice to the high dignity of the natural realm as reflecting the perfection of the Creator. Early liturgy was not rushed. It was celebrated with a spiritual relaxation hallowing time with quiet and silence. The harmony and peace of fixed prayer gave order and discipline to a Christian people facing the trials and the persecutions of the Roman Empire.

Dom Dominic Gaisford caught this atmosphere of serenity and assurance in his reflections on early worship in *A Touch of God:*

> I think, Lord, that what you give me and everyone in prayer is a new vision, or a new dimension. The people I am fond of and love, the things I like doing, the places I like, are in some tangible way different, added to, increased by you. . . . The people and places and activities which I love and like become different in you. . . . Lord, . . . you know what I mean, when I say that your abiding presence — yes, that's it Lord, prayer is your abiding presence made real.[12]

10. Romano Guardini in Bernard I. Mullahy, "The Spirit of Poverty," *Worship,* 27 (1955), 229.

11. Emil Brunner, *Christianity and Civilization* (New York: Charles Scribner's Sons, 1948), vol. 1, 102.

12. Dominic Gaisford, *A Touch of God,* quoted in Esther de Waal, *Seeking God: The Way of St. Benedict* (Collegeville, Minn.: The Liturgical Press, 1984), 156. For more on the eucharistic humanism of early Christianity see Werner Elert, *Eucharist and Church Fellowship in the First Four Centuries* (St. Louis: Concordia, 1966); Josef A. Jungmann, *The Early Liturgy to the Time of Gregory the Great* (Notre Dame: University of Notre Dame Press, 1959); David N. Power, *Unsearchable Riches: The Symbolic Nature of Liturgy* (New York: Pueblo, 1984); J. H. Srawley, *The Early History of the Liturgy* (Cambridge: Cambridge University Press, 1947).

Because the eucharist was understood as an act that embraced all of human life, men and women freely wove their crucial personal experiences and the ongoing history of their daily lives into the prayer of intercession at the eucharist. Worship was extended into processions that wound through surrounding streets so that more people would know themselves included in the church's joy. Celebrations of the eucharist blessed the daily experiences of giving birth, planting crops, and gathering food. The early church apparently did not know of any separate marriage service. The "fulfillment" of marriage by two Christians was their partaking together of the eucharist. As every aspect of life was gathered into the eucharist, so matrimony received its seal by inclusion in this central act of the community.

The liturgical year, the round of feasts lifting up events in the life of Jesus and his disciples, began to mark secular time and the seasons. Week by week and year by year reminders of the mighty acts of God were integrated into calendars and customs. On the feast of the epiphany, long associated with the baptism of Christ, rivers and boats were blessed. At the feast of the purification candles that would be used in the home for the next twelve months were brought to church. In these ways early worship reached into the total environment in which human beings seek their fulfillment.

This recurring round of celebration and feast reminds us that the gospel in the first centuries was not a collection of harsh restrictions and moralistic commandments, but glad tidings to all men and women of good will. From the first, the Lord's Supper was conceived above all as an act of thanksgiving that the benefits of the new age that began with the resurrection of Jesus from the dead — life, wholeness, freedom, and peace — can be realized now, on this earth, through the working of God's Holy Spirit in the lives of all who believe this good news. Hence the reason that *eucharist,* the giving of thanks, came so universally to be used to refer to Christian worship. Thanksgiving was the only response deemed possible before the fact of divine activity extended toward the human race in Jesus.

Augustine

One of the last and greatest of the fathers, Augustine, provided concrete suggestions for how worship might serve as a source of peace and good-will as the Roman Empire fell apart amid the chaos of the fourth and fifth centuries. Augustine was an immensely learned classical humanist of the fourth century who had become a leading professor at three ancient centers of learning before he was thirty-two. Like Paul he underwent a conversion to Christianity as a mature adult. For Augustine, this crucial change in his life took place at Milan in August 386, and he became one of the most tireless workers on behalf of Christ. He was elected a bishop in North Africa, where he served until his death in A.D. 430.

Augustine's activities as a bishop show him to have been a sensitive and completely dedicated pastor to his flock, yet he somehow found time to write a whole library of books, some of which are among the great books of all time. His advice was constantly sought, and dispensed, in letters and handbooks. Of the latter the *Enchiridion* is the oldest theological textbook for lay people. For more than a thousand years after his death, Augustine was a veritable mine of ideas and undoubtedly the dominant figure in the development of Christian thought. He was a model and guide for later pilgrims and reformers like Luther, Calvin, and Pascal.

The letters of Paul provided the point of departure for many of Augustine's most provocative discussions, and yet after his conversion he lost none of his previous humanism; he just Christianized it. He explored, for instance, the relationship between God and the human being, and thus his work is of special importance for any study of Christian humanism. Augustine's teaching on human community experienced in worship exerted a great influence. In sermons and in letters of advice to distant congregations, Augustine insisted that the way in which the church possessed the Spirit at the table of Christ was not as a "many" of single individuals, nor as a "sum" of elite moralists, but as a corporate "we," a solidarity of the faithful that transcended individual personalities.

Augustine used the New Testament language of the vine and the branches to convey his understanding that this solidarity is based upon a shared life of worship:

> The vine and the branches live the same life and feed upon the same sap, work together for the bearing of the same fruit. They form one sole being. Their action is one.[13]

For Augustine the Lord's Supper was the supreme action by which each Christian came into his or her own as a member of Christ's body and

---

13. Augustine, quoted in Abbé Angers, *The Doctrine of the Mystical Body of Christ* (New York: Benzinger Brothers, 1931), xv; see also G. G. Willis, *St. Augustine's Lectionary* (London: SPCK, 1962).

experienced union with the community. "There you are upon the table," he said to new communicants at Easter, "There you are in the chalice."[14] Augustine means here that in the eucharist the defiled image of God is restored in men and women by the reception of Jesus, the one archetypal image; and humankind, renewed and gathered into one, is presented to the Father as the "one new man."

It is not strange to Augustine that the eucharist should have this power of laying hold of human life, of grasping the material realities of it. For he saw that here in this act of worship it was the whole perfect life of Jesus that was broken and given. The purpose of God in human creation is fulfilled for Augustine in the eucharist. And though he did not think that God spoke exclusively through this means of grace, the word and sacrament of worship are the central and normal media through which God continues to communicate to the believing heart.

Against the background of the decay of classical civilization and its values, Augustine saw two societies competing for human allegiance, the City of God and the City of the World. Informed of the advancing barbarian invasions and realizing that the end of the Roman world was at hand, Augustine began his monumental *City of God* shortly after the sack of Rome by the Goths in A.D. 410.

Here he evokes the vanishing world of pagan worship, with temple prostitutes and temple sodomites who "against all shame of man and woman went with anointed heads, painted faces, relaxed bodies and lascivious paces up and down the streets of Carthage." He also portrays the vulgar feats of pagan priestly showmen.[15]

The *City of God* maintained that the vision of human life realized in Christian eucharistic worship offered something better and more enduring for the family, for the parish, for society, and for international solidarity than the dying classical worship could afford. These are some of the points Augustine makes:

1. *Family.* Families that live according to the liturgy will understand their lives in the spirit of pilgrims and not seek security in material goods. The gospel of God's love is the only solid basis of a true humanism in the family, which safeguards the dignity of each individual personality. Humility is the unambiguous sign of Christian love in the family, just as love

14. Augustine, *Sermon 272.*
15. Cited in Henry Chadwick, *Augustine* (Oxford: Oxford University Press, 1986), 96-106.

for the unworthy is its most genuine expression. These traits markedly distinguish the Christian family from the secular.

2. *Parish.* Augustine praised the church at Carthage for providing money and food when believers fell ill. He noted that talents, gifts, and common goods were shared to build up the local body at Alexandria. In the parish, human work of every kind should be a duty of solidarity, a means of social service, never at the expense of other members of the community. Worship reveals that we are God's instruments for the transformation of the whole fabric of local human life. We recognize our sisters and brothers, as well as Jesus, in the breaking of bread.

3. *Society.* An intelligent understanding about sin, conveyed in the lessons of the liturgical year, is necessary to preserve the world from putting unjustified confidence in the efficacy of the moral law. Every human attempt to abolish wars and wickedness by a moral majority is doomed to failure because of the fact of human sinfulness. Where the love of God is at work, members of society are bound together.

4. *International Solidarity.* Augustine never forgot that the Christian community existed within but apart from the Roman Empire. He once said that secular governments are nothing but large-scale robbery schemes, and so to him no particular economic or political system was ordained of God. Augustine was pleased that the church had developed a universal discourse in her prayer. Liturgy, though entirely a human creation, was not the product of a single artist or of one class or of one country or generation. It was formed by varied, anonymous hands over many generations. The "we"-forms of early prayer were no sham device; they pointed to an age when out of all peoples the church was building up the peace of the house of God.

As his life neared its end, Augustine wrote to a young Christian of his experience of a life shaped by liturgical prayer: "Begin then to praise now, if thou intendest to praise for ever. . . . Praise and bless the Lord thy God every single day, so that when the time of single days has passed, and there has come that one day without end, thou mayest go from praise to praise, as 'from strength to strength.'"[16]

16. Cited in Esther de Waal, *Seeking God,* 156.

Benedict

By the sixth century the Roman Empire had completely crumbled. Economic prosperity waned, cities disappeared, and trade and commerce slowed to a trickle. In the early sixth century, according to tradition, Benedict, a layman who was part of the last generation of the old Roman world, withdrew from the decaying city of Rome to the wild and inspiring hermitage of Subiaco in order to be closer to God in the wilderness.

The *Rule* of Benedict, developed in central Italy around A.D. 530 for use later at his monastery of Monte Cassino, laid out a pattern of Christian life for this wasted environment. In time Benedict would be known as the father of a monastic tradition that has been devoted to the ideal of community for almost fifteen hundred years, and along with this ideal had developed also a sense of a special responsibility for the liturgy. It was not long before nuns too began following Benedict's *Rule* in communities of women.

The *Rule* reflects the experience of the five previous centuries of Christian living in its stress on liturgy as the center of religious community. Benedict united all of his monks before God eight times a day in the liturgical prayer of the divine office. According to Benedict, Jesus had sanctioned ceaseless prayers of praise, blessing, and thanksgiving, and without an active community of worship, the monastery would have no reason to exist. Both conversion of the individual and the communitarian character of the church were perfected through liturgy.

Benedict's *Rule* taught ancient monks and nuns the love of a good and Godly world that was to be reshaped through dedicated prayer. A contemporary Christian woman has written that still today Benedict's "*Rule* is telling me that ultimately praying is living, working, loving, accepting, the refusal to take anything or anyone for granted but rather to try to find Christ in and through them all."[17]

Human work tempered by the rhythm of constant worship and nourished by the living water of the liturgy became an homage offered to God associated with the redemptive work of Jesus Christ. The monastic man or woman at labor was thought of as a partner with God in bringing creation to perfection. In Benedict's vision of a renewed society, a new paradise, work ceased to be regarded as a curse, the result of primeval human disobedience, but rather was welcomed as another mode of serving God and the human community.

17. Ibid., 152.

Prayerful work in the monastic library and *scriptorium* contributed significantly to the advancement of Christian humanism. Those intending to worship with heart and mind had to be taught reading and chant. In the *scriptorium* the monks produced magnificent volumes fit for use in the divine presence: psalters, Gospel books, Bibles, and sacramentaries that are among the most beautiful books ever produced. Because monastic worship required variety to enhance devotional life, hymns were composed to express the faith of the community in poetic form. Times of day, seasons of the year, persons of the Trinity, and the mysteries of belief were commemorated in hymns both spiritually penetrating and emotionally moving. The wonders of the cross, the gifts of the Spirit, and the love of the brethren are all expressed in hymns of astonishing power and beauty. They constitute an enduring legacy and an incomparable treasury of Christian humanism.

Benedictine monasteries spread throughout Latin Christendom and eventually absorbed most rival systems, including Celtic monasticism. Until the twelfth century the *Rule* was the standard for all Christians who chose to live some kind of community life. In their writings, in their buildings, at their finest moments, monks and nuns revealed a splendid Christian humanism, the integration of the worldly and the godly, the human and the divine. Worship in common was central to this humanism because the liturgy constantly sensitized the members of the community to the glory of the created order. This in turn helped develop a love of beautiful music and of new artistic — especially architectural — creations. It is no accident that Gothic architecture and Gregorian chant, two of the sublime creations of the medieval spirit, came out of the monastic service of the liturgy.

As monasticism evolved, the humanistic element became more pronounced, as through worship and study the religious sought not only to improve their knowledge of sacred texts but to enrich their personalities as well. By refining their human faculties in this way, "Benedictines" sought to become better men and women and thus give glory to God.[18]

18. On monasticism, humanism, and worship see Jean Leclercq, *The Love of Learning and the Desire for God: A Study of Monastic Culture* (New York: Fordham University Press, 1961); Rowan Williams, *The Wound of Knowledge: Christian Spirituality from the New Testament to St. John of the Cross* (London: SPCK, 1979); Claude J. Peifer, "The Relevance of the Monastic Tradition to the Problem of Work and Leisure," *American Benedictine Review,* 28 (1977), 373-96; and Johann Adam Moehler, "Bruckstücke aus der Geschichte der Aufhebung der Sklaverei," *Theologische Quartalschrift* (1834), 61-136, 567-613.

Gradually the reach of the monastery permeated the secular community, and finally all of European society came under its influence. Early medieval society came to be in many respects a monastic society even in secular life. The monasteries instructed Europe in how to organize civil life and provide material aid, and they thereby enlightened, ordered, and rendered more humane the lives of millions. Because the monks and nuns regarded the tools and products of their daily labor as though they were sacred vessels of the altar, they spread throughout the continent a high regard for the religious significance of all meaningful manual labor, a factor that played a role in the gradual ending of slavery in the West. This high regard for the status of the mundane was a distinctly new contribution of Christian humanism, an attitude not to be found in the pagan world. Secular callings now came to demonstrate a religious dimension and a social purpose, symbolized, for example, in the liturgy of a coronation. The public works of medieval society, whole populations of towns building churches and reclaiming waste areas, were a powerful witness to Christian communalism and the monastic teaching that the gifts of God belong in common to all.

"Throughout All Ages World without End"

At the end of his influential book on *The Shape of the Liturgy,* Dom Gregory Dix reprints the epitaph from a poorly carved rustic monument of the fourth century, "Here sleeps the blessed Chione, who has found Jerusalem for she prayed much."[19] Nothing else is known of Chione, a peasant of the forgotten world of Christian Asia Minor. All that survives of her after sixteen centuries is that she prayed in such a way that her neighbors felt sure that she must have found Jerusalem.

Dix goes on to suggest that it is precisely because worship became so embedded in the life of Christian people, coloring personal turning-points, marriage, sickness, death, and rest, that the Christian eucharistic vision became intricately woven into subsequent Western history. Dix reminds us in a famous passage that worship has occurred "in every conceivable human circumstance, for every conceivable human need from infancy to extreme old age, from the pinnacles of earthly greatness to the

19. Dix, *Shape of the Liturgy,* 751.

refuge of fugitives":[20] Pope Leo celebrating eucharist on the day he went out to meet Attila and save Rome; another Pope Leo doing the same when he crowned Charlemagne in A.D. 800 and Europe was born; King Charles I likewise on the morning of his execution when medieval England came to its final end; Columbus as he set out for America; soldiers repeating the action on the beach at Dunkirk in 1940; an exiled Russian bishop celebrating today in a modern Soviet labor camp near Murmansk.

This eucharistic vision of life was often lost sight of; nevertheless, it is a unique contribution of Christianity to the tradition of Western humanism. The sacred character previously associated with buildings and temples consecrated to cultic purposes was transformed in the New Testament to the assembled community of men and women, and for nineteen centuries Christianity has stressed the transforming power of God's presence in human lives rather than in structures of brick and mortar. The human congregation had not been the essential element in the sacred temples of pagan Greece and Rome, buildings and rites that honored the deity but made no provision for the people.

In the worship of Judaism the situation was different. In common with much of the ancient world, Israel had its house of God, the Tent of Presence in the wilderness or the temple at Jerusalem which only the priest would enter while the praying assembly remained outside. On the other hand, the house of God was never so important as to undermine the significance of the people Israel, consecrated to God and called to holiness. Moreover, from Israel Christianity learned valuable lessons about worship, including the profound idea of God's continuing presence with the people, whether they were "on the road" (the tent) or "at home" (the temple).

Even as the church borrowed heavily from the symbols and practices of Jewish worship, it forged its own new direction with reference to the central tenet of God's presence with the community. Because of the incarnate Christ and the indwelling of the Holy Spirit, Christianity not only bore witness, with Judaism, to the presence of God in the worshipping assembly but also maintained that the very life of God was transmitted to the believing assembly through its participation, its *koinonia*, in the body and blood of Christ. On the basis of its experience of God's presence in its midst in a personal way through Christ, the church then appropriated lively images of the divine habitation in the Jerusalem temple from the Hebrew

20. Ibid., 744-45. For more on the eucharistic humanism of Dix see Kenneth W. Stevenson, *Gregory Dix Twenty-Five Years On* (Bramcote: Grove Books, 1977).

Bible and applied them to its fellowship. Thus, for example, the figure of the church as a house or temple of living human stones recurs throughout Christian literature.

In meditating on this revolutionary step forward in the history of humanism in his *First Letter to the Corinthians* of A.D. 96, Clement of Rome included a powerful concluding prayer that proclaims at its climax the awesome fact that God's holiness comes close to the earth in the lives of men and women at prayer. God's glory is in them and they are God's fitting worship. "If we compare what [Clement] has written here with what we know of town and community life, the societies, schools, etc. of that time," wrote Adolf von Harnack in his famous study of Clement in 1929, "the tremendous difference strikes us at once, and we remember the words of the apostle Paul to the Philippians: 'You are children of God without blemish in the midst of a crooked and perverse generation, among whom you are seen as lights in the world'" (Philippians 2:15).[21]

For hundreds of years Christians have learned the meaning of their humanity through the simple action of meeting together to participate in the holy meal, the Lord's Supper. Protestant, Catholic, and Orthodox believers have always approached the table of the Lord with appropriate awe and humility, sensing that there they breathed for a moment the air of the world to come and touched the hem of divinity's garment. One does not question the universal reverence associated with the eucharist, but the discussion above has been suggesting something that may be new for most modern worshippers. It proposes that the eucharist is not only communion with the divine world but a participation in the new humanity being fashioned by Jesus Christ. To join one's fellow Christians at the holy table is to affirm their humanity and one's own, and to receive the life of God for the human journey.

21. Adolf von Harnack, *Das Schreiben der Römischen Kirche an die Korinthische aus der Zeit Domitians* (Berlin: W. de Gruyter, 1929), 102-3.

Chapter 8

*Eucharistic Humanism
Lost and Regained*

B y the thirteenth century Christian humanism had moved from the
monasteries to the newly revived European cities, and there it found
its home in the Gothic cathedrals and especially the scholastic universities.
University humanists championed study, the acquisition of languages, and
careful thinking in individual minds and hearts. Secular wealth and improved economic conditions in the flourishing cities of Italy and Germany
nurtured a public emphasis on individual pursuits. By the end of the
fourteenth century, Christian humanists were seeking their inspiration
primarily in classical Greek and Latin literature, with its emphasis on the
dignity and freedom of the individual. Christian humanism no longer
centered on the ideals of worship and community.

Early Christianity had assumed the community as a given, but in
the European culture of the late Middle Ages the individual was the given
and the community was a goal to strive toward. The venerable tradition
of Christian fellowship in the eucharist, with its implications for humanism
and society, had receded far into the background.

In late medieval theology the eucharist became a vehicle of piety
for the individual soul rather than a community action. In the fifteenth
century a book that tried to restore Augustine's teaching that the people

are the body of Christ was condemned as "offensive to pious ears."[1] Interest in the relationship between the sacramental body of Christ and the "mystical" body that is the church had fallen by the wayside. "Watching" and "hearing" became the only role of the laity at worship. In many places, as in Westminster Abbey, the rood screen that represented the crucifixion had become a real wall separating the altar from the people. The thirteenth-century idea that the canon or eucharistic prayer of the mass was reserved for the priest alone was extended in the fourteenth century to the whole mass. Now much of the Lord's Supper was celebrated in silence, with only the priest receiving holy communion. More and more the physical posture of the laity became distinct from that of the priest: the celebrant stood, but the people knelt.

By the sixteenth century, paintings of the Last Supper did not evoke a common meal but conveyed an individual, psychological emphasis, the most famous example being Leonardo da Vinci's scene of the disciples asking, "Lord, is it I?" The numerous chapels and altars that began to clutter churches in this period were an outgrowth of the emphasis on the mass as an efficacious offering for individual merit, and they further obscured the communal dimension of worship and life. The eucharist became a good work to be performed by offering a stipend or by mere attendance, an automatic device for obtaining favors, spiritual and temporal. Churches with thirty-five to forty-five altars were no rarity. In about the year 1500, the Church of St. Mary at Gdansk and the Cathedral at Magdeburg each had forty-eight altars. Altars were constructed in the organ loft, under the pulpit, behind columns and pillars. In Breslau at the end of the fifteenth century no fewer than 236 priests were attached to two of the town's churches, solely as "altar priests" whose only duty was to say masses for the souls of departed individuals.

The decline of eucharistic humanism did not develop in a vacuum isolated from a metamorphosis in the secular world. A number of interactions of the secular world and the world of the church contributed to the mutation of the liturgical tradition of Christian humanism. While these dynamics are of great interest, we cannot pause to examine them in detail here, but only list them: the focus on the clergy alone at worship, the influence of the Roman imperial court on the liturgy, the enormous growth of the church and the need to devise a religion that appealed to the vast

---

1. The Council of Basel (1439) in Godfrey Diekmann, *Come, Let Us Worship* (Baltimore: Jelicon Press, 1961), 15.

and poorly catechized populations of Europe, and the transformation of monasticism into a pillar of the status quo all played their part. As a result of these processes that extended over a millennium, the laity came to be present at worship simply as passive recipients of the spiritual benefits bestowed by the clergy. Over the course of the Middle Ages the old sense of the eucharist as a model of daily living for the mass of ordinary Christians was lost.

The people of God became a silent, stationary mass, watching the clergy, kneeling while the bishop or priest stood, declining more and more even to eat the consecrated bread. In the minds of most theologians by the year 1000 the praise and thanksgiving of the eucharistic offering had little or nothing to do with the people's participation.

This eroded theology of the eucharistic sacrifice, new concepts of leadership and authority in the church, and the increasingly dominant role of the clergy are three reasons why the intense consciousness of human solidarity experienced by the early Christians in their worship was lost. Moreover, monasticism, the institution that had once embodied the old patristic humanism, lost the balance between prayer and work as it declined into an era of "spiritual rusticity" and became, in most cases, a puppet of the secular state or a powerful, and unjust, economic force in its own right.[2]

Luther and Calvin on the Eucharist

Martin Luther (1483-1546) and John Calvin (1509-1564), commonly regarded in the popular mind as champions of individualism, criticized the late medieval mass not only as clergy-dominated but also as individualistic. It may come as a surprise to many that the Reformation of the sixteenth century in Germany and at Geneva initiated a great revival of the eucharist and of the humanistic implications of community worship. The Reformation espoused a social humanism. Luther and Calvin asserted once again the Christian humanistic tenet that men and women become complete only in relationship with other human beings.

"God has created man so that he may be a creature of fellowship,"

2. The classic treatment of the decline of monasticism in England is David Knowles, *The Religious Orders in England*, 3 vols. (Cambridge: Cambridge University Press, 1948-1959).

wrote John Calvin.[3] Early Lutheran and Calvinist worship was so ordered as to make fellowship once again a real experience of human life, with concrete implications for social and economic relationships. Communion-fellowship, the great heritage of Augustine, was revived. In the sixteenth century, Christians had the chance to become aware once again of their supernatural oneness in the eucharist.

The sixteenth century was an age of uncertainty and ferment. The peoples of Europe had to cope with an unprecedented combination of plague, war, voyages of discovery, and rapid inflation, all occurring simultaneously and all interacting. Along with commercial expansion came rising prices. The peasant, the small landholder, and the small merchant were preyed upon by money lenders and ambitious politicians, who readily found ways to evade the laws of church and state. It was precisely because Christian men and women needed to reform society as well as the church that Luther and Calvin distinguished their corporate "evangelical humanism" from the individualistic humanism of Renaissance Italy. Italian humanists had fostered a deep appreciation of private life, the retirement of the gentleman scholar from the concerns of the world; Petrarch once advised a correspondent to be true only to himself. Over against this privatism the reformers once again posited a humanism of the Christian community.

Though Luther was not a humanist in the strict sense, he was well acquainted with classical authors and the Christian humanists of the first five centuries of the church, especially Augustine. What Luther took from humanism was an appreciation for education and learning, especially the study of languages as a tool with which to exegete Scripture. Calvin considered himself more of a humanist than Luther. He wrote a humanistic commentary on the pagan Seneca's *De Clementia,* published in 1532. In the 1539 edition of his *Institutes of the Christian Religion,* Calvin introduced a new section describing humanistic studies as God's gifts. He said that learning, the precise use of languages, and the use of primary sources all have a role in God's kingdom.

While he would not turn his back on the humanists of his time, Calvin criticized them because they did not take religion seriously enough and because they lacked a social dimension. The self-centeredness, the noisy self-sufficiency, the easy accommodation to the comforts of the rich, and the neglect of humility in contemporary Italian humanists incurred Calvin's

3. André Biéler, *The Social Humanism of Calvin,* trans. Paul T. Fuhrmann (Richmond, Va.: John Knox Press, 1964), 17. See also Quirinus Breen, *John Calvin: A Study in French Humanism* (Grand Rapids: Wm. B. Eerdmans, 1931).

wrath. Luther and Calvin both found the Lord's Supper to be a source for Christian humanism that could speak to their age.

Eucharist and Community in Martin Luther: 1519-1546

From his first mass, when he dashed in fear from the altar, through all the sacramental battles of the Reformation, the eucharist was an essential part of the spiritual journey of Martin Luther. Though he held that the human being is justified *solely* by God's grace, Luther expected that eucharistic worship would flow spontaneously from a Spirit-led life. For Luther, the eucharist is above everything else the "act of confession before God that we are Christians."[4] The "church orders" of the sixteenth century assume that the regular Lutheran Sunday service will be a full eucharist, with sermon and the communion of all present celebrated at 8:00 A.M.

This worship was to be the expression of the whole church, however, not just the local clergy. Luther did not abolish the priesthood; he said that every Christian is a priest to other believers. The mass "is a communion of the faithful with each other."[5] There is in the Christian congregation no official function other than the one that every Christian in principle possesses. Luther looked upon the whole congregational action as consecratory at the eucharist, not just the words of institution pronounced by the presiding minister. He preferred the biblical word "congregation" to describe the church precisely to underline the principle of lay fellowship that was one of the cornerstones of the Reformation. Luther maintained that an individual must find the Christian life in a congregation at worship. "In this Christian church day after day [God] fully forgives my sins and the sins of all believers," writes Luther in his *Small Catechism*. Discussing the benefits of the Lord's Supper Luther writes that "in the sacrament we receive forgiveness of sins, life, and salvation. For where there is forgiveness of sins, there is also life and salvation."[6]

4. Yngve Brilioth, *Eucharistic Faith and Practice,* trans. A. G. Hebert (London: SPCK, 1965), 122. On the centrality of the eucharist to Luther see also Vilmos Vajta, *Luther on Worship* (Philadelphia: Muhlenberg Press, 1958), and Hermann Sasse, *This is My Body* (Adelaide: Lutheran Publishing House, 1977).

5. Roland H. Bainton, *Christianity* (Boston: Houghton Mifflin, 1987), 248.

6. Martin Luther, *The Small Catechism, A New Translation* (Intersynodical Catechism Committee, 1960), 21, 38.

In his practical liturgical reforms Martin Luther believed that he was setting the church free from the elitism of the world of scholastic theology and that he was recovering the emphasis on Christian fellowship he had found in Paul and Augustine. Where the singular had crept into prayers, Luther changed the form back to the plural in his *Formula Missae* of 1523. The *Formula Missae* gave the communion cup once again to the people. The *German Mass* of 1526 gave them back their own language in worship. Another great contribution of the Lutheran Reformation to the liturgy, vernacular hymns, opened up other new possibilities for congregational participation. The church orders drawn up for Reformation principalities kept the altar, but changed its position so that the presiding minister might face the people as from behind a common table. "No mass without communicants" is the principle of every one of the sixteenth-century Lutheran church orders.

Luther's extended sermon-treatise of 1519, "Concerning the Blessed Sacrament of the Holy and True Body of Christ," emphasized that from the eucharistic eating and drinking a real earthly fellowship arises. Luther particularly valued the restoration of the "kiss of peace" exchanged in the congregation after the breaking of the bread, because this was a worthy preparation for life in the world. In these and other ways Luther sought to return to Augustine's notion that fellowship in worship bears fruit in "humanistic" social action on earth. In explaining further why the term "communion" is applied to the eucharist, Luther points out, as Augustine had, that the service signifies not merely a communion between the individual soul and God, but a closer union among all the members of the body of Christ, outside the church building as well as inside it.

Luther united his voice with Augustine and cried out, "O sacrament of piety, O sign of unity, O bond of charity!"[7] The humanistic message of Luther was clearly this: at the altar the human being does not become less but more of a person. At the altar the Christian begins to realize that full development of selfhood comes within and through creative fellowship with other persons. Only in the sharing of the experience of the altar or table with others, and sharing the tasks which flow from that experience,

7. Martin Luther, "A Treatise Concerning the Blessed Sacrament of the Holy and True Body of Christ and Concerning the Brotherhoods," *Works of Martin Luther* (Philadelphia: Muhlenberg Press, 1943), vol. 2, 9-31. On Luther's specific reforms see "Concerning the Order of Public Worship," in *Works of Martin Luther* (Philadelphia: Fortress, 1965), vol. 53, 7-15 and 51-90; and "The German Mass," *Luther's Works*, vol. 53, 61-90; and Luther A. Reed, *The Lutheran Liturgy* (Philadelphia: Fortress Press, 1947).

does an individual believer grow into the full stature of Christ. The eucharist is the sacrament of growth.

The eucharist unites the citizens of a city in a human solidarity that transcends every distinction of class, social standing, sex, age, and even ecclesiastical rank. There can be only one Christian estate, even though there may be different offices. Yet this liberation in Christ incurs obligations. Luther returned to Augustine's theme of the *City of God* to illustrate the social obligations that communion-fellowship imposes:

> As the citizen, who is received into the fellowship of the city, shares in its freedom and its privileges, and enjoys its protection, so the Christian receives power and hope from the spiritual fellowship into which he is incorporated through the sacrament. This fellowship is like a city where every citizen shares with all the others the name, honor, freedom, trade, customs, usages, help, support, protection and the like, of that city, and on the other hand shares all the danger.[8]

Luther distinguished two aspects of this sharing. The first is the sharing of burdens. The guilty conscience, the sense of sin, the wickedness of the world, the fear of death — all of these weigh down the individual. Frequent worship in common reminds us that our troubles are not private. Celebration of the eucharist encourages us to be of good cheer because we do not struggle alone: "Strong help and succour surround thee."[9]

The second form of sharing is the sharing of love. Believers can assume the burdens of one another because eucharistic fellowship leads to a community of love. The thanksgiving Collect of the *German Mass* of 1526 states that the Lord's Supper is to serve "unto firm faith in thee and fervent love among all of us."[10] Growth in this love makes us feel more strongly the unjust suffering of the innocent and needy. One of the most important gifts of communion for Luther is the gift of love for others.

What does worship have to do with Christian humanism? For Luther, it is in the eucharist that God's power to restore the lost *imago dei* is made manifest among women and men. When God meets the worshipping people, the life from God becomes a present reality. Communion

8. Luther, "A Treatise," 10-11.

9. Luther in Brilioth, *Eucharistic Faith,* 96.

10. Luther in Carl F. Wisløff, *The Gift of Communion,* trans. Joseph M. Shaw (Minneapolis: Augsburg, 1964), 171. See also David C. Steinmetz, *Luther in Context* (Bloomington: Indiana University Press, 1986); and Harvey A. Hoover, *Living the Liturgy* (Gettysburg: The Lutheran Theological Seminary, 1946).

renews and refreshes: there is cleansing and healing; there is the enabling power and wisdom to meet all kinds of difficulties at home and abroad; there is freedom from the bondage of sin and selfishness. Luther urged a frequent partaking of the sacrament of the altar lest one become cold and indifferent. In Luther's teaching it is the eucharist that is the concrete instrument for the formation of believers in the *humanitas* and *pietas* that Erasmus had said are central to Christian humanism.

Luther on the Eucharist and the Material Dimensions of Life

One example of the transforming power of eucharistic worship is related to the Christian understanding of the material dimensions of human life. Though Luther did not elaborate on this notion as much as John Calvin did later, he also maintained that Christians have "all things in common, both good and evil" because of eucharistic fellowship.[11] Luther writes: "By this sacrament all self-seeking love is uprooted and gives place to love which seeks the common good of all."[12] Though Luther admitted that few will practice "what it signifies," the eucharist should involve the actual gathering of food and material goods in the church and their distribution among Christians who are in need.[13]

Luther's eucharistic humanism, like that of Irenaeus, is part of a Christian faith in a God who is concerned with the welfare of the temporal world and the use of material means to better it. The eucharist stood for this incarnational balance of the material with the spiritual, so primary in the tradition of Christian humanism, even before Martin Luther. The "false separation" of matter and spirit in the teaching of the Swiss Reformer Ulrich Zwingli provoked Luther, for he saw there a threat to the doctrine of the Incarnation itself. In the late 1520s Luther defended the real presence of Christ at the eucharist against "the false idea of the spiritual presence" maintained by Zwingli.[14] Luther borrowed from Irenaeus the notion that the sacraments are not mere signs but material channels of divine presence,

11. Luther, "A Treatise," 14.
12. Ibid., 26.
13. Ibid., 17.
14. Luther in Brilioth, *Eucharistic Faith,* 107.

parallel to the Incarnation. "It is with the Sacrament as with Christ himself."[15] Luther's doctrine may be summed up in the one phrase which he wrote in the dust on a table before Zwingli, at the Marburg Colloquy in 1529, "The Lord means what he says. This is my body."[16]

Awe before the "incarnational" dimension of the eucharist shaped Luther's teaching on the setting of worship. The early Lutheran rites preserved much of the form of ancient worship because of an instinctive sense that dignity and solemnity could safeguard the reverence due to the Lord in his presence. The old ceremonies expressed the sacredness of the mystery of Christ present with his people on earth, and Luther dared not discard them. Vestments, altar candles, incense, and other physical aids to worship were retained in the Lutheran tradition. The chasuble, a special garment for the eucharist, and thuribles, or censers containing incense, were still in use at Lutheran Hamburg in the eighteenth century. Luther highly valued the teaching value of these signs as well as the customs of the liturgical year, and he preserved the round of liturgical feasts with their familiar domestic associations. The Lutherans also retained paintings and sculpture in their churches.

By defending the physical aspects of religion Luther sought to advance the goal of appropriating the gospel into every place of work and every home. The sacredness of the secular was reaffirmed in this way. All life was invested with meaning, and all work crowned with dignity. Luther asserted that the Christian's calling could be fulfilled in any vocation, not just a sacred one. The shoemaker can serve God at his bench as fully as the priest can at the altar. The Reformation gave "the common life" back to women and men. Men and women, in their turn, were to give their lives back to God.

All Christians are in "holy orders"; they are all obligated to serve as priests to their neighbors. This is the basis of Luther's criticism of later monasticism, that in its decadent stages it divided Christians into two classes, the "religious" or spiritual elite and the common horde. In his extended treatise *On Monastic Vows* of 1521 Luther assaulted the whole monastic system precisely because it had turned worship into a selfish quest for personal perfection and salvation that lacked a social dimension. One result of Luther's teaching was that monasticism became a victim of the Protestant Reformation. At the same time Luther transposed to the whole lay Christian community the tasks of providing for a humane culture once

15. Ibid., 101.
16. Werner Elert, *Eucharist and Church Fellowship in the First Four Centuries*, trans. N. E. Nagel (St. Louis: Concordia, 1966), 39.

performed by monasteries. Luther appealed, for instance, to the councilmen of the cities of Germany to establish Christian schools. No effort or expense was to be spared by Reformation communities in providing good libraries open to all. "Not over human beings, but over swine and dogs should persons rule who seek their own profit or glory" and fail to maintain the common good, Luther wrote.[17]

Luther links the long tradition of the human as a channel of the divine to his doctrine of common prayer and vocation. Vocation and the human who fulfills it are tools for God's continuing creation. In the *Large Catechism* Luther states that all creatures are God's hands, conduits through which he gives us all things. Characteristically, Luther adds a warning against turning away from God's mandate to work for the lifting up of the created order.

When work does not avail, when human strength no longer suffices, when the ordinary powers within creation do not suffice, prayer brings a new force into play. Being in need means that all earth's possibilities have been tried and found to be inefficacious. It is at those points that God enters and completes creation, and the door by which God enters to effect the new on earth is prayer.

The human response to God's creative and redeeming action is faith expressed in praise. Thus Luther attached great significance to hymnody in worship, and the importance of hymns after 1523 as vehicles of the Lutheran sense of human expression cannot be overstated. More than that, Luther understood hymns to be an important tool to shape people's thinking about living out the values learned in the eucharist. Luther's hymns were an important means for moving piety from the mournful, self-preoccupied mood of the Middle Ages toward a piety focused on the cheerful service of others.

Despite his preoccupation with the devil and with human depravity, Luther believed in a God of joy and a Christian life that is marked from first to last by joyfulness because heaven, in the love of God through Christ, has come to us. "We ought to sing, and give praise and thanks to God the Father, that He has allowed His dear Son to become like us, a man and our brother!"[18] A lover of flowers and drinking, of card-playing and good

---

17. Martin Luther, "To the Councilmen of All Cities in Germany That They Establish and Maintain Christian Schools," in *Luther's Works*, vol. 31 (Philadelphia: Fortress Press, 1962), quoted in *Readings in Christian Humanism*, ed. Joseph M. Shaw, R. W. Franklin, Harris Kaasa, and Charles Buzicky (Minneapolis: Augsburg, 1982), 324. See also "An Answer to Several Questions on Monastic Vows," *Luther's Works*, vol. 46, 139-55.

18. Martin Luther, "On the Councils and the Churches," *Works of Martin Luther*, ed. C. M. Jacobs, The Philadelphia Edition (Philadelphia: Muhlenberg Press, 1931), 5, 223.

company, Luther all his difficult days remained markedly inclined to a Christian cheerfulness rooted in the joy of worship.[19]

John Calvin and the Eucharistic Community: 1536-1564

John Calvin, a Frenchman, led a Swiss reform movement that eventually spread to Holland, to Scotland, into the Puritan party of the Church of England, and finally across the Atlantic to become for many generations the dominant force in North American Christianity. Calvin's thorough and logical *Institutes of the Christian Religion* (1536) had enormous influence on much of Christendom.

Calvin developed his social humanism in a eucharistic context. He saw questions of ethics and discipleship in the light of the church at worship. Calvin drew such a close connection in his own mind between the eucharist and daily living that he could write that believers "truly worship God by the righteousness they maintain within their society."[20]

For Calvin, the problem of the Lord's Supper was one of two great theological issues in his life, the other being the doctrine of predestination. In the fourth book of the *Institutes* he wrote on the eucharist in considerable detail. Though Calvin insists that the physical body of Christ remains in heaven, the celebration of the eucharist has for him a divine and saving power beyond the mere memorial or psychological significance it takes on in the theology of Zwingli. The eucharist is "filled with much power"[21]; the "matter and substance" of the sacrament is the Lord Jesus.[22]

The eucharist is the public testimony of the Christian life. Calvin

19. For a further exploration of the expression of Lutheran Christian humanism in hymns see Robert D. Hawkins, "The Liturgical Expression of Sanctification: The Hymnic Complement to the Lutheran *Concordia*," Ph.D. diss., University of Notre Dame, 1988.

20. William J. Bouwsma, *John Calvin: A Sixteenth-Century Portrait* (Oxford: Oxford University Press, 1988), 192.

21. John Calvin, *Institutes of the Christian Religion*, trans. Ford Lewis Battles (Philadelphia: Westminster Press, 1960), 4:14, 9. For an introduction to Calvin's teaching on the eucharist see David Willis, "A Reformed Doctrine of the Eucharist and Ministry and its Implications for Roman Catholic Dialogues," *Journal of Ecumenical Studies,* 21 (1984), 295-309; Brian Gerrish, "John Calvin and the Lord's Supper," *The McCormick Quarterly* (January 1969), 80-100; Ronald S. Wallace, *Calvin's Doctrine of the Word and Sacrament* (Edinburgh: Oliver and Boyd, 1953).

22. Brilioth, *Eucharistic Faith,* 168.

said, "I come to the eucharist in order to seek a witness that Jesus Christ is my life and that I am incorporated in him and that the life I have from him will be eternal."[23] Calvin, like Luther, believed that in the eucharist we enter into a living, dynamic relationship with Jesus who forgives, guides, comforts, and revitalizes us in the course of our worship. It is for this reason that he could refer to the Lord's Supper, as Luther did, as the sacrament of growth.

Calvin thus directed that the Lord's Supper should be celebrated as often as possible, at least weekly. Early Calvinist liturgies lead to the sacrament as the climactic moment in worship, as both their introductions and the structure of the services themselves make clear. Calvin even suggested that when friends, acquaintances, and neighbors gather at the home of a sick person the eucharist should follow naturally, according to the commandment of Christ. The *Institutes* reminded readers that in the early church it was the unvarying rule that no meeting should take place without a partaking of the Supper, and that this order remained in use for many centuries.

The earliest architectural arrangements of Calvinist churches reveal a corporate understanding of worship. The eucharist was understood by Calvin as the rite of a community; prayer is not so much a private act for him as it is a "sharing among all the faithful."[24] Calvin's own arrangements at St. Peter's in Geneva focused on a long communion table, surrounded on three sides by pews, at which the community actually gathered. At times Calvinist holy tables were set for as many as six hundred worshipers who received communion together sitting or standing. The simple, square American Puritan and English Nonconformist meetinghouses of the seventeenth century are evidence of the primacy of the community gathered in the presence of Christ following the Calvinist tradition. The entire congregation shared together in the music, since there were no choirs or organs. The eucharist was always celebrated by a company of believers, for it was neither a priestly act nor a multitude of private acts.

The humanistic implications of worship in common appear in the

23. Kilian McDonnell, *John Calvin, the Church and the Eucharist* (Princeton: Princeton University Press, 1967), 31-32.

24. Bouwsma, *Calvin,* 216. On the early corporate character of Reformed worship and its frequent celebration see Carlos Eire, *The War Against the Idols* (Cambridge: Cambridge University Press, 1986); Howard G. Hageman, *Pulpit and Table* (Richmond, Va.: John Knox Press, 1962); and James Hastings Nichols, *Corporate Worship in the Reformed Tradition* (Philadelphia: Westminster Press, 1968).

fourth book of the *Institutes* where Calvin maintained that men and women "cannot be welded together in any name of religion unless they are bound in some partnership of signs or visible sacraments."[25] Calvin's teaching is very clear: "It is necessary that all of us be made one body by such participation."[26] The source of this teaching is Augustine. Calvin quotes no one as frequently as Augustine in the sections of the *Institutes* treating the sacraments; in all his works, Calvin cites Augustine nearly 3,000 times.

In Calvin's regard for worship as a witness to the renewal of the earthly city, we discern the influence of the old Augustinian ideal of civic humanism linked to the Lord's Supper, as well as a confidence in the humanistic value of worship to train the mind, inculcate virtue, and shape character. The ideals of *humanitas* and *pietas* for Calvin focused on moderation, and in the eucharist he found a unifying balance of body and soul and matter and Spirit that had the potential to extened beyond the church and establish a greater social harmony. In worship the true character of human life becomes clear as the believer learns of the possibility of existence within the bounds of self-control, poised between freedom and limits. Christ's life poured out in the eucharist provides the appropriate symbol of humanity's potential.

Calvin on the Material Dimensions of Christian Community

Calvin related one aspect of this eucharistic balance to the material dimensions of the Christian community. "To each according to his needs, from each according to his capacities," said Karl Marx, and Lenin maintained that atheistic communism would attain its goal the day this ideal became a reality. Calvin expressed a Christian statement of this desire: "God wills that there be proportion and equality among us, that is, each man is to provide for the needy according to the extent of his means so that no man has too much and no man has too little."[27]

25. McDonnell, *Calvin*, 41. On the humanistic implications of Calvin's reform of worship see Kilian McDonnell, "Calvin's Conception of Liturgy," *Concilium*, 42 (New York: Paulist Press, 1969); and James Hastings Nichols, "Intent of Calvinistic Liturgy," in *Heritage of John Calvin* (Grand Rapids: Wm. B. Eerdmans, 1973).
26. Calvin, *Institutes*, 4:14, 9. On the source of this in the early church see Hughes Oliphant Old, *The Patristic Roots of Reformed Worship* (Zurich: Theologischer Verlag, 1975).
27. Biéler, *Social Humanism*, 8. For more on Calvin's social humanism see Robert M.

Without this, Calvin maintained, the spiritual fellowship of worship is mere religious illusion and a dangerous deception. Calvin's sermons are set against the insolent luxury of some who, without regard for the poverty of others, wasted the common patrimony that God had given for the good of all. He said, "God does not extend his hand to us that each may follow his own course but that we may assist others and help them to advance."[28]

In Geneva every Christian had an economic responsibility to share a part of his or her wealth with the poor, in response to Calvin's teaching on the temporal dimension of the eucharist. This was the origin of the austere life-style of later Calvinists that included such virtues as sobriety, industry, thrift, and the shunning of frivolous amusement. In Calvin's time the deacons of Geneva were charged with the responsibility for redistributing, freely, goods and services within the community. The Reformation at Geneva brought with it the establishment of a general hospital as well as other agencies for assistance to the sick, the aged, and the invalid. Later Calvin's asceticism would be secularized into the "Protestant work ethic" that glorified profit and saving, but this was a degeneration from an earlier social concern that had been rooted in the eucharist.

Calvin directed a second aspect of this eucharistic balance to the relation of the local church to the national and international community. Like Paul and Augustine, Calvin was very explicit about the universal reach of Christian humanism. A nationalism that tears at human society in the name of conformity is absolutely contrary to and hostile to Calvin's faith. In Christ there is no longer Jew or Greek, and Calvin tests the authenticity of a Christian church in the light of her spiritual judgment in this matter. A church's rejection of any confusion of church and nation is a mark of her authenticity.

Calvin fiercely opposed any attempt to set up the cult of the nation as a part of Christian worship. As Protestants were massacred in country after country, Calvin himself organized general collections for the relief of the destitute, climbing the winding stairways of Genevan buildings crowded with refugees to collect contributions for brothers and sisters in many nations.

This kind of social humanism was impossible to Calvin without

---

Kingdon, "Social Welfare in Calvin's Geneva," *American Historical Review,*76 (1971); and Richard M. Douglas, "Talent and Vocation in Humanist and Protestant Thought," in *Action and Conviction in Early Modern Europe,* ed. T. K. Rabb and J. E. Seigel (Princeton: Princeton University Press, 1969).

28. Bouwsma, *Calvin,* 216.

retaining a eucharistic focus in Christian life. The sacrament leads to this many-sided Christian love: "We are joined in one body and one substance" because of the eucharist.[29] It nourishes material love, gives witness to spiritual love, and discerns the ties of communal love in the unity of Christ's body. Thus it is with reason that Calvin so often calls the sacrament the bond of love, *Caritatis vinculum.* The eucharist by signs and example moves us to devote ourselves to the welfare of others. The bread in the sacrament, as it is baked out of many small grains so blended together that one cannot be separated from another, symbolizes "that we are united and bound together in such a unity of souls that no dissension or quarrel may divide us."[30]

Contrasting Anglican and Roman Catholic Reforms

Roman Catholics and Anglicans approached the late medieval wall separating worship from life in more conservative ways than Luther and Calvin. The liturgy of the Church of England was reformed by the Archbishop of Canterbury, Thomas Cranmer, who led a committee that prepared two Books of Common Prayer under King Edward VI in 1549 and 1552. Cranmer's first eucharist, which retained much of the medieval order, including altar candles, vestments, and incense, supplied 95 percent of the wording of the Prayerbook of 1662 that remains the standard of the English Church and has shaped the worship of the worldwide Anglican Communion.

The Council of Trent (1545-1563), whose canons were to govern the Roman Catholic Church for the next four hundred years, undertook its liturgical task as one of correction and purgation. Though Trent removed superstitious and apocryphal texts and unfitting ritual from the celebration of the mass, the council mounted a general defense of ceremonies and vestments, and it anathematized those who declared material signs in worship to be provocations to impiety. The means the council adopted to accomplish liturgical reform was the formulation of a uniform Latin missal promulgated through the worldwide church under Pope Pius V in 1570.

29. Calvin, *Institutes,* 4:14, 9.

30 Brilioth, *Eucharistic Faith,* 166. On the international political implications see Michael Walzer, *The Revolution of the Saints: A Study in the Origins of Radical Politics,* (Cambridge, Mass.: Harvard University Press, 1965).

Catholic styles of worship, whether Roman or Anglican, took the human community seriously. The community was the medium through which the presence of God continued to be communicated. The eucharist also stressed the divine accommodation of the mixed spiritual and material nature of men and women. Both of these themes were in keeping with the incarnational tradition of Christian humanism. Anglicans and Roman Catholics followed an ordered rite that enabled a religious community to approach God together. Moreover, the structure and content of both Anglican and Roman liturgies were designed to consecrate the whole of life to God. Anglican and Roman ritual provided a visible expression of the eucharistic tradition that served masses of women and men in the succeeding centuries.

Thomas Cranmer and the Book of Common Prayer

The nature of the holy community was to Anglicans profoundly nationalistic. The Book of Common Prayer conveyed the deep sense of the whole English nation on its knees, united by the prayerbook to kin laboring in Virginia or gathered in English enclaves throughout the world. The old monastic ideal of the worshipping community was transferred to the nation as a whole. That church and nation are coextensive is explicitly stated in Cranmer's prayers for the monarch and by his provision of a type of worship comprehensive enough to include an entire nation: saints and sinners, beginners and mature Christians. Prayerbooks printed in 1549, 1552, and 1559 were widely distributed by the Tudor government so that their texts would become the familiar possession of the English people. The eucharist was translated into a language "understanded of the people." The common repetition of the Kyrie, Creed, Confession, Sanctus, Lord's Prayer, and Gloria in English united priest and people in a new sense of national solidarity.[31] Now there could be in Anglican worship a continuing dialogue

31. Horton Davies, *Worship and Theology in England: From Cranmer to Hooker, 1534-1603* (Princeton: Princeton University Press, 1975). Two works that place Cranmer in the context of nationalism are P. N. Brooks, *Cranmer in Context* (Minneapolis: Fortress Press, 1989), and the classic account by E. G. Rupp, *Studies in the Making of the English Protestant Tradition* (Cambridge: Cambridge University Press, 1947); see also "Communion and Commonwealth: The Book of Common Prayer," in J. E. Booty, ed., *The Godly Kingdom of Tudor England* (Wilton, Conn.: Morehouse-Barlow, 1981), 139-216.

between clergy and laity, an ongoing liturgical conversation that could render less rigid the difference between clergy and laity in carrying religious values into the daily life of the English nation, a fact that would profoundly shape English history during the next centuries.

During the 1550s, some English altars were replaced by tables placed endwise in the choir of the church to symbolize one community gathered at the eucharist. Heads of households were now expected to lead devotions in their own homes modeled after the liturgy of the prayerbook. The godly parent became at family prayers a real parent-in-God, passing on to his or her children such values as the spirit of simplicity, respect for others, and orderliness and dignity in life, values that are characteristic of Anglicanism at its best. A deep note of thanksgiving for newly found Christian fellowship sounds through the prayers of Cranmer's book. The Collect of Thanksgiving that closes his English eucharist is perhaps the finest expression of the mystery of Christian fellowship of the sixteenth century:

> We are very members incorporate in the mystical body of all faithful people. Assist us with thy grace, that we may continue in that holy fellowship, and do all such good works as thou hast prepared for us to walk in.[32]

Cranmer was not a liturgical scholar in the modern sense. But a reading of his prayers is convincing evidence that he was the greatest liturgical writer of the sixteenth century. Humanism contributed to this achievement in the form of two ideals that shaped Cranmer's career: *eruditio* and *persuasio*.[33]

First, *eruditio* or erudition. From the time he entered Jesus College, Cambridge, in 1503 at age fourteen Cranmer was trained in the new humanist method of studying languages, and he quickly mastered the three tongues of scholarship: Latin, Greek, and Hebrew. The future archbishop

---

32. *The Book of Common Prayer* (New York: The Church Pension Fund, 1945), 81. On Cranmer's liturgical reforms see two works of Geoffrey Cuming, *A History of Anglican Liturgy* (London: Macmillan, 1982), and *The Godly Order* (London: SPCK, 1983); and also P. N. Brooks, *Thomas Cranmer's Doctrine of the Eucharist* (London: Macmillan, 1965).

33. The masterly exposition of these two concepts in Reformation humanism is found in Bouwsma's *Calvin*, 113-27. On the humanist context of Cranmer see J. K. McConica, *English Humanists and Reformation Politics* (Oxford: Clarendon Press, 1965); M. Dowling, *Humanism in the Age of Henry VIII* (London: Croom, Helm, 1986); and A. Fox and J. Guy, *Reassessing the Henrician Age: Humanism, Politics and Reform 1500-1550* (Oxford: Basil Blackwell, 1986).

used the tools of textual criticism to extricate the spirit of the liturgy from the labyrinths of the old medieval service books so that it could speak again to the men and women of his own age.

Second, Cranmer set out to exploit the power of language through the *persuasio* or persuasion of the Italian humanists to reform the world to godliness. He became convinced of the ability of liturgical speech to move the feelings of a congregation and to stimulate hearers to action: "And if any would judge this way more painful, because that all things must be read upon the book ... if those men will weigh their labor with the profit in knowledge, which daily they shall obtain by reading upon the book, they will not refuse the pain, in consideration of the great profit that shall ensue thereof."[34]

When Cranmer emerged a quiet scholar from a fellowship at Jesus College at the age of forty to step onto the national and European stage, a violent and ruthless world of dictatorial monarchs, his extraordinary talent as a liturgical writer with a humanist background was a timely gift to the Church of England. A few years earlier his talent would have found no outlet, for the Latin mass had been virtually unchanged for centuries; a few years later radical Protestant activists in England would have moved beyond the point of accepting a fixed and traditional liturgical style of public worship. What singular combination of humanist impulses and appropriate response to a "time out of joint" made Cranmer a liturgical writer of lasting influence?[35]

First, he created a style of vernacular liturgical prose — sonorous, dignified, beautifully suited to shaping the habits and imagination of an entire nation — contained in a single book. Cranmer's combination of "book" with "common" and "prayer" was revolutionary, and its success was so complete that even after four hundred years Anglicanism more than any other tradition is a church of a book of worship. Even hymnals were relatively late in coming to other world families of churches.[36]

34. "Preface," *The First Book of Common Prayer* (1549); on Cranmer's language and the influence of humanism see S. Brook, *The Language of the Book of Common Prayer* (London: Andre Deutsch, 1965); and two essays in D. S. Armentrout, ed., *This Sacred History* (Cambridge: Cowley Publications, 1990): Stephen W. Sykes, "Cranmer on the Open Heart," 1-20; and Guy F. Lytle, "Prelude to the Condemnations of Latimer, Ridley, and Cranmer: Heresy, Humanism, Controversy, and Conscience in Early Reformation Oxford," 222-42.

35. H. Boone Porter, "Cranmer and Our Liturgy," *The Living Church* (November 26, 1989), 12; and G. Rupp on Thomas Cranmer in *Six Makers of English Religion, 1500-1700* (London: Hodder & Stoughton, 1957).

36. See James F. White, *Protestant Worship: Traditions in Transition* (Louisville: John Knox Press, 1989), 94-116; and Marion J. Hatchett, *The Making of the First American Book of Common Prayer* (New York: Seabury Press, 1982).

Second, he wrote prayers susceptible to a richness of meaning and interpretation. Great prayers, prayers intended for all sorts and conditions of persons, repeated thousands of times during a lifespan, must offer different shades and levels of meaning capable of balancing the needs of the individual Christian with the aims of the larger community.

Third, Cranmer went beyond Luther and Calvin in printing and widely distributing devotional forms that could actually establish and maintain connections between basic theological values and the needs and concerns of a nation. Cranmer as archbishop underlined the essential relationship between the public virtues of justice, practical wisdom, and courage and the instruction and personal participation in the life of God available in the eucharist. Fostering the causal relationship between prayer and work is the whole point of public worship to Cranmer: "Almighty God, you have created the heavens and the earth, and made man in your own image. Teach us to discern your hand in all your works, and to serve you with reverence and thanksgiving: through Jesus Christ our Lord who with you and the Holy Spirit reigns supreme over all things now and forever."[37]

In this respect the carefully calculated balance in The Book of Common Prayer between worship and work reminds us of the Benedictines. The moderation of the prayerbook was not likely to encourage the martyr or any form of extremism. One of Cranmer's Collects puts the ideal of a moderate Christian humanism in this way: "O Almighty and most merciful God, of thy bountiful goodness keep us, we beseech thee, from all things that may hurt us; that we, being ready both in body and soul may cheerfully accomplish those things that thou wouldst have done; through Jesus Christ our Lord."[38]

It is ironic, then, that of all the reformers, it was Thomas Cranmer who was imprisoned, tried, and burned at the stake for heresy in 1556. On the day of his burning a Catholic bystander expressed something of what Cranmer wished his legacy in the reform of worship to be: "His

---

37. Quoted in Esther de Waal, *Seeking God* (Collegeville, Minn.: The Liturgical Press, 1984), 113. It was Richard Hooker who wrote in greater detail on the connection of the prayerbook to English society; see the most recent edition of Hooker with bibliography on this point: A. S. McGrade, ed., *Richard Hooker: Of the Laws of Ecclesiastical Polity* (Cambridge: Cambridge University Press, 1989).

38. The Collect for Trinity XX, quoted in de Waal, *Seeking God,* 97; on the Benedictine influence in Cranmer see Robert Hale, *Canterbury and Rome, Sister Churches* (New York: Paulist Press, 1982).

friends sorrowed for love; his enemies for pity; strangers for a common kind of humanity whereby we are bound one to another."39

The Council of Trent and Catholic Worship Reform

Many historians of the liturgy once agreed that in the sixteenth century Roman Catholics abandoned the official corporate worship of the church as a primary vehicle for the faith life of the believer. Underlying this was a widespread assumption that the bond of common prayer could not and did not exist in the Latin church as it did — as a result of Cranmer's achievement — in Elizabethan England. Today there is a new interest in the contributions the Council of Trent made to insure that the liturgy would once again be a source of spiritual life for Catholic Christians into the seventeenth century and beyond, through its clarification of doctrine and reform of rites.40

The Council of Trent (1545-1563) dealt specifically with abuses in the liturgical practices of the Roman church, and it discussed the theology of the eucharist twice, in 1547 and again in 1551. The 1547 deliberations began at the city of Trent at the foot of the Alps and were continued at the old university town of Bologna where the council had fled to escape the plague. When the Roman Catholic bishops reconvened in 1551, they saw eight chapters and eleven canons of the Tridentine decree *On the Eucharist* through to completion.

This document defines the mass with a precision never before accorded it in any official document of the Roman Catholic Church. Trent's doctrine of worship is set against the multiple interpretations of the Reformers that we have surveyed. The bishops assert the real and substantial presence of Christ in the bread and wine of the mass, not his virtual presence

39. J. Strype, *Memorials of the Most Reverend Father in God, Thomas Cranmer* (Oxford: Oxford University Press, 1848), vol. 3, 255.

40. The most important article to relate humanism to Catholic liturgy in the sixteenth century is A. L. Mayer, "Renaissance, Humanismus und Liturgie," *Jahrbuch für Liturgiewissenschaft*, 14 (1934), 123-70. The most complete bibliography of new work on the Council of Trent and its reform of worship can be found in John O'Malley, ed., *Catholicism in Early Modern History: A Guide to Research* (St. Louis: Center for Reformation Research, 1988), particularly the chapter by Niels Rasmussen, "Liturgy and Liturgical Arts," 273-98.

as Calvin had taught, and they name Christ's presence as "transubstantiation" as opposed to Luther's doctrine, which some have called "consubstantiation."[41]

Despite the fact that many of the bishops and theologians at Trent were intellectually the products of the last days of Renaissance humanism — their speeches were permeated with allusions to the works of Cicero, Plato, Horace, Virgil, and Suetonius — the council is usually regarded as a reaction against the humane ideals of the early sixteenth century. Yet the council's doctrine of transubstantiation is just one example of a Tridentine decree that in fact served to preserve a tradition of Christian humanism for the future.[42]

Trent related transubstantiation to the doctrine of the Incarnation, one of the foundations of Christian humanism. The bishops said, "In the sacred sacrament of the holy Eucharist, after the consecration of the bread and wine, our Lord Jesus Christ, true God and man, is truly, really, and substantially contained under the species of these sensible things."[43] The bishops go on to say that the eucharist is the chief means whereby the Incarnation of God in Christ continues to be extended to all humanity — and beyond, into the natural creation.

The significance of the mass for humanism may be summarized as follows: the image of God in us is continually revitalized in the receiving of the sacrament of Christ's body and blood. The mass is the unveiling in time,

41. Lutherans themselves do not hold to a doctrine of "consubstantiation." They prefer to speak of the real presence of Christ "in, with, and under" the bread and wine of the sacrament. Four studies in English of the eucharistic doctrine and worship reform of Trent can be found in Jaroslav Pelikan, *The Christian Tradition,* vol. 4, *Reformation of Church and Dogma (1300-1700)* (Chicago: University of Chicago Press, 1984); Reinhold Theisen, *Mass Liturgy and the Council of Trent* (Collegeville, Minn.: The Liturgical Press, 1965); and two articles in Paul C. Empie and T. Austin Murphy, eds., *Lutherans and Catholics in Dialogue I-III* (Minneapolis: Augsburg, 1974): "Luther and Roman Catholicism on the Mass as Sacrifice"; and "Doctrine of Transubstantiation from Berengar through the Council of Trent," 45-124.

42. The relation of humanism to Tridentine figures is discussed in Nikolaus Pevsner, *Studies in Art, Architecture, and Design* (London: Thames and Hudson, 1968), 11-33; and Vicente Muñoz Delgado, "Lógica, ciencia y humanismo en la renovación teológica de Vitoria y Cano," *Revista española de teología,* 38 (1978), 205-71. The background is set in John O'Malley, *Praise and Blame in Renaissance Rome, ca. 1450-1521* (Durham: Duke University Press, 1979).

43. *Decree Touching the Most Holy Sacrament of the Eucharist of the Council of Trent,* chap. 1, quoted in *Readings in Christian Humanism,* 348. See also A. Duval, *Des Sacrements au Concile de Trente* (Paris: Editions du Cerf, 1985); and J. Delumeau, *Catholicism Between Luther and Voltaire: A New View of the Counter-Reformation* (London: Burns and Oates, 1977).

through succeeding ages, of the process initiated by God in Christ — the reassembly and the lifting up of the ruined and scattered human race. The direct link between altar and Incarnation led the Trent bishops to formulate their teaching that the bread and wine at the eucharist actually do become body and blood, just as God actually did become fully human in Jesus Christ.[44] It must be kept in mind, however, that many non-Tridentine Christians also affirm Christ's real presence in the bread and wine without positing that the elements change in substance.[45] For Anglicans, Lutherans, Calvinists, and the Orthodox, for example, the humanistic benefit of the Incarnation as expressed in Christ's sacramental presence does not require the idea of transubstantiation.

When viewed on its own terms as a contribution to Christian humanism, Trent's doctrine of transubstantiation makes of the human beings gathered at the mass collaborators with Christ in the process of restoration. Human hands renew Christ's sacrifice at the altar and make possible the spreading abroad of its benefits. Human prayers at the mass become a channel of God's purposes, which, like streams of goodness, flow from the altar out into the world to meet its needs. Our privilege as women and men who celebrate worship is to keep this stream of goodness flowing and to become ourselves fit channels of grace. From the mass we receive the further capacity of grace to order the disordered elements of human life into a pattern that more closely approximates Christ's perfect humanity.

Trent thus dared to speak of human cooperation with God in the mass — human cooperation with God is the great theme of the council. This proximity of God to the human, of heaven to earth, was vividly portrayed in the lavish architecture, costly furnishings, colorful pageantry,

44. Christian humanism and Trent's doctrine of transubstantiation are discussed in three works of Frederic Hastings Smyth, *Manhood Into God* (New York: Round Table Press, 1940); *Discerning the Lord's Body* (Louisville: The Cloister Press, 1946); and *Sacrifice: A Doctrinal Homily* (New York: Vantage Press, 1953).

45. In their confessional statement of 1577 called *The Formula of Concord* the leading Lutheran theologians in Germany explicitly rejected the Roman Catholic doctrine of transubstantiation "when it is taught in the Papacy that in the Holy Supper the bread and wine lose their substance and natural essence, and are thus annihilated; that they are changed into the body of Christ, and the outward form alone remains." *The Formula of Concord, Summary Content {Epitome}*, VII, "Of the Lord's Supper," in *Concordia Triglotta: Libri symbolici Ecclesiae Lutheranae* (St. Louis: Concordia, 1921), 813. In the earlier, affirmative discussion of the article on the Lord's Supper the Lutherans stated: "We believe, teach, and confess that in the Holy Supper the body and blood of Christ are truly and essentially present, and are truly distributed and received with the bread and wine." See *Epitome*, 809.

and rich music that later surrounded the Tridentine liturgy. After Trent Catholic art expressed the "humanistic" message of the mass: that Jesus signifies the utmost in human goodness, human nobility, and human compassion. This is in stark contrast to the Christian art of some earlier epochs in which Jesus is portrayed as a remote being, possessed of mysterious superhuman powers. Baroque art underlined the central place of the human personality and its senses in the Christian religion. We need think only of Bernini's statue in downtown Rome of St. Teresa of Avila in almost sexual religious ecstasy or Pope Paul V's exuberant splashing fountains built above the city at about this time to be reminded of the truth of this fact by works of art in only one European capital.[46]

After Trent the Catholic world underwent a probing renewal from within, a renewal that owes much to the reforms of doctrine and worship initiated by the council. This renewal bore fruit both in the public life of the church and in the private spirituality of individual saints that surfaced in the next century. It continued the incarnational balance of matter and spirit that had been a central concern of the sixteenth-century bishops.

Blaise Pascal in France is a product of that renewal. His biblical reflections in the *Pensées* (1670) are informed by his assiduous daily attendance on the liturgy, an attendance that flowed into service of the poor and the public, not to mention his imprudently insistent advocacy of justice to minorities. Another example is Teresa of Avila herself in Spain who wrote sublime pages on the eucharistic presence of Christ, but also concerned herself with economic justice and judicial fairness. Bernini was right in choosing Teresa of Avila as the symbol of the Catholic Christian humanism of her age: Teresa, who was so caught up in the intensity of worship that observers said they saw her rise into the air from the steps of the altar; the same Teresa, so alive with practical initiatives, business acumen, diplomatic ability, and common sense that she became a dominant political figure of her age.[47]

---

46. A. L. Mayer, "Liturgie und Barock," *Jahrbuch für Liturgiewissenschaft*, 15 (1935), 67-154; Richard Krautheimer, *The Rome of Alexander VII, 1655-1667* (Princeton: Princeton University Press, 1985); and R. Wittkower and I. Jaffe, eds., *Baroque Art: The Jesuit Contribution* (New York: Fordham University Press, 1972).

47. On humanism and liturgy in the seventeenth century see F. Ellen Weaver, "Liturgy for the Laity: The Jansenist Case for Popular Participation in Worship," *Studia Liturgica,* 19 (1989), 47-59, and "Jansenist Bishops and Liturgical-Social Reform," in R. Golden, ed., *Church, State and Society under the Bourbon Kings of France* (Lawrence: Kansas University Press, 1982), 27-82; and Ph. Sellier, *Pascal et la liturgie* (Paris: Presse universitaires de France, 1966).

Those heroes and heroines of the sixteenth and seventeenth centuries whom we have named in these pages, Luther, Calvin, Cranmer, Teresa of Avila, and Blaise Pascal, would have found it impossible to worship together in their time. Part of their legacy is that pluralism in worship has been the Christian experience of four centuries, although, on its positive side, pluralism may have provided a wider set of options to the people of God in their attempts to produce a more worthy worship. At the same time, we are struck by the uncanny similarity in the common values they all sought to express in different ways in their worship: the importance once again of joining worship to work; the church upheld as community — whether a congregation, a local democracy, a nation, or an international hierarchy; and the central witness of the Incarnation to the unique stance of the human in God's plan of salvation, a role unique in world religions. All of this had been evident in the early church; now it returned again in the sixteenth century. Why did this happen?

The Reformation of the sixteenth century was the most traumatic event in the history of the Western church, and with its seismic shifts came widespread clamor for reform from all sides. Italian humanists, northern humanists, biblical reformers, Catholic reformers, all had one thing in common: they sought to "return to the sources" of ancient times. Inevitably the liturgy was one of those sources.

The humanists' contribution to the renewal of worship was the impetus they gave to the study of the ancient texts of the liturgy and to the eucharistic writings of the Greek and Latin fathers. Such reading in the Catholic camp led to the attempt to restore the scrupulous observance of the rite of the mass. Among Protestants it created pressure for a reform of the rite itself in order to bring it into line with much earlier liturgical understanding and practice and with the pastoral and evangelistic needs of the day. But on both sides there was a recapturing of the central message of Christian worship that we surveyed in the previous chapter: that divine power is at work at worship re-creating a flawed world, that the chief image of divine power at the eucharist is suffering love, and that the loving purposes of God are expressed through women and men gathered in praise and adoration.

Chapter 9

Worship and Work in the Machine Age

In the seventeenth and eighteenth centuries the ideals of eucharistic humanism that emerged in the Reformation never came to mean for Lutherans, Calvinists, Anglicans, and Roman Catholics what they might have and should have meant. Only in a few places did important exceptions emerge, such as at the communities of Port-Royal in France or Little Gidding in England. It is estimated that in the seventeenth and eighteenth centuries Lutherans took holy communion only twice a year, having forgotten Luther's call for "often" in the *Large Catechism,* and the preaching of the Word became the focus of Lutheran worship. Ante-communion nearly became the norm for Sunday; both clergy and congregation regarded the sacrament as a routine to be gotten through quickly to arrive at the chief business of the day, the sermon. The eucharist became for most seventeenth- and eighteenth-century Lutherans "a devotional luxury," although it continued to be celebrated frequently in some German cities, such as Hamburg and Leipzig, until the Enlightenment.

Nowhere in Calvinism did a weekly eucharist establish itself. Four celebrations a year was the rule by the middle of the seventeenth century. Only the first Sundays of March, June, September, and December were set apart for the Lord's Supper, and hence the meaning of the liturgical year was, for all practical purposes, lost in the Calvinist churches. Year after year, as in Lutheranism, the sermon came to be longer and longer and to dominate worship more and more. As the Calvinist celebration of the eucharist came to surround itself with a dark penitential caste, it lost its social dimension.

As had happened among the Lutherans and Calvinists, so the eucharist soon lost its place as the chief Anglican service. It was treated with less honor and became a mere appendage to morning prayer, while the musical glories of the Anglican cathedral tradition were lavished on morning prayer and evening prayer. During the English Restoration of the 1660s, some efforts were made to maintain a daily eucharist in some cathedrals and London churches, but these were exceptions. Almost all other Anglican parish and cathedral churches celebrated the eucharist three times a year, or four times at the most.

Once again the role of the English laity in worship became one of "hearing." The invariable question for those coming home from church was, "Whom did you hear?" or "Who preached?" In some parishes the laity were instructed "not to interrupt the parson nor to argue or walk about."[1] A clerk in a black gown would sit at a reading desk opposite the pulpit and make responses in the liturgy for the congregation. The greatest Anglican architect of the seventeenth century, Sir Christopher Wren, referred to his churches as "auditories." Not the altar but the pulpit received special attention in Wren's churches with elaborate sounding boards and rich carvings surmounting the place where the sermon was delivered. Wren designed his galleries and pews with an understanding that the congregation would remain passive and stationary throughout the Anglican rite.

In the Roman Catholic Church in the seventeenth and eighteenth centuries "hearing mass" was one thing while "going to communion" came to mean something quite different. In actual pastoral practice it was clear that even at mass the people's communion had nothing essential to do with the praise and thanksgiving of the eucharistic offering. The assembled congrega-

---

1. Kathleen Philip, *Victorian Wantage* (Oxford: K. Philip, 1968), 72. A number of studies provide details about the position of the eucharist among Protestants in the seventeenth and eighteenth centuries. For Lutherans, see Friedrich Kalb, *Theology of Worship in Seventeenth-Century Lutheranism* (St. Louis: Concordia, 1965), and Guenther Stiller, *Johann Sebastian Bach and Liturgical Life in Leipzig* (St. Louis: Concordia, 1984). For Anglicans, see W. Jardine Grisbrooke, *Anglican Liturgies of the Seventeenth and Eighteenth Centuries* (London: SPCK, 1958), and G. W. O. Addleshaw and Frederick Etchells, *The Architectural Setting of Anglican Worship* (London: Faber and Faber, 1948). For the Reformed churches, see Ronald S. Wallace, *Calvin's Doctrine of the Word and Sacrament* (Edinburgh: Oliver and Boyd, 1953), and Duncan Forrester and Douglas Murray, *Studies in the History of Worship in Scotland* (Edinburgh: T. & T. Clark, 1924).

tion had no active voice in the mass prayers at all; the servers or the choir took over all the people's dialogues, acclamations, and doxologies in the mass. Nor was the congregation's assistance considered essential to the celebrant's action. When a change in this state of affairs was suggested to a French bishop he replied, "The Christian people are not obliged to understand or even be acquainted with liturgical rites. When we have saved religion, which is perishing, then it will be time to talk about worship for the people."[2]

Recovering the People's Worship

The rebirth of liturgical community and a renewal of eucharistic humanism among Anglicans, Lutherans, Roman Catholics, and Calvinists began in the nineteenth century in part as a Christian response to the coming of the industrial world. (A parallel development, which we will not examine here, occurred in the Russian Orthodox tradition in the twentieth century.) In the early church worship had represented a symbolic articulation of Christian values. The sixteenth century saw a return to this early tradition of Christian humanism, and though it was lost for many generations, it was recovered again in our machine age. A number of Christian thinkers from diverse places and cultures found ways to relate the ordered worship of God to human beings as they existed in the dehumanizing conditions of an increasingly industrial society.

The recovery of a eucharistic model of the human community came about because many Christian observers marked the alienation of spirit from matter and of the individual from the community as the industrial revolution advanced. The industrial revolution essentially replaced human and animal labor with machines, and it included the organization of machine work into the factory system. Industrialization began in England in the eighteenth century and had spread by the 1850s to the northern United States and by the 1870s to the German Rhineland. Patterns of life were transformed in every industrialized society. Ancient crafts were replaced by machines. The majority of Europeans and Americans were no longer farmers but city dwellers.

2. Bishop Jean-Jacques Fayet of France, quoted in R. W. Franklin, "The Nineteenth Century Liturgical Movement," *Worship*, 53 (1979), 15. On the eucharist in Catholic piety during this period, see as an introduction to the terrain Owen Chadwick, *The Popes and the European Revolution* (Oxford: Oxford University Press, 1981), and F. Ellen Weaver, "Women and Religion in Early Modern France: A Bibliographic Essay on the State of the Question," *The Catholic Historical Review*, 67 (1981), 50-59.

Life in the new industrial city made the world of the Spirit seem dim and distant. Materialism was the keystone of the industrial revolution. Nineteenth-century capitalists prided themselves on the creation of a new "acquisitive man" for an economically focused society. Materialism shows through the culture of the industrial age in a myriad of ways: in the displacement of natural materials by man-made materials — concrete, steel, and glass, in new construction; in the industrial city itself, where hundreds of thousands of all classes hurried past one another as though they had nothing in common but brutal indifference, the unfeeling isolation of each in his or her own materialistic self-seeking. The popular impression was conveyed in the industrial city that religion had been discredited and that it was no longer necessary to trouble oneself about the Christian estimation of the human person and the human condition.

Community also inevitably declined in the factory world. The rigorous new discipline of the factory removed women and men from their families and from their rural parish communities. In London in 1833 the churches had room for only one-tenth of this transplanted industrial population, and sixty-four English parishes in working-class districts were without resident clergy. Workers complained that they were mere numbers toiling for the profit of an unknown millionaire, while capitalists preached "the gospel of work," "self-help," "self-reliance," "free enterprise," and "free trade."

Throughout the nineteenth century some voices protested the dehumanizing effects of the factory. We hear this protest in John Ruskin's *The Stones of Venice* of 1851:

> The great cry that rises from all our manufacturing cities, louder than their furnace blast, is that we manufacture everything there except men. To brighten, to strengthen, to refine or to form a single living spirit, never enters into our estimate of advantages.[3]

The protests were also there in 1917 when J. L. and Barbara Hammond's *The Town Labourer* provided a classic description of the relation of the industrial revolution to humanism:

3. John Ruskin, quoted in E. P. Thompson, *William Morris: Romantic to Revolutionary* (New York: Pantheon Books, 1976), 34. As a way into the monumental literature on industrialization as a force for dehumanization see Alasdair MacIntyre, *Marxism and Christianity* (Notre Dame: University of Notre Dame Press, 1984); Hugh McLeod, *Religion and the People of Western Europe 1789-1970* (Oxford: Oxford University Press, 1981); E. P. Thompson, *The Making of the English Working Class* (New York: Vintage Books, 1963); and Robert Tucker, *Philosophy and Myth in Karl Marx* (Cambridge: Cambridge University Press, 1967).

The depreciation of human life was the leading fact about the new system for the working class. The human material was used up rapidly. At the end the working class, which was now contributing not only the men but the entire family, seemed to be what it was at the beginning, a mere part of the machinery without a share in the increased wealth or the increased power over life that machinery had brought.[4]

Historians of Christian humanism may be excused for faulting the churches for their virtual paralysis in the face of the new economic system. Only a few ecclesiastical voices were raised in protest. In the Church of England E. B. Pusey (1800-1882) had the courage to challenge modern Christians to "grapple with our manufacturing system as the apostles did with the slave system of the ancient world if by God's grace we would wrest from the principalities and powers of evil those portions of his kingdom, of which, while unregarded by the Church, they have been taking full possession."[5] Within Lutheranism N. F. S. Grundtvig (1783-1872) of Denmark expressed his hope that worship would reinforce a sense of community solidarity to counter the destructive influence of the industrial capitalism being imported from England.

Gradually some other avenues were opened to recover the benefit of the Christian humanist tradition in the machine age. The relationship between worship and factory work became an explicit theme in the Benedictine liturgical revival (1833-1938) within the Roman Catholic Church. Before World War I Dom Lambert Beauduin of Belgium pointed out that a *comprehending* participation in the eucharist had the power to lift workers for a moment from the misery of their surroundings.

In the Reformed tradition, a striking parallel to these movements has been the Iona Community of the Church of Scotland, founded in 1938 by George F. MacLeod. The community has worked for the reestablishment

4. J. L. and Barbara Hammond, *The Town Laborer,* quoted in *Readings in Christian Humanism,* ed. Joseph M. Shaw, R. W. Franklin, Harris Kaasa, and Charles Buzicky (Minneapolis: Augsburg, 1982), 367. There were many movements of humanism that rose in the face of the dehumanizing effects of industrialization. Some key works that may serve as an introduction to these are E. P. Thompson, *William Morris: Romantic to Revolutionary* (New York: Pantheon Books, 1976); Raymond Williams, *Culture and Society 1780-1950* (New York: Harper & Row, 1966); Nikolaus Pevsner, *Pioneers of Modern Design* (London: Penguin Books, 1974); John F. Kasson, *Civilizing the Machine* (London: Penguin Books, 1976); F. W. Roe, *The Social Philosophy of Carlyle and Ruskin* (New York: Columbia University Press, 1921).

5. E. B. Pusey, *The Councils of the Church from the Council of Jerusalem to the Council of Constantinople* (Oxford: Rivington, 1857), 4-5.

of a weekly holy communion in Presbyterian churches. Out of his frustration in serving an industrial parish during the great depression of the 1930s MacLeod came to see that evangelism must arise out of corporate worship.

The advent of the industrial system is chief among several historical forces that prompted the search for liturgical community and the restoration of full lay participation in the eucharist in many nations and churches during the last century and a half. Pusey, Grundtvig, the Benedictines, and MacLeod spoke of the eucharist as the power to redeem the industrial social order. They emphatically did not understand worship as an escape; it was for them, rather, the pattern of community that God has ordained in the midst of a world where humans have become strangers to one another, caught in economic circumstances that deprive them of their full stature as God's children.

These figures of the nineteenth and early twentieth century were again able to speak of the eucharist hallowing daily life and work. An illustration of this is the way in which the offertory, the taking of representative elements from the secular context and making them ready for the sacred, became a focus of worship. For the first time since the Reformation era there was a rediscovery of prayer as a social act with humanistic implications. With good reason, then, we have singled out these movements as playing a significant role in bearing one tradition of Christian humanism from the early industrial era down to our own day.[6]

The Church of England: The Oxford Movement and Its Parishes, 1833-1900

The Oxford Movement (1833-1845) began as a Catholic revival within the Church of England. In the face of the disdainful frowns of evangelicals, who stressed salvation by faith alone, and the sneers of English rationalists, among whom the sacraments had fallen into neglect, the leaders of the

6. On the liturgical movement and humanism, see Aidan Kavanagh, "Liturgical and Credal Studies," in Henry W. Bowden, ed., *A Century of Church History* (Carbondale: Southern Illinois University Press, 1988), 216-44; Thomas F. O'Meara, "The Origins of the Liturgical Movement and German Romanticism," *Worship,* 59 (1985), 326-42; E. B. Koenker, *The Liturgical Renaissance in the Roman Catholic Church* (Chicago: University of Chicago Press, 1954); and R. W. Franklin, "Humanism and Transcendence in the Nineteenth Century Liturgical Movement," *Worship,* 59 (1985), 342-53.

Oxford Movement proclaimed that religion unnourished by a visible church with its sacramental system could not long maintain vital spiritual life in an age of secularism and revolution. On July 14, 1833, John Keble (1792-1866), a high church Oxford divine, preached a sermon denouncing "National Apostasy" before English assize judges gathered in the Oxford University Church. Keble stressed that a visible church is essential to the survival of Christianity in modern times and that bishops in the apostolic succession are necessary. The church, he said, is a spiritual organism deriving its life and its authority from Jesus Christ and his apostles and their successors and not from the British crown, the laws of Parliament, or the actions of the sixteenth-century reformers. In other words, Keble argued that the established church was not the *Protestant* Church *of* England, but the *Catholic* Church *in* England. The Oxford Movement was an attempt to return the church to a character consistent with the best in its Catholic past, including those elements of Christian humanism that have been a recurring part of the tradition.

From September 1833 John Henry Newman (1801-1890), a fellow of Oxford's Oriel College, fashioned the Oxford Movement's *Tracts for the Times* into instruments for a second, Catholic reformation. In his incisive *Tracts,* which he published until 1841 and which earned the label "Tractarian" for the movement, Newman upheld the Church of England as a "divine" or "ecclesial" institution with a social mission to the people of England. Against evangelical views of faith that had often diminished to little more than self-regard, Newman wrote that Christ has lodged his blessings in the body of the church collectively to oblige men and women to meet *together* if they would gain grace each for himself or herself. "The body is not made up of individual Christians, but each Christian has been made such in his turn by being taken into the body,"[7] Newman wrote.

E. B. Pusey took action after September 1833 to express this recovered communal dimension of Anglicanism through a revival of eucharistic worship linked to a campaign for building parish churches in the new industrial cities of England. The established church had based its power and its privileges upon an alliance with the country gentry. Pusey had

7. John Henry Newman, quoted in Alf Härdelin, "The Eucharist in the Theology of the Nineteenth Century," *Eucharistic Theology Then and Now* (London: SPCK, 1968), 81. On Newman's treatment of Christian humanism see Vincent Ferrer Blehl, *John Henry Newman: A Bibliographical Catalogue of His Writings* (Charlottesville: University Press of Virginia, 1978).

grown up among the landed aristocracy, and he had been appointed Regius Professor of Hebrew at Oxford in 1828 by the Tory Duke of Wellington when the previous incumbent in the chair had died from breathing too much dust in Oxford's Bodleian Library, a sort of scholars' black lung disease. In September 1833 Pusey took the unprecedented step for a country Tory of advocating the construction of a church every day of the year amid the brutal social conditions of the mill towns.

Pusey developed a considerable understanding of urban dehumanization in his visits to London. There he sought to find signs of God's presence; he found the joy of children to be such a human witness to the divine. Here is an interesting passage from his commentary on Zechariah, touching what he felt as he walked the London streets:

> In the back-streets and alleys of London, the irrepressible joyousness of children is one of the bright sunbeams of that great Babylon, amid the oppressiveness of the anxious, hard, luxurious, thoughtless, care-worn, eager, sensual, worldly, frivolous, vain, stolid, sottish, cunning faces which traverse it. God sanctions, by His Word here . . . our joy in the joyousness of children, that He too taketh pleasure in it, He the Father of all.[8]

From 1835 to 1853 Pusey spent considerable time in the mill town of Leeds, whose distressing scenes of misery and poverty in a population of 123,000 were memorialized in Friedrich Engels's *The Condition of the Working Class in England* (1844). In a course of sermons preached to some of the wealthiest congregations in England, Pusey portrayed men and women falling from community into isolation in Leeds. He described the emergence of a new, dehumanized economic individual cut adrift from the ties that make for sound physical and mental life.

Pusey related this loss of English organic community to the growing divergence of the rich from the poor and the cruel conditions of factory work: "New luxuries have invaded us. We *will* not limit our self-indulgence; and so in order to obtain it cheaply, we pare down the wages of our artisans."[9] Pusey did not shrink from pointing to the industrial system as the source of the alienation of class from class and of the people from their work. He

8. E. B. Pusey, *Commentary on Zechariah*, quoted in *St. Peter's Parish Magazine* (January 1900), 13.

9. Pusey, quoted in his standard biography, H. P. Liddon, *Life of Pusey*, vol. 3 (London: Longmans, Green, 1898), 171. For more analysis of Pusey's views on the industrial revolution see R. W. Franklin, "Pusey and Worship in Industrial Society," *Worship*, 57 (1983), 386-411.

presented industry as a force that was doing much to lessen the stature of men and women as beings created in God's image.

Revising parish worship and building churches in factory districts and slums was the way Pusey reminded the laboring masses that they were surrounded and embraced by God in creation. To Pusey the times required very visible communities of faith to do this. The old Anglican establishment — the episcopal palace, the country parsonage, the bare worship — would never make a breach in the dehumanizing factory conditions and could never lay hold of an industrial population. Revival of the eucharist was an essential part of any renewal of Christian fellowship in the city, and a rich liturgy could dramatize vividly the Christian understanding of the true nature of humankind, that workers were not despised "hands" worthy of less care than a manufacturer's spindles, but God's daughters and sons.

The Regius Professor of Hebrew sold his wife's jewels and publicly auctioned his horse and carriage in 1837 to fund "eucharistic" metropolitan churches. By 1838 Pusey could write to Newman that they were advancing to "correct the stupidity with which people look on at such skeletons of the true fabric [of the Church]."[10]

The Human Community at the Lord's Table

Pusey's growing conviction that the city required eucharistic community was nurtured between 1825 and 1840 by the lectures and monographs of the Berlin Protestant church historian Johann Augustus Neander. Neander set before Pusey the incarnational teaching of the patristic church, by then forgotten in England even though it had been partly revived at the Reformation and again in the seventeenth century.[11] The intense consciousness

10. Ms. letter of E. B. Pusey to J. H. Newman, August 15, 1838, Pusey House, Oxford. Four recent studies relate the Puseyites to movements to establish social justice: Perry Butler, ed., *Pusey Rediscovered* (London: SPCK, 1983); Kenneth Leech and Rowan Williams, eds., *Essays Catholic and Radical* (Milton Keynes: Bowerdean Press, 1983); Geoffrey Rowell, *The Vision Glorious* (Oxford: Oxford University Press, 1983); and Louis Weil, *Sacraments and Liturgy* (Oxford: Basil Blackwell, 1983).

11. Johann Augustus Neander (1789-1850), ecclesiastical historian at Berlin, was responsible for popularizing in many countries the eucharistic humanism of the early church in such works as *History of the Planting and Training of the Christian Church* (Edinburgh: T. & T. Clark, 1842).

of human solidarity expressed in the writings of the fathers; the fellowship, sharing, and corporate celebration the early church experienced in its liturgical worship; especially the essential vision within the patristic church that it was a community propagating itself in opposition to the dominant pagan power: these were all lessons that Neander taught Pusey.

Central to Pusey's understanding of the early church were the patristic focus on the Incarnation of Jesus, the church as his abiding Incarnation, and the humanism implicit in the Word becoming "flesh." For Victorian society in particular, Pusey drew out the communal implications of the fathers' teaching relating "the religion of the Incarnation" to the modern visible church and its sacraments of baptism and eucharist. As he read the fathers from Justin Martyr through Augustine, Pusey perceived that throughout salvation history God had chosen certain women and men as members of a given community, "a people." One enters the orbit of God's "people" through baptism. One continues in this living, organic relationship with others by taking nourishment, Christ's body and his blood, at the eucharist.

Pusey followed the early patristic writer Irenaeus in stressing throughout his Oxford sermons and lectures that man and woman are made in the image of God, formed to receive the divine likeness. Adam and Eve in the garden "reflected the Maker's will, as clear water gives back the face of Heaven." The believer, particularly now amid the harsh dislocations of modern times, is commissioned anew in the midst of corporate worship to live toward this intended heavenly vision of the human.

Pusey saw that God's vision of the human challenged the stereotyped roles of men and women in patriarchal Victorian society. Under that vision women could be freed to lead lives of public service, and men could feel unrestrained in showing such characteristics as warmth, tenderness, mercy, and sacrifice on behalf of others. It follows naturally that the Puseyites organized religious communities in which women exercised public leadership, a rarity in the nineteenth century, and that they offered celibacy as an acceptable alternate form of priestly life for Anglican men. Pusey wanted his skeptical contemporaries to be reminded in vivid ways that it is the eucharist that even now brings us into contact with this re-creating and liberating image of the human given us in the Incarnation. In the eucharist, as in the Incarnation which is part of the same mystery, Christ takes our nature into himself so that "in Him it is In-Godded, Deitate." The humanism of the Incarnation is "a depth of mystery unsearchable . . . that God . . . should take into

Himself what is not God; one must stand speechless with awe at so amazing a mystery."[12]

By 1843 Pusey's study of the fathers issued in this interpretation of the gospel for Victorian society: the good news about Jesus is that faith in him establishes a living, organic relationship with others. The eucharist can become this bond of fellowship, but only if the English recover a belief in the Real Presence and grasp again the intimate link of the Incarnation with the Lord's Supper. The goal was to join this sense of the Real Presence to a communal understanding of the church; the result would be Christian action intended to humanize people caught in the rigors of the industrial revolution. William Gladstone, the great liberal British prime minister who was also influenced by Pusey, wrote a hymn, "O lead My Blindness by the Hand," that expresses this goal: "We who with one blest Food are fed, Into one body may we grow."[13]

Pusey sustained the development of a colorful ritual at worship as a form of Catholic evangelism and as a basis for social action in the dark industrial towns, rites that engaged the population as a whole with Christian teaching on the nature of the human. The drab industrial context required that every sense be engaged in this teaching, and ritual was not introduced into a parish until it was first carefully explained to the congregation. For the Puseyites, active participation in worship — through bodily gestures, singing hymns, joining in responses and processions, and frequent communion — was the primary way a parish and its people witnessed to the values of Jesus Christ in the modern city.

One district in England was taken over almost entirely by the Puseyites. That was the East End of London, a quarter of abject poverty where

12. E. B. Pusey, *A Course of Sermons on Solemn Subjects, Preached in St. Saviour's Church, Leeds* (Oxford: J. H. Parker, 1845, 1847), 265; Pusey, *Sermons During the Season from Advent to Whitsuntide* (Oxford: J. H. Parker, 1848), 58-59, 64-65. This theme is analyzed in detail in Andrew Louth, "Manhood into God: the Oxford Movement, the Fathers and the Deification of Man," *Essays Catholic and Radical,* 70-80; and in A. M. Allchin, *Participation in God: A Forgotten Strand in Anglican Tradition* (Wilton, Conn.: Morehouse-Barlow, 1988). On Puseyism and new definitions of men's and women's roles, see two articles by John Reed, "A Female Movement: The Feminization of Nineteenth-century Anglo-Catholicism," *Anglican and Episcopal History,* 57 (1988), 199-238, and "Giddy Young Men: a Counter-cultural Aspect of Victorian Anglo-Catholicism," *Comparative Social Research,* 11 (1989), 209-26.

13. *The English Hymnal,* 1933, no. 322. For the extent to which Gladstone might be described as a Puseyite humanist see Perry Butler, *Gladstone: Church, State, and Tractarianism* (Oxford: Oxford University Press, 1982). On other Puseyite humanists Stewart Headlam, Henry Scott Holland, and Charles Gore see Robert Woodfield, *Catholicism: Humanist and Democratic* (London: Theology for Modern Man, 1954).

factories, workshops, warehouses, and docks crowded the banks of the Thames. The Puseyite pioneer in the East End was Charles Lowder (1820-1880). The docks became his missionary district in 1856, and Lowder chose liturgical worship as his means of evangelization and action. The populace scoffed when they saw the eucharist celebrated for the first time with incense, vestments, and processions; these "ritualist innovations" prompted riots in the East End in 1859. A mob attacked Lowder's mission, seized him, and almost succeeded in throwing him off a dockbridge. His choir was assaulted with pea shooters when they appeared in the street in "popish rags" — that is, their surplices. This is evidence of how uneasy Victorian society was with the vision of liberation from economic, political, and sexual oppression that the Puseyites expressed visually in their celebration of the eucharist.

But gradually there was a change. Lowder taught the people to make God's house their home through active participation in worship. A sense of warm familial involvement was encouraged among the East End worshippers by means of processions, singing, and other common liturgical actions. Those who worshipped in this manner came to feel themselves "members of one another."[14] A church was put up in 1866 to accommodate 700 communicants. The London dockers came to love and glory in this Church of St. Peter, London Docks. To many it was their only quiet retreat. St. Peter's was God's house, but it had become theirs through their worship, and it became a symbol of their pride in their advancement as a people in the face of harsh economic conditions.

The Eucharist and the Christian Vision of Human Life

Against a one-sided Puritan spirituality that had deprecated the body and its senses and portrayed material externals as signs of hypocrisy in religion, Pusey held up the sacramental life as a way to recover the lost and noble heritage of Christian humanism in the community of Christ. For the Puseyites, the eucharist lent new significance to earth as well as to eternity, to matter as well as to spirit, a new view of what it was to be a woman as well as a man. In their parishes justice for the human community began

14. Maria Trench, *Charles Lowder* (London: 1882), 165. Two recent surveys of London Puseyite parishes are L. E. Ellsworth, *Charles Lowder and the Ritualist Movement* (London: Darton, Longman and Todd, 1982), and Michael Reynolds, *Martyr of Ritualism* (London: Faber and Faber, 1965).

to flow in real ways from the eucharist: funds for workers' compensation, funds for worthy burial, and distribution centers for clothing, food, and other necessities. From 1840 to 1900 the bond between worship and Christian humanism was vividly dramatized in Puseyite parishes in commercial districts.

For example, in Leeds, in the West Riding of Yorkshire where short-stapled wools were used in the manufacture of hand-spun woolen yarn and cloth and where the population had risen from 53,000 in 1801 to 123,000 in 1831, Pusey himself built and supervised a church that was an experiment to determine whether these goals could become actuality. The clergy Pusey appointed to Saint Saviour's Leeds spoke out with blunt passion about lives ground down in the continual din of revolving wheels, the glare and blaze of furnaces, and the choking clouds of smoke and flax dust. Their sermons were indictments of mill owners who treated workers as hands or machines and not as brothers and sisters in Christ.

But it was the liturgy at Saint Saviour's that unfolded images of the new life to which the workers were beckoned by the gospel. Here the mill hands were welcomed as honored guests into a house surrounded with jewels and diamonds: bread and wine were shared equally, the water of baptism was poured out with great dignity on the poorest, and all were summoned to participation by splendid music and the pomp of processions.

And this vision of heaven was firmly tied to earthly institutions. From 1848 money was given daily to the poor at the vicar's door, and classes for men and women were held each weekday evening. There were day schools for boys, girls, and infants — for all who could pay two pence per week. The parish endowed a fund to provide workers with compensation when ill, and another to provide worthy funerals for members of the parish. There was a savings account established for the purchase of clothing and a library of 1,000 volumes for the workers.

In 1848, a year of widespread European revolution, a visitor from the country saw and recorded how worship at Saint Saviour's effectively proclaimed a humanism and a liberation inspired by the power of Christian faith:

> A poor woman and her two children were baptized during the Eucharist. All the clergy and all the choir made a procession to and stood round the Font. We could not have done more honour to the Queen's children and their sponsors, but we did not put to shame the tattered rags and mean

appearance of these poor people. They were not at all out of place in this splendid house. I never witnessed one of the powers of the church more forcibly — that of raising up the poor — and by inference I felt another of the powers — that of pulling down the rich.[15]

A second example — and there are scores of others — of sacramental life leading to human renewal in nineteenth-century England is offered by the town of Wantage. When the new Puseyite vicar, William John Butler, arrived in 1847, Wantage lay "almost outside the pale of nineteenth-century civilization," even though the industrial revolution had begun to make an impact here as well.[16] There were no paved roads or oil street lamps. Pubs flourished at every corner, and the open sewage ditches were not cleaned. The public grammar school had been discontinued in 1832.

The eucharist became the impulse behind Butler's widespread re-form of the town. He preached on "the need of the Sacrament of the Lord's Supper to restore the armour of God among us." First it was necessary to bring "the beauty of holiness to the town" by establishing public and regular celebrations of the sacrament at an altar placed prominently in the crossing of the parish church, after the town fire engine had been removed from the Lady Chapel.[17]

From this altar Butler and his congregation moved outward to institute secular change. He contracted with a gas company to lay pipes for the gas lighting of the town by thirty-seven lamps. The church built a drainage system to reduce the occurrence of typhoid. The streets were paved. By the end of two decades the church in Wantage was managing twenty-one institutions, and at least 750 young people were being trained in its schools.

Wantage, with its elaborate parish operations and vigorous and fearless vicar, became a model Puseyite parish and a training ground for other priests and prelates. The revitalization of an entire town provided evidence that eucharistic principles could be translated into better living

15. Ms. copy of a letter of James Davies to his mother, November 7, 1848, Pusey House, Oxford. For more on this parish see Stephen Savage and Christopher Tyne, *The Labours of Years* (n.p., 1965), and Nigel Yates, *The Oxford Movement and Parish Life: St. Saviour's Leeds 1839-1929* (Leeds: W. N. Yates, 1975).

16. Sir Arthur Quiller-Couch, *Memoir of Arthur John Butler* (London, 1917), 343. On Butler's transformation of Wantage see Kathleen Philip, *Reflected in Wantage* (Wantage: K. Philip, 1970) and *Victorian Wantage* (Oxford: K. Philip, 1968).

17. W. J. Butler, ms. "Parochialia," June 30, 1847, 24; ms. sermon, Friday after Ninth Trinity Sunday, 1849, 90. Butler's published works are *Ignorance the Danger of the Church* (London: W. Butler, 1890) and *What Is Our Present Danger?* (London: W. Butler, 1891).

conditions for the English public. Wantage became symbolic of a kind of apostolic zeal that had been reborn in the nineteenth century.[18]

W. G. Sawyer, who carried Puseyism north to Yorkshire, recalled at the end of his life, "I went for one day, and stayed for five and a half years. Whatever little work I may have been able to do in the Church of God has mainly been the result of the training I received at Wantage."[19] Charlotte Yonge the novelist put down her impressions of this almost forgotten example of Christian humanism in the machine age:

> Nothing struck me so much as the zest, life, and spirit which pervaded everything. The early service, the merry breakfast, the schools, the parish visiting, the midday dinner with the curates, the classes, the evening visits to parishioners, all concluded by a supper as lively as the former meals had been. There was something brilliant and something quaint about it all. One felt that there was a very atmosphere of high intellect and refined taste — not very many books — Classics and Fathers.[20]

The Pusey influence left its mark on nineteenth-century English parish life, but the effective pairing of worship and social protest was continued in the revived Anglican religious orders. Above all, the Society of St. John the Evangelist (1863) and the Society of the Sacred Mission (1894) transformed the experience of the Puseyite parishes into a new monastic tradition that would influence the Anglican Communion into the twentieth century. The influence can be seen, for example, in A. G. Hebert, the most important twentieth-century Anglican to relate worship and society.

Hebert was drawn to the Society of the Sacred Mission in 1914 because he felt "an outstanding feature of modern life is the lack of true human community — the loneliness and isolation of the individual in the modern town where people do not know their neighbors."[21] Hebert restated the message of Pusey for the twentieth century: the Incarnation as

18. Wantage as a model of Christian humanism is discussed in Community of St. Mary the Virgin, *Butler of Wantage* (Westminster, 1961).

19. A. J. Butler, *Life and Letters of William John Butler* (London: Macmillan, 1897), 93. On these models in the twentieth century see Donald Gray, *Earth and Altar: The Evolution of the Parish Communion in the Church of England to 1945* (Norwick: Alcuin Club, 1986), Peter Jagger, *A History of the Parish and People Movement* (Leighton Buzzard: The Faith Press, 1970), and W. S. Pickering, *Anglo-Catholicism* (London: Routledge, 1989).

20. Butler, *Life and Letters*, 237, 287.

21. A. G. Hebert, ms. "The Liturgical Movement," Archives of the Society of the Sacred Mission, Kelham.

the coming of God in the flesh for the redemption of our actual bodily life and our social relations. Encouraging lay participation in the eucharist around a free-standing table, Father Hebert envisaged a worldwide revival of this active participation of the laity in Roman Catholic, Orthodox, Lutheran, Anglican, and Reformed churches. He believed that "God is already beginning to lead us back to a Christianity that shall be at once evangelical, Catholic, and modern."[22]

The Church of Denmark: N. F. S. Grundtvig, 1839-1900

The Puseyites and their descendants had counterparts in other churches and other nations. One such was Bishop Nikolai Grundtvig (1783-1872) of Denmark. Grundtvig and Pusey met on several occasions and also exchanged letters. In a variety of ways Grundtvigianism in the Danish Church was a development paralleling the Oxford Movement in the Church of England.[23]

Nikolai Grundtvig was what is termed a "ten-talent" man, but there was something eccentric about his makeup. His career in the church was so turbulent that he could not keep a regular pastorate until 1839. On three occasions he was the victim of a mental breakdown. In the last occurrence, when he was eighty-three, Grundtvig began to address the queen mother of Denmark from the pulpit as the Queen of Sheba, who had come to hear the wisdom of Solomon. This extravagant sense of public mission was an integral part of Grundtvig's personality.

At the age of fifty-six, in 1839, Grundtvig was appointed pastor in the Vartov home for the aged in the inner city of Copenhagen. There he served for the next thirty-three years, gathering about him a congregation of disciples who experienced with him a renewal of fellowship in worship. From the simple sanctuary of the Vartov home emerged a Grundtvigian Party, some of whose members rose to high office and directly influenced the political and religious life of Denmark.

Grundtvig made four trips to Britain between 1829 and 1843. There he observed first-hand the roaring din of industrial society, and the

22. A. G. Hebert, *Intercommunion* (London: SPCK, 1932), vii.
23. On Pusey and Grundtvig see P. G. Lindhardt, "Grundtvig and England," *The Journal of Ecclesiastical History*, 1 (1950), 207-24; F. Aubrey Rush, "Letters from England: Grundtvig Writes Home," *The Norseman*, 11, 263-70.

visits made a deep impression on the Danish pastor. He said later that he had gone to England in quest of ancient manuscripts and had returned as a prophet. He embarked upon a mission to reshape the contemporary evolution of his nation.

Grundtvig and his party proclaimed that believers still encountered the incarnate Jesus in modern times, above all in baptism and the Lord's Supper. The Grundtvigians helped turn aside the Danish government from its policies of expansion and war to concentrate instead on the welfare of the people. The party worked for the intellectual and spiritual awakening of Danish artisans and small farmers, to avoid the fate of their counterparts in other industrializing countries. The Grundtvigians guided Denmark along a different path to modernization.[24]

Grundtvig took seriously the call for worthy temporal conditions that the physical elements of the sacraments dignified. He was concerned about the waste and greed of the industrial society developing around him. Through the Christian Cooperative Movement he fostered folk arts and crafts, weaving, carpentry, folk dancing, and story telling to counter the destructive influence of the industrial capitalism being imported from England. This movement preserved craft traditions and handwork within the sacramental context of the parish. Grundtvig's cooperatives emphasized simplicity and authenticity and a preservation of the delight of working with one's hands, working close to the natural rhythms of the earth.

Grundtvig discovered a craving for human fellowship in many places he visited. All over Europe men and women were longing to share a common life. He was sharply opposed to, and wanted to begin a reaction against, the dominant individualism of his time. In the 1832 introduction to a volume on Nordic mythology, he defined the fellowship needed in modern society as "folk-life." For Grundtvig, "folk-life" meant an existence that is not a matter of private concern alone; it is a community life that finds its earthly home in the created world. Grundtvig was a literary scholar and poet who delighted in the myth, ritual, fantasy, and celebration of the common people. There he discovered vital aspects of a nation's well-being and legitimate vessels of truth not to be discarded with the coming of modernization. Grundtvig experienced the presence of God in the wisdom

---

24. The two best introductions to Grundtvig in English are Johannes Knudsen, *Danish Rebel* (Philadelphia: Muhlenberg Press, 1955), and P. G. Lindhardt, *Grundtvig: An Introduction* (London: SPCK, 1951). Also to be mentioned is a study translated into English from Danish: Hal Koch, *Grundtvig*, trans. Llewellyn Jones (Yellow Springs, Ohio: The Antioch Press, 1952).

and mythology of the Nordic peoples. "Folk-life" is a "living word" for Grundtvig, "a pleasing habitation of the Lord."[25]

In his humanistic "folk high schools" (forty-one were established all over Denmark between 1844 and 1870) Grundtvig sought to nurture the "folk-life" of his people. The folk high schools were his secular weapon in forging a unique Danish pattern of modernization, in direct contrast to the German model evolving to the south that emphasized rapid industrialization and a large-scale military buildup. Grundtvig called the existing Latin preparatory schools in Denmark and the University of Copenhagen "schools of death," because they forced people into the shape required to fit into the artificially fabricated, dehumanizing jobs offered by modern society. In the academies, he maintained, the human personality was sacrificed to work.

The purpose of the folk high school was to awaken a zest for life — "for life whole and complete" — in the context of bonds of friendship between craft masters and students.[26] Grundtvig was less interested that students have formal instruction than that they have close personal communication "with honest craftsmen."[27] A Grundtvig disciple wrote of the folk high schools: "We wish our students to leave us with the desire to devote themselves to the tasks of life and to use with understanding the means which life offers."[28] Grundtvig's schools, laying their stress on what is stimulating and vivid, aroused a feeling for the lovely and noble things of human life and stimulated students to work at making them a reality.

Life nourished in the schools had to be sustained. For Grundtvig, this was accomplished by participating in the Lord's Supper. Grundtvig's concern for the cultural progress of the Danish people was intimately linked to his interest in advancing their religious maturation. He was convinced that in the Lord's Supper, God, the Creator and Giver of life, has provided

25. E. L. Allen, *Bishop Grundtvig: A Prophet of the North* (London: James Clarke, 1944), 82; Johannes Knudsen, *Selected Writings of N. F. S. Grundtvig* (Philadelphia: Fortress Press, 1976), 33. On Grundtvig as humanist, see Llewellyn Jones, "Grundtvig as a Scandinavian Precursor of Humanism," *The Humanist*, 1 (1953), 34-36; Johannes Knudsen, "Revelation and Man According to N. F. S. Grundtvig," *The Lutheran Quarterly*, 10 (1958), 217-55; Kaj Thaning, "Das Menschliche und das Christliche bei N. F. S. Grundtvig," *Kontroverse um Kierkegaard und Grundtvig* (Berlin, 1966), 50-80.

26. G. Everett Arden, *Four Northern Lights* (Minneapolis: Augsburg, 1964), 97. On the humanism of the folk high schools, see C. Hartley Grattan, "The Meaning of Grundtvig: Skill plus Culture," *The Antioch Review*, 18 (1958), 76-86; Holger Begtrup, *The Folk High Schools of Denmark* (London: Oxford University Press, 1936).

27. Allen, *Grundtvig*, 81.

28. Ibid., 84.

the means by which life is undergirded and strengthened at its very deepest levels so that it might come to its highest fulfillment in social activity.

When Grundtvig emerged upon the religious scene, the Danish church was dominated by individuals and parties who ignored public worship. Groups of earnest folk were being gathered together for self-examination and devotion outside church services. Others emphasized distributing and reading the Bible in homes. In the *Attack Upon Christendom* that occupied him in the months before his death in 1855, the Danish philosopher Søren Kierkegaard had maintained that the marks of Christian living are found only in a strong personal and ethical discipleship guided by the teachings of Jesus.

But the congregation was central to Grundtvig's understanding of the faith and to his Christian humanism. The Vartov church in Copenhagen became the center of a remarkable congregational life that spread its influence through the whole Danish church and became the embodiment in practice of Grundtvig's new emphasis upon Christian fellowship. Because of his experience at Vartov, Grundtvig, like Luther, began to use the word "congregation" rather than "church" to describe God's people, and the congregation became the basic unit in his understanding of Christian reality. In its worship the parish comes to understand the full humanity intended for it; therefore Grundtvig was concerned that the entire congregation participate fully in the liturgy and that women be more actively involved in the leadership of worship. Grundtvig reminded his contemporaries of the historic tradition of eucharistic fellowship at worship that the Lutheran churches had abandoned.

He envisioned a series of free congregations loosely bound to the state church where the Danes would gather to explore and practice new life-styles. He wanted to make the parish the center of life in every town and village in Denmark. Public activities such as planting a parish garden would be powerful witnesses to a shared eucharistic vision of life that balanced spiritual advancement with the preservation of natural beauty. Grundtvig encouraged parishes to be involved in projects of reforestation and land reclamation.

At a significant point in his life Grundtvig had made what he described as an "unparalleled discovery": that Christianity had been preserved not by the Bible nor by the theologians, but by the "living word" from God and the "living word" of the Christian congregation in the creed and in the sacraments.[29] "No book can confer life, not even the Bible. The Christian community is no mere reading club; it is a fellowship of faith

29. Arden, *Four Northern Lights*, 106. See Toivo Harjunpaa, "Grundtvig and his Incomparable Discovery," *The Lutheran Quarterly*, 25 (1973), 54-70.

begotten and preserved through the spoken word as this goes down from generation to generation."[30] The human community, not the Book, was the channel of God's revelation.

He came to see that it is impossible to build the church on the Bible, but that rather we must place the Bible in the church: we must place the open Bible on the altar, and not imagine that we can construct the altar on the Book. It is in the celebration of the sacraments and within the congregation that we hear God's Word to us, God's creative Word, which brings into being the church, the new people of God.

This "unparalleled discovery" — the Word in worship first and then the Bible — came from Grundtvig's reading in Irenaeus, the influential father of the second century who also inspired Luther and Pusey, and it represents in many ways a return to the earliest insights of Luther. For Luther, too, the Bible only comes to life and is fully understood as God's Word when it is received by faith in the congregation. Similarly, Luther taught that in the Holy Supper we have the fullest assurance of Christ's presence with us.

The eucharist is thus the soil in which the Christian community must be planted to grow, if it is not to wither and die. To realize our own true humanity, to become "truly human" is to develop God's gift of humanity in a eucharistic fellowship, within a particular people of God in a specific parish. Such a parish is not of the state, government, or nation. It comes into being through the "living word" present in baptism and the eucharist and in the "Amen" spoken by the congregation at the creed. In this way the creative power of God is entrusted to women and men "to make all things new."[31]

Grundtvig's message gradually led to a restoration of eucharistic fellowship in Denmark. By the end of his life the eucharist had become again the regular form of worship in the Danish church, celebrated twice every Sunday or festival in the town churches, and at "High Mass" in the country churches. In these circumstances God came to be grasped as a new source of energy for the times, and the Grundtvigians addressed God in new energetic forms — poems, folk-dances, and folk songs. Grundtvig successfully integrated the traditional products of the folk-life of the people into their worship through the use of weaving, carving, and carpentry to brighten the worship space and through songs and dance to bring joy to

30. Allen, *Grundtvig,* 66.

31. On Grundtvig's liturgical theology, see A. M. Allchin, "Grundtvig: An English Appreciation," *Worship,* 58 (1984), 420-33, and "Grundtvig's Catholicity," *N. F. S. Grundtvig* (Copenhagen: The Danish Institute, 1983), 11-21.

the church. He also called for the ordination of virgins and widows (oddly, not married women) so that God's feminine as well as masculine qualities could be articulated by preachers.

Grundtvig wanted worship to reinforce a sense of solidarity not only among the living but also with the dead. He wanted to make people aware of a human continuity that reached back to the apostles. To do this he revived the liturgical year and wrote hymns for all the days in the church calendar. Congregational singing was one of the essentials of Grundtvig's liturgical reform. He understood the power of community singing to weld the members of a group together and strove to build a singing church rather than a church of sermon tasters. He saw that the Christian education of many members in country congregations would come more effectively through the hymnbook than through preaching. It was no accident that Grundtvig was the greatest Scandinavian hymnwriter of all time; he wrote 2,000 hymns, and his *Song-Book of the Danish Church,* in five volumes (1837-1881), contained new versions of the hymns of the whole Christian church. These hymns were grouped around the great liturgical festivals to foster in the common people a love of the church and its services. In a singing congregation Grundtvig saw the Holy Spirit of God actively nurturing human hearts.

Through his hymns Grundtvig succeeded in creating an atmosphere of festal celebration in the congregation. These tremendous and joyful songs of praise, intended to be sung by the whole people of God, were so radically new that the authorities for a long time prevented their inclusion in the official hymnal of the Danish state church. Kierkegaard derided Grundtvig as a "bellowing blacksmith" who did not understand "the true tone of a hymn," which in Kierkegaard's opinion should give expression to the intimate suffering of the individual as he or she, in quiet sorrow, becomes reconciled to God. To Kierkegaard "Grundtvig is, was, and continues to be a noisemaker who will be unpleasant to me even in eternity."[32]

But today Grundtvig's hymns are sung by everyone in the Danish church, and some appear in the hymnals of other churches. Few would deny the vitality and vigor with which these songs even in our own time still express the reality of the church as the place where through the power of the Spirit we hear God's Word to us in the eucharist and through our participation in it are ourselves able to go out in the Spirit to renew all legitimate forms of human endeavor and to act as agents of reconciliation.

32. Henning Høirup, "Grundtvig and Kierkegaard: Their Views of the Church," *Theology Today,* 12 (1955), 330.

Above all, the hymns celebrate Sunday as the day of rejoicing and triumph in which we enter into the victory of our Lord. One of the finest expressions of the theme of Christian humanism in worship is a hymn well known among Danish congregations. In the strength of its lines we hear not only Grundtvig, but something of Luther and the fathers speaking again in the machine age:

> Sunday morning from the dead
> Jesus arose in triumph,
> Every Sunday's dawn
> Now brings healing to death
> and wonderfully recalls
> all the life of the Lord.
>
> Thousand-tongued the Lord's words
> are then reborn throughout the world:
> Wake now from sleep and sloth
> every ear which can hear.
> Arise, soul from the dead
> and greet the dawn of Easter.
>
> Every Sunday makes death shudder
> and makes darkness tremble underground,
> For there where Christ gives light and glory
> the Word of life speaks in giant-tones,
> and with joy of victory does battle
> with the king of death and power of darkness.[33]

The Roman Catholic Church in France, Germany, Belgium, and the United States: The Benedictine Liturgical Revival, 1833-1979

A reawakened sense that public worship is meant for all the people and the investigation of the social implications of worship also began to revive in the Roman Catholic Church in the nineteenth century, but it proceeded

---

33. *Danske Salmebog,* no. 372. See two articles of A. M. Allchin, "The Hymns of N. F. S. Grundtvig," *The Eastern Churches Quarterly,* 13 (1959), 129-43, and "Grundtvig's Translations from the Greek," *The Eastern Churches Quarterly,* 16 (1961), 28-44.

in a different direction from that taken by the Anglicans and the Lutherans. The Roman Catholic liturgical revival began primarily as the work of Benedictine monks.

In the Church of England and the Church of Denmark, frequent celebrations of the eucharist and increased corporate participation of the laity appeared first in the parishes. For French and German Benedictines, rebuilding the fabric of human life called for the restoration of liturgical worship first in the monasteries. But the Roman Catholic liturgical revival also came to include a translation of the old Benedictine ideals of worship and work out of the monastery and into the church at large. The monks found the mass to be a source of renewal for all the church. The nature of the monastery, an institution that is a center both of learning and of daily life, shaped the Catholic liturgical revival along a creative middle way that was at once conservative in that it looked back to the fathers for models of worship, and progressive in that it sought to create a revived community life for the laity, the expression of Christianity most suited to the human needs of the industrial age.

The abbot of Solesmes in France, Dom Prosper Guéranger (1801-1875), grew up amid the chaos of political and industrial revolution in western France. Guéranger perceived that rebuilding the fabric of life called for the restoration of common worship everywhere. Abbé Guéranger convinced his followers from 1833 to 1875 that this restoration was the chief duty of modern monks. Guéranger had discovered that liturgy combats individualism; for the first time in centuries, prayer was again for a Benedictine monk a social act with implications that reached beyond the monastery.

In order to make the liturgy live again, Guéranger taught that it must be the prayer of all the people. In the third volume of his massive *Liturgical Institutions* (1851) Guéranger invited the clergy to provide the people a vital knowledge of the church by encouraging their intelligent participation in the liturgy. He urged parish clergy to consider that it is chiefly by what the people *do themselves* in church that they are educated in the meaning of the whole of life in the light of the church's sacred actions. Guéranger sought to give everyone a stake in religion. He did not defer to certain segments of the population; all classes were taught to feel at home in church, not to come merely for the doling out of sacraments. Social solidarity in the parishes, for Guéranger, had to be founded on worship.

The paradox of Guéranger's career is that, though the movement he founded was regarded as reactionary, it had within it elements that evolved into an expression of Christianity well suited to industrial conditions. He taught that although the community must not reject existence in the contemporary world, men and women could transcend the choking life of materialism only by reaching beyond a system of values whose end lies in the physical. The community is formed by that act of reaching beyond. That act is the liturgy of the mass.

Guéranger understood the eucharist to be a means to address one of the greatest problems of the nineteenth century, the domination of a materialistic civilization that divided life into a secular sphere and an increasingly unimportant and "otherworldly" spiritual sphere. The ties established in the eucharist between the church and ordinary household objects were valuable symbols, as were processions that carried a religious presence into places of work in a century that underestimated the spiritual value of labor. A revived liturgical year could symbolically hallow specific times in an age when employment schedules and technology had created nightless days and seasonless years.[34]

The leadership of the liturgical revival passed from abbey to abbey and from country to country. In the nineteenth century, monks and nuns were harassed by a sense of being tolerated rather than welcomed and felt they had to prove their worth in public works of zeal rather than in prayer. This served to quell the revival in some places where it had begun to blossom. But the international character of Benedictine monasticism made it possible for ideas to migrate out of countries in which the Roman Catholic liturgical revival had become threatened and distorted by anti-monastic prejudices. By the 1860s the center of the liturgical revival had moved to the Benedictine abbey of Beuron on the edge of the Black Forest in southern Germany. There the *Mass Book of the Holy Church* was published in 1884; for the first time, a missal included translations and explanations of all the mass prayers for the laity. By 1906, some 100,000 copies of this so-called Schott Missal had been sold. In 1939, about 1,650,000 impressions were in use in Germany alone.

Political persecution directed at monks in Germany after 1870 forced the Beuronese revival into abbeys in Belgium and the Austrian Empire, but this did not separate the Beuronese liturgical movement from

34. On Incarnation, eucharist, and humanism in Dom Prosper Guéranger, see Cuthbert Johnson, *Prosper Guéranger: A Liturgical Theologian* (Rome: S. Anselmo, 1984), and two articles by R. W. Franklin that place him in the context of other movements surveyed here, "The People's Work: Anti-Jansenist Prejudice in the Benedictine Movement for Popular Participation in the Nineteenth Century," *Studia Liturgica,* 19 (1989), 60-77, and "Guéranger: A View on the Centenary of His Death," *Worship,* 49 (1975), 318-28.

the context of industrial dislocation in Germany. At the Beuronese monastery of Maria Laach, Abbot Ildefons Herwegen wrote in the 1930s that if worship were restored to a corporate act of the whole Christian people it would be able also "to free society from its earthly bonds, to lift it from the misery of the present."[35]

Herwegen's colleague Dom Odo Casel taught at Maria Laach that "the world into which the liturgy introduces us is not a world in its own right, standing aloof from the world of ordinary living. A liturgical life is a life of true humanism, for it is a life concerned with fostering the true interests of human beings as they actually exist in the real order."[36] The liturgy to Odo Casel expressed an authenticity, austerity, simplicity, and dignity that worked to overcome the dehumanizing aspects of the industrial world.

At the Beuronese monastery of Mont-César in Belgium, other links were forged between worship and humanism on the eve of the First World War. The central figure at Mont-César was Lambert Beauduin. Before becoming a monk, Beauduin had lived for eight years with factory workers in a radical district of Liége where he experienced firsthand the hard life that was the common lot of industrial workers. He perceived that by participating in the eucharist, workers could be lifted for a moment from the dehumanizing character of their surroundings. Beauduin's Christian manifesto was *The Piety of the Church* of 1914:

> From the first centuries to our own day, the Church has ever given to all her prayers a spirit which is profoundly and essentially collective. . . . By means of living the liturgy wholeheartedly, Christians become more and more conscious of their supernatural fraternity.[37]

Beauduin demanded that the Catholic Church not hide from the contemporary industrial world of machine work but meet it and transform it through the people's work, the liturgy, so that the world of the sacraments, the world into which the liturgy introduces us, could bring the new life of

---

35. Ildefons Herwegen, "The Nature of Religious Art," *Liturgical Arts,* 1 (1931), 1-6.

36. Louis Bouyer, *La vie de la liturgie* (Paris: Editions du Cerf, 1956), 327-29.

37. Lambert Beauduin, *La Piété de l'Église* (Louvain: Abbaye du Mont-César, 1914), 18. For more on the eucharistic humanism of Beauduin, see Sonya S. Quitslund, *Beauduin: A Prophet Vindicated* (New York: Newman Press, 1973); and Bernard Botte, *From Silence to Participation: An Insider's View of Liturgical Renewal,* trans. John Sullivan (Washington, D.C.: The Pastoral Press, 1988).

the resurrection into the sphere of factories, machines, shops, and strikes. In the factory world Beauduin came to the conclusion that the old individual interpretation of Christian ethics had become irrelevant in the face of the brutal facts of daily life. Little moral homilies did not change human conditions or actions or attitudes in any sphere of collective behavior. Beauduin sought to reestablish a social perspective on Christian ethics and provide for a broader and deeper conversion, but what would be its source?

In 1906 Beauduin entered the Benedictine abbey of Mont-César, and there he came into contact with fourteen centuries of monastic living and its stress on the liturgy as the center, not the periphery, of the Christian life. There he adapted the unique educational and publishing resources of the monastery to the needs of the parish. He often worked through the night, kept awake by a pot of hot black coffee brought to him by one of his brother monks, writing inexpensive liturgical guides, reviews, and pamphlets for lay people. He popularized in the early twentieth century Benedict's old vision of a renewed Christian society that no longer saw work as a curse but rather as a gift of God in the service of the human community. Human work tempered by the rhythm of constant worship and nourished by the living waters of the liturgy became a monastic ideal shared by Lambert Beauduin with his contemporaries who were not monks.[38]

The Liturgical Movement Comes to America

The words and works of Lambert Beauduin cast a spell over Dom Virgil Michel (1890-1938), a young American monk. After studying with Beauduin in Rome in 1924, and with other liturgists at Solesmes and Beuron in 1925, he returned to America with a "new" discovery: that the church gives us "a proper concept and understanding of what society should be like [and] it puts this concept into action in its worship and wants us to live it out in everyday life."[39]

38. Weekly inexpensive liturgical guides, reviews, and pamphlets were issued by Beauduin with the help of confreres at Mont-César. In 1909 *La Vie liturgique,* a weekly paper, began to be distributed in Belgium, and in 1910 it was carried into Holland. The faithful received books edited by a staff of monks in the *Petite bibliotheque liturgique* series after 1912. The whole monastery was mobilized for these endeavors.

39. Paul Marx, *Virgil Michel and the Liturgical Movement* (Collegeville, Minn.: The Liturgical Press, 1957), 205. Two other studies of this point are Jeremy Hall, *The Full*

When Virgil Michel returned to his home, St. John's Benedictine Abbey in Minnesota, the historic mission of Michel and St. John's was now to transplant the recovery of public worship already accomplished in Denmark, England, France, and Germany to the United States. In 1926 Michel organized two projects that were to become permanent forces in American Catholic and Protestant churches: the journal *Orate Fratres* (later renamed *Worship*) and the publishing house Liturgical Press. By 1929, *Orate Fratres* was circulated in twenty-six countries. Liturgical Press distributed an especially noteworthy volume, *A Short Breviary for Religious and Laity*. *A Short Breviary*, anything but short, adapted the entire divine office to the needs of the lay person, just as the *Mass Book* of Beuron had provided translations of all the eucharistic texts. Over the years, tens of thousands of lay people from all across America purchased *A Short Breviary*, and by 1980 more than 400,000 copies had been sold. Through such publications St. John's sought to enable all people to take an active part in the official worship of the church and thereby transform American parishes, convents, and monasteries into living communities.

During the Great Depression of the 1930s, *Orate Fratres* explicitly emphasized the Christian humanism implied in worship. Virgil Michel looked out from Minnesota across a land grown hard, cynical, and sinister. One-fourth of American families were on relief. *Orate Fratres* addressed more than the problem of unemployment in American life. Of the quality of life Michel wrote:

> The greatest of the evils is perhaps the depersonalization of man, the reduction of man to a mere cog in a machine. The greatest evil of bourgeois capitalism is the harm it has done to man himself, to dehumanize and depersonalize man most completely.[40]

Michel encouraged local social action inspired by a eucharistic model. He never considered the liturgical revival to be merely a new way

---

Stature of Christ: The Ecclesiology of Virgil Michel (Collegeville, Minn.: The Liturgical Press, 1976), and R. W. Franklin and Robert Spaeth, *Virgil Michel: American Catholic* (Collegeville, Minn.: The Liturgical Press, 1988).

40. Marx, *Virgil Michel*, 312. Some of Michel's essays on eucharistic humanism are collected in *The Social Question: Essays on Capitalism and Christianity by Fr. Virgil Michel* (Collegeville, Minn.: Saint John's University, 1987), and his position is analyzed in Emerson Hynes, "Social Thought of Virgil Michel," *American Catholic Sociological Review*, 1 (1940), 172-80, and Kenneth R. Hines, "Eucharist and Justice: Assessing the Legacy of Virgil Michel," *Worship*, 62 (1988), 201-24.

to recite the psalms or to offer the mass. Taking the liturgy seriously implied that each Christian must have satisfying secular work in surroundings becoming to human beings. Worship in common should lead to secular cooperation in parish credit unions, parish grocery, gas, and burial societies, and worker participation in management, ownership, and profits.

Like the Puseyites and the Grundtvigians, Virgil Michel saw a connection between the new vision of human life offered in the eucharist and a Christian challenge to gender stereotypes as defined by secular society. He insisted to his contemporaries on the fundamental equality of Catholic laywomen and -men in codiscipleship. He reminded Catholics of the order of deaconesses in the early church who helped in the administration of baptism, instructed the community during times of persecution, and prepared catechumens for the sacraments. In every way possible he encouraged women to participate in the church's worship and to take on positions of lay leadership since they shared, as members of the Savior's body, in the same priesthood as laymen.

Michel encouraged the apostolic leadership of three women in particular. Ellen Gates Starr was a cofounder, with Jane Addams, of Hull House, the pioneer settlement house for workers' families established in Chicago. Father Michel recruited her for his movement and relied on her as the leader of the liturgical movement among Catholics in the Chicago area.

Dorothy Day was another distinguished woman who found a friend in Virgil Michel. When the leftist tendencies of her Catholic Workers' Movement drew fire from the church hierarchy in the 1930s, Father Michel wrote letters in her defense. Whenever he could he visited her Houses of Hospitality where lay people brought the message of Jesus to the streets by feeding the poor and housing the homeless. In the Houses Father Michel would preach on the mass as the source of social renewal.

Catherine de Hueck Doherty was a third woman whose leadership was championed by Father Michel. Along with four other lay people, she founded Friendship House in the Toronto slums in the 1930s. Their work among the unemployed poor, including blacks and communists, was met with disapproval from the hierarchy and with either indifference or ridicule by other laity. Discouraged, Doherty considered abandoning the project when one morning in 1935 Virgil Michel came into her empty storefront on Portland Street. He took a seat on an old broken chair and spoke to her from the depths of his own suffering and experience of poverty. He reminded her of the apostolic vocation of Catholic women and of worship as the basis of the Catholic woman's quest for justice, both within the church and outside it.

In the end Virgil Michel and St. John's Abbey urged Christians who had been given such a radical new vision of human life through the liturgical renewal not to withdraw into a movement apart but to take an active place in their local parish church. These American Benedictines held that new life could come to every congregation, however routinized into hardened forms it may have become. Above all, it was the parishes and their members who had to make the case for Christian humanism by living the gospel radically, by developing in parishioners a critical attitude toward the church's acceptance of the status quo in the industrial culture surrounding them, and by making others aware of the dehumanizing aspects of this culture. The parishes needed to foster skills so that men and women could survive in the industrial world as effective and active Christians, capable of making a substantial impact on their church and their society.[41]

Many American Catholics were critical of this emphasis, from morticians threatened by the new simple funerals to bishops who banned *Orate Fratres* from seminary libraries and St. John's monks from their diocesan pulpits. One critic was Sister Antonia McHugh, president of the College of St. Catherine, who wrote:

> The Liturgical Movement centered at St. John's, which aims to diffuse social charity and understanding through increased lay participation in the official worship of the church is something with which I will have nothing to do. The thought of connecting the psalms with socially activated prayers is too irritating to be considered. The whole commotion is doubtless of German origin.[42]

In truth, not surprisingly St. John's became a haven for radical Catholics from 1930 to 1961. Activists such as Dorothy Day and Bar-

---

41. Readers interested in the issues surrounding Christian social reconstruction in the parish will want to find Virgil Michel's book *Christian Social Reconstruction* (Milwaukee: Bruce, 1937), and the following pamphlets all published in 1936 by the Wanderer Printing Company of St. Paul: *Ideals of Reconstruction, Labor and Industry, Money and the Common Good, The Nature of Capitalism,* and *Reconstruction Schemes*. On the eucharist and women, see Virgil Michel, "The Liturgical Movement and the Catholic Woman," Central Verein of America, *Annual Report* (1929), 58.

42. Helen Angela Hurley, *On Good Ground* (Minneapolis: University of Minnesota Press, 1951), 261. To Irish bishops on the East and West Coasts, Michel's liturgical works were merely "a meeting of a bunch of Germans out in the Midwest."

oness Catherine de Hueck took the social implications of worship to new audiences and fresh endeavors, fueling new struggles for racial and economic justice. When Virgil Michel died at forty-eight, Dorothy Day wrote that "to us at the Catholic Worker, Father Virgil was a dear friend and adviser, bringing to us his tremendous strength and knowledge, for he had such faith in the people, faith in their intelligence and spiritual capacities. . . ." Years after Michel's death, the Baroness de Hueck recalled him as he appeared in the early 1930s: "He was young, but he was carrying a flame within him. . . . Perhaps I mean fire, the fire that renews the face of the earth."[43]

The revolutionary Abbey Church completed at St. John's in 1961 gave concrete expression to these ideals. The Bauhaus architect Marcel Breuer used factory materials of concrete, steel, and glass to provide the abbey with a great open church where monks and laity together could assemble for corporate worship. Breuer's design unifies monastic choir, altar, and congregation into one space through the rhythmic repetition of starkly modern elements. To many this church suggests a harsh factory, which only becomes alive and warm when the people fill it up with the common work of worship. Yet this was Breuer's artistic parable of the meaning of the liturgical revival. Breuer was convinced that the Benedictine monks, with their ancient traditional Christian family life, could offer contemporary society both meaningful and attractive standards.

The rediscovery of the communal dimension of the Roman Catholic Church and the revival of liturgical worship culminated in the Second Vatican Council (1962-1965), among the most important religious events of modern times. The revolutionary idea permeating the council and its documents is that the Christian church is more than a clerical hierarchy, and certainly much more than the legal arm of prelates, but is in fact one people of God. To this people as a whole, not just to pope, bishops, and clergy, belong all the rights and obligations of a full role in the public worship and life of the church.

This new understanding of the church at Vatican II was expressed in the 1960s and 1970s in a global emphasis on liturgy and common action flowing from worship. In the Roman Catholic Church, eucharistic liturgy had become once again a setting for the fellowship of humankind: for in

43. Dorothy Day in *Orate Fratres*, 13 (1939), 139; Catherine de Hueck Doherty, *Not Without Parables: Stories of Yesterday, Today and Eternity* (Notre Dame: Ave Maria Press, 1972), 104.

the words of the council, the liturgy is "an instrument for the achievement of social union and unity."[44]

The Church of Scotland: The Iona Community, 1938-1990

The story of the Iona Community in the Church of Scotland begins in 1938, the year of Virgil Michel's death, in the Scottish parish of Govan. Govan had been a country village until the industrial expansion of Glasgow swallowed the village up in the neighboring metropolis. The economy of Govan came to depend on shipbuilding, and in the 1930s shipbuilding, along with other heavy industries in Scotland, was cruelly hit by the Depression. Govan suffered as few other places did. Eighty percent of the people of the parish were unemployed between 1933 and 1938.

George MacLeod (born in 1895) had come to be minister of the old parish of Govan in 1930, at the beginning of the worst period of the Depression. He came from Edinburgh, from the parish of St. Cuthbert's, one of the city's largest and most famous churches. His father was a prominent Presbyterian layman who headed a bitter anti-Roman Catholic campaign in Scotland in the early twentieth century. In his eight years in Govan, MacLeod distanced himself from the heritage of his father. His greatest achievements were in the sphere of public worship: in the beauty, power, and relevance that he brought to the revitalization of worship; in his ability to make women and men find in prayer a meaningful activity in the midst of economic hardship.

He provided corporate worship for the unemployed and corporate work for them as well: the unoccupied men of the parish relaid the graveyard and the grounds around the Govan church, and opened the area as a green space free for all the residents of Govan to use. Another of the prophetic things that MacLeod did was to take over an old disused mill in the hills to the south of Glasgow. By the labor of unemployed men and women the mill was turned into a youth hostel for the use of their sons on the weekends.[45]

44. Peter Foote, ed., *Vatican II's Dogmatic Constitution on the Church* (New York: Macmillan, 1969), 6. See also John Carmody, "Eucharistic Worship, Radical Contemplation, and Radical Politics," *Occasional Papers of the Institute for Ecumenical and Cultural Research*, 20 (1983), 1-8.

45. The history of the Iona movement and the reform of worship instigated by it can be found in T. Ralph Morton, *The Iona Community Story* (London: Lutterworth Press,

In 1938 George MacLeod resigned his charge in Govan and settled on the island of Iona off the coast of Scotland. During the early middle ages, in A.D. 563, St. Columba had founded an influential monastery on Iona, but after the Reformation there had been no religious community on the island and the abbey buildings had fallen into ruins. MacLeod brought a dozen young men with him to Iona; half were craftsmen, and the other half were young ministers of the Church of Scotland who had just finished their theological training. In the course of rebuilding the ancient ruined abbey MacLeod's company set about to discover for themselves something of the Christian way of life of the old monastic community and how its values might become relevant again in the twentieth century. The restored Iona community grew to include 2,000 associates.

The form of the modern Iona community was based on three convictions that placed before the Church of Scotland the tradition of Christian humanism in worship. The first conviction was that the way to new life in the church would be found only by people living and working together. "Living together" meant sharing the whole of life. "Working together" did not mean cooperating for a short time on some marginal task that made no great demands. It meant working together on a job for which the whole church community paid. The second conviction of Iona was that only by living and working together could clergy and laity come to appreciate the full nature of the Christian faith, "the faith whole and complete." Only through common action would understanding come.

The third conviction was that worship is the chief form of Christian common action. MacLeod even preferred to reinstate the old Scottish word for eucharist: *action*. After 1939 the Iona community made its greatest impact on visitors to the island through the worship services in the restored abbey church. As a large, freshly baked loaf was consecrated, visitors could look out the arched windows behind the altar to notice large seabirds dipping into the sea as the celebrant prayed, in lilting Scottish accent, about "the wind which batters these walls."

Through this common experience of prayer, life on Iona was shared with others from the Scottish mainland. The appeal and strength of the abbey worship was that it was the act of a continuing, working community.

1960); Frederick Quinn, "Iona: A Celtic Treasure," *The Living Church* (June 1990), 10; John M. Barkley, "The Liturgical Movement and Reformed Worship," *Church Service Society Annual,* 31 (1961), 13-21; and George B. Burnet, *The Holy Communion in the Reformed Church of Scotland, 1560-1960* (Edinburgh: Oliver and Boyd, 1960).

The thirty or so men and women who labored on the island and who came to the daily services in their overalls and working clothes led the services together and then went straight from the abbey to their daily tasks. The center of this abbey worship was the celebration of the eucharist in the Reformed tradition.

The Iona Community lifted up before the Church of Scotland insights from Christian humanism about the eucharist that we have already described as returning among Lutherans, Anglicans, and Roman Catholics in the machine age. The first was a sense that the worship of the church must express and be seen to express the fullness of the Christian faith. The kind of worship we offer to God has a great deal to do with how we convey God's message to others; in MacLeod's phrase, "Mission will not work again till our worship is put right."

It was a goal of the Iona movement to establish the eucharist as the regular and weekly form of Presbyterian worship, so that Scottish congregations could be built up into effective communities of service and love. The unemployed and outcast were the very people with whom the church, if true to her master, should be specially concerned. One thing the lonely and poor needed was to feel wanted, and the one thing the church should be able to give them was a sense of belonging to a human community. Without eucharistic worship, which is the corporate work of the whole people of God and not just the preacher, there was no real Christian foundation to offer help to other human beings.[46]

MacLeod's emphasis did not introduce anything new into the Presbyterian tradition, for we have already noted that Calvin sought to recover a social humanism by making the sacrament the normal center of worship on the Lord's Day, as in Scripture, celebrated in the presence of the entire congregation, not in a small, quiet aside after the main service is over. And a second insight of Iona came from Calvin as well: that the eucharist symbolizes the church's tie to all who surround her. MacLeod put the reformer's message this way, "Jesus the carpenter, the friend of shepherds and of fishermen showed us God by being human."

Because of this fact of the Incarnation, when we remember Jesus at the Lord's Supper we also bring to mind a web of human relationships also sym-

46. George F. MacLeod, *We Shall Re-Build: The Work of the Iona Community on Mainland and on Island* (Glasgow: The Iona Community, 1944), 24. For more of this message in detail see three books of George F. MacLeod, *The New Humanity Now* (London: The Fellowship of Reconciliation, 1965); *Only One Way Left: Church Prospect* (Glasgow: The Iona Community, 1961); *Speaking the Truth — In Love* (London: SCM Press, 1936).

bolized by the bread and the wine. During the Great Prayer of Thanksgiving these elements are consecrated, reminding us that our human lives and relationships may be similarly transformed. The passing of the bread and wine challenges what our relationships may be like in day-to-day affairs. To George MacLeod the passing of the elements is a model in miniature of the vision of Christian humanism: "Better off, to less well-off; saint to sinner; young to old, we all have to share Christ to one another; or crucify Him by refusing to share."[47]

In 1951, the General Assembly of the Church of Scotland voted to take the Iona Community under its jurisdiction and at the same time acknowledged the wisdom of more frequent celebrations of the Lord's Supper among Presbyterians. Over the next decades, more and more Presbyterians across the world heard of Iona's mission of worship and work and wanted to be part of it. Today three thousand men and women support the community from every corner of the globe.

The Iona Community still defines itself as seeking new and radical ways of living the gospel in today's world. Its theology remains incarnational, rooted in the doctrine of Word-become-flesh. The conviction that God became human in Jesus Christ means for the Iona community that there can be no division between the spiritual and the material, prayer and politics, worship and work. George MacLeod said it best: "Iona is a place where the veil between earth and eternity is particularly thin."[48]

Iona has made the case for Christian humanism through worship; it crystallized on its windswept island a tradition that stretches on both the Protestant and Catholic side back to the Reformation, and then even farther back to the church the apostles left us. Worship revealed to the Scots what it has given to the generations: a richer understanding of Jesus Christ and how he is now acting in the world, how he redeems space and time and how believers might follow him best into the future.

The very momentum of living the liturgy on the island developed at

47. MacLeod, *We Shall Re-Build*, 56, 89. The Iona message is explained in two books by T. Ralph Morton, *Community of Faith: The Changing Pattern of the Church's Life* (New York: Association Press, 1950); and *The Twelve Together* (Glasgow: The Iona Community, 1960).

48. Barbara Chaapel, "A Vast and Beautiful House of God." *Princeton Theological Seminary Alumni/ae News,* 26 (1987), 13-16. The task of restoring Iona's ancient abbey was completed in 1967 by the Very Reverend Lord George MacLeod. Two recent studies of the Iona Community and its founder are both by Ronald Ferguson: *Chasing the Wild Goose* (London: Collins, 1988), and *George MacLeod, Founder of the Iona Community* (London: Collins, 1990).

Iona a conviction that a genuine liturgical life must move out into culture and human relationships, that those who participate must seek a reconstruction of the social order. The liturgy on the island turned hearts from self-seeking to a sharing of goods; it challenged comfortable ways of living that accepted without question the status quo. In its worship the Iona Community became a sign of the justice and peace that God wills for the whole of humanity.

The Churches of North America Today: Reading the Signs

How are we to interpret this sign to the churches of North America in our own day? The Christian Right must consider how its neglect of the Lord's Supper may be responsible for a dangerous individualism that weakens its witness. It separates the media clergy from their audience, believers from their local communities, and the experience of worship from the problems of daily affairs in the social realm. These are matters of great concern. The services of the historic Reformation churches and the Catholic churches in many regions of the United States have been pushed off the air. On our screens and radios worship is dominated by preachers, the community is secondary, and the eucharist is absent.[49]

Particularly worrisome is that a misunderstanding of the role of the laity in liturgy, against which the New Testament was set and the Reformers preached, has returned again in the era of television evangelism. As in the ancient temple and the medieval cathedral, now on our screens the laity are mere spectators. "Watching" and "hearing" are virtually all they have to do at worship.

In addition, an increasingly large number of conservative churches are moving from their old homes in the inner city to the security of the suburbs. Rather than challenging the dehumanizing aspects of industrial society, these "superchurches" are constructing entirely new ecclesiastical centers sleekly adapted to the machine age. These "Christian centers" are often similar in design to neighboring corporate headquarters, and they are carefully adapted to the demands of the machine, especially in making

---

49. On television, worship, and the Christian Right see Robert W. Jenson, "The Hermeneutics of the Electronic Church," *American Academy of Religion* (Dallas meeting, November 1980); and Corwin E. Smidt, *Contemporary Evangelical Political Involvement* (Calvin College Conference on Christianity and Politics: University Press of America, 1989).

it possible to choreograph worship services to meet the demands of broad-casting.

In this worship adapted to the machine age it is the preacher who is at center stage, a performer surrounded by klieg lights and cameras. His image is projected on giant screens, but the Lord's Supper is nowhere to be seen. The participation of the "congregation" — which is really an audience — is a minor part of the performance. There could be significant gains for the Christian witness to our society if the still powerful leaders of the Religious Right were to analyze the misplaced emphases of their worship in the light of the humanism of the Incarnation as revealed in the eucharist.[50]

To the liberal and mainline churches we would like to say that many of its parishioners still do not have the faintest notion of what the liturgy teaches about God or the human person or the nature of society or the person of Jesus Christ. It is possible to argue that its success in the past was at times achieved through easy compromise with the secular social order, which has not been altered by the values of Christianity. These churches still exist in the midst of a competitive society that sets individual against individual, sanctions painful economic restrictions, and fosters forms of popular culture that deliberately exclude the transcendent.

In both traditions, secularization has occasionally coopted worship through reliance, even though for worthwhile goals, on popular musical performances and on secular settings for worship such as football stadiums that are overwhelmed by their association with competition, aggression, and violence. An entire generation has grown up in some churches deprived of the history and tradition of Christian symbolism in music and art.

There is a danger that in reappropriating any of the past achieve-ments we have summarized in these pages we are tempted to justify

---

50. Of the growing appeal of the themes of eucharistic humanism to American evangelicals and Protestant conservatives see Rodney Clapp, "Remonking the Church: Would a Protestant Form of Monasticism Help Liberate Evangelicalism from its Cultural Captivity?" *Christianity Today* (August 12, 1988), 20-21; and three works by Robert Webber: "Ecumenical Influence on Evangelical Worship," *Ecumenical Trends,* 19 (1990), 73-76; *Worship Old and New* (Grand Rapids: Zondervan, 1982); and *Evangelicals on the Canterbury Trail: Why Evangelicals are Attracted to the Liturgical Church* (Waco: Word, 1985). For an Orthodox perspective on the eucharist and Christian humanism, see three books by Alexander Schmemann: *The Eucharist — Sacraments of the Kingdom* (Crestwood, N.Y.: St. Vladimir's Seminary Press, 1987); *For the Life of the World: Sacraments and Orthodoxy* (Crest-wood, N.Y.: St. Vladimir's Press, 1973); and *Introduction to Liturgical Theology* (London: Faith Press, 1966).

clinging to old ways that have ceased to give life. At the very heart of Christian humanism is a call to see Christianity as a shared faith that can never be the possession of any one generation or any one century, a faith expressed in a eucharist that binds into one solidarity eighty generations since Jesus himself instituted it. Pusey and Grundtvig, Luther and Irenaeus each beckons us forward to see in Christian worship a compassionate perspective on humanity and the world, with resources of faith and hope to be applied to the quest for human fulfillment in the future.

PART IV

DOING THEOLOGY IN
CHRISTIAN HUMANISM

Chapter 10

God and the Human Scene

The worship of God presupposes knowledge of God, and that is the concern of theology. A community of faith is strong when it has a serious interest in theology. Such was the case with the Iona Community in Scotland where each of the insights of Christian humanism developed in the community was the fruit of careful theological reflection: the corporate character of the church, faith at work in ordinary human activities, pastoral concern for the outcasts, and worship centered in the eucharist.

Christian humanism is not the same thing as theology, but the two are closely related since both stem from the gospel of Jesus Christ. Theology takes on the intellectual assignment of making clear the meaning of the gospel as expressed in the doctrines of the church, while Christian humanism pursues the cultural task of relating Christian beliefs to all spheres of human existence. Theology says, "This is what the church means by its doctrine of God." Christian humanism asks, "If that is the church's doctrine of God, how can it enrich the human situation?"

Theology and Revelation

The term *theology* is formed from two Greek words, *theos,* meaning God, and *logos,* which can mean word, thought, or reason. Theology then is speaking about God or thinking about God. Some define theology simply as "talk about God," which is reduced to the phrase, "God-talk." However we understand it, we have to remember that theology is a human activity. It is human thinking and talking about God. As human activity, theology cannot be perfect or final. Theology does not offer the same completeness and perfection found only in God.

The doing of theology depends on God's prior actions. If humans are to think and talk about God, God must disclose something about the divine mind, will, and intentions in a way that enables humans to comprehend God's purposes. Theology begins with the premise that God has revealed a fundamentally loving disposition toward the human race through acts of creation, providence, and historical guidance made known in the life of ancient Israel and, in the Christian view, brought to final clarity in the life, death, and resurrection of Jesus Christ, the Son of God and true human.

God's revelation to humankind is conveyed along three main channels, all of them inviting human participation and response. One channel is that of *religious experience.* The ancient Israelites came to know God and to trust in the divine word because God had entered into their history to liberate, protect, and guide them. The disciples of Jesus had the experience of being in the company of Jesus in a variety of real human situations, and on the basis of those encounters and observations they drew certain conclusions about the God into whose service Jesus called them. Today, too, people have religious experiences as God continues to act in the world. Theology seeks to understand what such experiences may signify about God.

The second channel for God's revelation to humans is *the Bible,* the Hebrew Bible growing out of Jewish experience and the New Testament books written by first-century Christians. Too often, in some circles, the Bible is accorded a status that tends to remove it from the human realm entirely. But the Bible arises from human experience of God's action. Over the centuries the Bible has rightly been given an authoritative status, not because of its perfection as a book, but because in a singular way it points its readers to decisive events in the history of God's actions among and on behalf of human persons.

The Bible's authority is also seen in the fact that the ancient events it speaks about have a continuing implication for the future. For example, God's freeing of the children of Israel from Egyptian bondage is a sign to the human community in every generation not only that God wants people to be free but also that God does something to secure human freedom. Similarly, the New Testament's story of Jesus is the enduring witness to God's love and power to give life and salvation to all people, despite human folly, sin, injustice, and even death itself. Therefore when people avail themselves of the Bible's message they participate in a personal way in God's current revelation.

None of this is difficult to detect in the biblical records, but many Bible readers have been taught to look only for signs of the divine and the miraculous in Scripture, the human elements being regarded either as incidental features or as occasions for deploring human failings. But the genius of the Bible is the claim that God expresses a loving purpose for humanity in and through human persons and circumstances. The Bible is utterly candid and realistic about human sinfulness but at the same time totally confident concerning the power of God's forgiving and healing love.

The student of humanism will notice that at the very end of the Bible, the seer's vision of the holy city is not of something in a remote heaven, but rather of a city "coming down out of heaven from God." Likewise, the voice heard by the seer declares that God comes to be with humankind. "He will dwell with them, and they will be his people" (Revelation 21:3). From Genesis to Revelation, the Bible is consistently attentive, not simply to God, but to God in relation to humanity.

The third way in which revelation comes to human beings is through *the tradition* of the believing community. Tradition means "that which is handed down." Judaism has the Talmud, a living tradition through which God continues to speak. Among Christians, Roman Catholic and Eastern Orthodox believers have been more appreciative of the role of tradition in revelation, faith, and theology than most Protestants have. That situation is changing within the modern ecumenical movement, however, as Protestants too are realizing, for example, that their insistence on the priority of Scripture over tradition is itself a tradition, something handed down from the reformers of the sixteenth century.

In its own whimsical way, the "Tradition" song in the popular musical "Fiddler on the Roof" has probably helped many people catch a glimpse of how tradition works in a community. In communities of faith, the reality of God and God's gifts can be made known through traditions that are not necessarily based on the Bible. A familiar case in point for Christians is the Christmas tree which, though having absolutely no basis in Scripture, serves as one of the focal points for the celebration of the birth of Jesus.

Doing theology is a human activity. Theology depends on revelation, which is a divine activity. But since revelation takes place through religious experience, through the Bible, and through tradition, it necessarily engages the human community in a variety of ways as it responds to the revelation. The community hears, remembers, obeys, and seeks to understand what is received. This chapter will concentrate on how twentieth-century theology has been moving toward an understanding that explicitly relates God to the nature and needs of humanity. Such an understanding, that God is involved in human affairs, assists Christian humanism in its task of relating theology to culture.

In the section immediately following, "The Question about God," we make the point that the theology of the latter part of this century has moved away from the old tendency to picture God as remote and unrelated to the world. Instead, God is understood as being in a close relationship with humanity.

Later, under the heading "God and the Secular Mind," we observe that contemporary theologians are no longer willing to follow the old liberal path of adjusting statements about God to the whims of a collapsing secular culture. They are now insisting with a new boldness that the God of the Bible is still the sovereign Lord over all, though the divine sovereignty may be exercised in quiet ways that defy the expectations of the secular mind.

Finally, the last part of the chapter takes up the topic "God and Public Life." Here the main point we make is that God's power cannot and should not be perceived as merely something that nurtures the private religious needs of individuals, but rather as a creative and redemptive force in the public forum. Persons of faith have a right and an obligation to speak out on public issues, lending the insights of religion to the betterment of the common good. Such participation is not coercion nor any threat to the separation of church and state. It is a legitimate contribution toward the humanizing of society.

The Question about God

Theology as human thinking about God has both a wide and a narrow meaning. In its wider sense theology deals with such topics as God, creation, revelation, evil, the person and work of Christ, the Holy Spirit, salvation, the church, and the last things or eschatology. In its narrow and more specific sense, theology has to do with the meaning of God. "The central task of theology," writes theologian John B. Cobb, Jr., "is the formulation of a doctrine of God."[1]

The major thrust in the formulation of a doctrine of God today is to relate "God-talk" to human experience. Daniel Migliore says as much as he begins his book *The Power of God*:

> Even if neglected or avoided for a time, the question about God never entirely dies out. That is because it has its roots in everyday human experience. . . . It arises not at the periphery but at the very center of our common human life.[2]

Langdon Gilkey underlines certain "givens" in human life that point to divine reality: the sense of joy in living, the sense of vitality, the awe people feel at the wonder and beauty of life, the sense of purpose which draws out human powers. These come from beyond. They are not fabricated by humans; they are given. Similarly, sociologist Peter Berger writes about "signals of transcendence" observed in day-to-day life that seem to point beyond "natural" reality. He mentions the human propensity for order, for example, as illustrated by a mother's reassuring word to a frightened child in a dark room that "everything is all right."[3]

These examples from ordinary human experience show that the question of God is not solely a matter of interest to theologians and church people. It is societal and public; it arises, as Migliore says, "at the very center of our common human life."

So it is in a recent theological development, the liberation theology of Latin America. It develops its concept of God "from below," from the experiences of political and economic oppression which threaten to dehumanize its victims. As the poor, powerless people in the Christian basic communities of Latin American countries have drawn together to read their Bibles, worship, and analyze their miserable condition, the power of the gospel has given them new hope. They have discovered that God is the liberator of the oppressed, the God of the poor, and their

1. John B. Cobb, Jr., *God and the World* (Philadelphia: Westminster Press, 1976), 19.
2. Daniel L. Migliore, *The Power of God* (Philadelphia: Westminster Press, 1983), 15.
3. Peter L. Berger, *A Rumor of Angels: Modern Society and the Rediscovery of the Supernatural* (Garden City, N.Y.: Doubleday, 1970), 55.

companion as they gird themselves to gain freedom from poverty and oppression.

Black theologians feel constrained to shape a theology based on black experience. For some black theologians Christ is the "Black Messiah." Feminist theologians offer another strong example of doing theology in the light of a particular set of human experiences. They protest against sexist language about God in the Scriptures, in the historic theology of the church, and in the prayers and hymns of Christian worship. They speak of a God who is not to be perceived exclusively as a masculine deity but rather as one whose nature encompasses femininity as well — a view reminiscent of the nineteenth-century Christian humanism of N. F. S. Grundtvig.

The theology of the past often made God seem very abstract and remote from the human scene. *The Westminster Shorter Catechism,* adopted in 1729 and familiar to generations of Presbyterians, asks the question, "What is GOD?" and supplies this answer: "God is a Spirit, infinite, eternal, and unchangeable, in his being, wisdom, power, holiness, justice, goodness, and truth." Similar understandings of God can be found in the catechisms of other Christian groups. Such language suggests a formidable God, an exalted being whose dazzling perfection is the direct opposite of what human beings are. People hear that God is almighty but they are weak. God is holy but they are sinful. God knows everything but they are ignorant. God is spiritual but they are bodily. God is eternal but they are mortal.

Hearing such God-talk, many people understandably shrink away from God. If God is so distant and forbidding, isn't it only common sense to avoid such a being? Some may do so out of fear, dreading an all-revealing presence, but others may have been so conditioned by such talk about a great, powerful, but distant God that they finally turn away out of sheer disinterest. Why concern oneself with a deity so obviously unrelated to anything close to actual human concerns?

Another reaction to certain traditional forms of God-talk goes to the other extreme. Instead of a fearful, or bored, neglect of God there can be an indulgence in unfitting familiarity with the ruler of the universe. The singing of "My God and I go through the fields together" may not inflict lasting harm on anyone's religion but it fosters the impression that God is relevant in this world only as a friendly companion for the individual. Pious businessmen declare that God is their partner. Their prayer breakfasts combine salvation and commerce with equal gusto. Coaches and athletes unabashedly implore God to help them win the big game. The basketball player makes the sign of the cross before a free throw attempt.

The football player kneels quickly in the end zone after scoring a touchdown. The experience of war gave rise once to the devout slogans "God is my co-pilot" and the famous "Praise the Lord and pass the ammunition."

There is nothing wrong with the desire to be close to God. Christian humanism supports the impulse to know God's presence in the midst of work and play and strongly affirms those experiences in which God is known as close friend and companion. The danger is that the biblical concept of God is distorted, either by picturing the deity as far removed from the life of human persons or by reducing God's significance to that of a docile magician ready to gratify every human desire.

Such distortions can be avoided by learning from one of the church's great teachers. In his *Small Catechism* Martin Luther explained the first article of the Apostles' Creed in a way that honors both divine dignity and human trust. Addressing the statement, "I believe in God the Father Almighty, Maker of heaven and earth," Luther explains it as follows:

> I believe that God has created me and all that exists. He has given to me and still preserves my body and soul, my mental and physical powers.
>
> He provides me with food and clothing, home and family, daily work, and all I need from day to day. God also protects me in time of danger and guards me from every evil.
>
> All this he does out of fatherly and divine goodness and mercy, though I do not at all deserve it. Therefore I surely ought to thank and praise, serve and obey him.
>
> This is most certainly true.[4]

Luther's "God-talk" strikes a good balance between an appreciation of the creative sovereignty of God and God's intimate concern for human beings in the midst of their mundane existence. The language can be understood by priests, theologians, lay persons, and children. Luther's teachings about God retain their validity in our own time when the conspicuous feature in the doctrine of God has become the emphasis on God's close engagement with the human world.

In the work of Karl Barth (1886-1968), possibly the most important theologian of the present century, one can trace a clear line from the majestic, awe-inspiring, and almost intimidating picture of God to a conception of God's partnership with human beings. Following Augustine, Luther, and

4. Martin Luther, *The Small Catechism* (Intersynodical Catechism Committee, 1960), 17.

Calvin, Barth grounded his entire theological effort on the self-revelation of God in Jesus Christ as that revelation is attested to in the Bible.

Through a series of great theological writings, at the heart of which was his massive *Church Dogmatics,* Barth gained the reputation of being the chief spokesman for the conception of God as the awesome, totally transcendent being known only through the revelation in Christ. Fired by the rediscovery of the world of the Bible and the sovereign God of the biblical witness, Barth and others emphasized the *deity* of God. This God was, in Barth's words, "a God absolutely unique in His relation to man and the world, overpoweringly lofty and distant, strange, yes even wholly other."[5]

Reclaiming the transcendent God of the Bible was a necessary counter to the old liberal theology of pre–World War I days, a type of thinking that glorified human experience while it took God for granted as a kind of genial older relative to whom one pays formal respect. As Barth said of that theology, "Here man was made great at the cost of God."[6]

But Barth's theology was like a bell that awakened the world as it tolled the glory of God. For a period of more than forty years, from 1919 to around 1960, the Barthian theology of the Word of God proclaimed the powerful, self-revealing God of the Bible, the God of Abraham, Isaac, and Jacob, who is ultimately and decisively disclosed in the person of Jesus Christ. In one of his books Barth wrote concerning the Bible and its content: "We have found in the Bible a new world, God, God's sovereignty, God's glory, God's incomprehensible love. Not the history of man but the history of God!"[7] In a similar context Barth wrote, "The Bible tells us how God has sought and found the way to us."

Then in 1956, when Barth had reached the age of seventy, he announced a change of direction when he delivered a lecture with the surprising title "The Humanity of God." Looking back at the earlier change, the break with the old liberal theology, Barth insisted that he and his colleagues had not been wrong in upholding God's deity when that had been needed, but they had not followed that point through "to the true word concerning His humanity."[8] Barth's main point in "The Humanity of God" is that God's deity includes humanity.

5. Karl Barth, "The Humanity of God," trans. John Newton Thomas, in *The Humanity of God* (Richmond, Va.: John Knox Press, 1960), 37.

6. Ibid., 39.

7. Karl Barth, *The Word of God and the Word of Man,* trans. Douglas Horton (New York: Harper & Row, 1957), 45.

8. Barth, "The Humanity of God," 42.

Who God is and what He is in His deity He proves and reveals not in a vacuum as a divine being-for-Himself, but precisely and authentically in the fact that He exists, speaks, and acts as the *partner* of man, though of course as the absolutely superior partner. He who does *that* is the living God. And the freedom in which He does *that* is His deity. It is the deity which as such also has the character of humanity.[9]

As a Christocentric theologian, Barth develops the idea of the humanity of God by focussing on the coming together of God and humans in Jesus Christ. "It is when we look at Jesus Christ that we know decisively that God's deity does not exclude, but includes His *humanity*."[10]

What then is the humanity of God, as Barth sees it? It is God's "free affirmation of man, His free concern for him, His free substitution for him,"[11] all of which shines through in Jesus' parables of the kingdom. In the stories of the father and the lost son, the good Samaritan, and the king who shows mercy on the insolvent debtor, one sees how human God is.

In the mirror of this humanity of Jesus Christ the humanity of God enclosed in His deity reveals itself. Thus God is as He is. Thus He affirms man. Thus He is concerned about him. Thus He stands up for him.[12]

One of the consequences of God's humanity seen in Jesus Christ is the need to take seriously and affirm the church. Those who have obtained knowledge of the humanity of God must "thankfully acknowledge *Christendom, the Church,*" writes Barth, and "take part in its life and join in its service."[13] One of the major themes of this present book, to be illustrated further in the next chapter, is that the humanism of the Christian tradition finds embodiment in history as a specific fellowship of men and women. As God in affirming humanity creates the church, human beings respond by taking part in its life, there to discover more fully their own humanity.

From Barth's 1956 statements on the humanity of God down to the present, theological thought has continued in the direction of formulating a doctrine of God as one who affirms humans. Existentialist theology stressed active participation in life rather than theorizing about the nature

9. Ibid., 45-46.
10. Ibid., 49.
11. Ibid., 51.
12. Ibid.
13. Ibid., 62.

of reality, thereby accenting human responsibility and choice. The so-called "death of God" theology of the 1960s was, in its own way, a call to human beings to assume responsibility for their lives in a world come of age. The theology of hope, process theology, liberation theology, and feminist theology have all had the aim of speaking about God, not as a distant power either terrifying or innocuous, but as the God who can be known by people in the midst of their earthly walk. Recent theology teaches that the effective presence of God enables persons to realize in a deeper way what it means to be human. God and the human creation belong together.

God and the Secular Mind

Any doctrine of God that is faithful to the biblical record and the central theological tradition will affirm God's universal sovereignty over all things as creator and Lord. The doctrine of God that has been gaining ground throughout this century is one that refuses to trim God's authority to fit a secular mold. It affirms the God who plunges into the moving stream of human history to save and fulfill creation. Such a doctrine understands the exercise of divine sovereignty as being something other than the sheer overpowering of all opposition by heavenly force. The model of God's kingly rule in action is Jesus, who chose not to summon twelve legions of angels but obediently went to the cross. The risen Lord told the apostle Paul, "My power is made perfect in weakness" (2 Corinthians 12:9). Such New Testament texts yield a doctrine of God as one who works in and through the historical process, enlisting the energies of human partners toward the accomplishment of God's will.

The church with its congregations, theological seminaries, and publications has its own forum for the discussion of the doctrine of God and how it can undergo a change in emphasis from time to time. Informed church people, their pastors, and theologians know about such things, but what about secular culture, the world outside the church? Do theological matters have anything to do with the world "out there?"

The answer to the latter question is an emphatic Yes. Even as theology focuses on the doctrine of God, it must also clarify the meaning of faith for believers and explain the church's teachings to the world. This latter function is called "apologetics." In making an "apologia" to the world, theology makes clear the grounds for the beliefs of the church. Such an "apologia" is a positive declaration, having nothing to do with "apologizing" in the popular sense. Rather, the "apologia" aims to show what the church's doctrines can mean for the typical "man and woman in the street."

Today a number of contemporary theologians are going about the apologetic task in a new spirit. Instead of devising a theology that will be agreeable to the modern secular mind or to secular humanism, they are challenging the presumed authority of the secular view of things. Instead of rounding off the sharp edges of the Bible's message in an attempt to answer the objections of the secularists, skeptics, and atheists, some theologians, including erstwhile liberals, have taken the offensive against the secular worldview. This is an important trend to note, particularly at a time when secular humanists in the academic community were increasingly intolerant of ideologies other than their own.

In his book *Discerning The Way,* Paul Van Buren takes a hard look at what Western culture in the twentieth century has proven to be and asks, "How can we bow down and worship before the standards of this culture?" In a sobering paragraph he sketches some of the features of recent history that call into question any impulse to worship at secularism's shrine.

Reviewing such grim realities as "the slaughter of World War I," totalitarian regimes, "the horrors of World War II," oppression of the Jews, "the nuclear devastation visited on Japan," sufferings inflicted on the Vietnamese and Cambodians, plus widespread pollution and international terror, Van Buren then asks, "After all this, what earthly reasons can there be for this supposed confidence in our culture which our liberal apologists seem to have?"[14]

Van Buren's charge is both against secular culture and the theologians of the past who have tried to accommodate theology to that culture. The same is true with Thomas C. Oden, for nearly thirty years an active participant in liberal causes. In his book *Agenda for Theology* Oden charges that "The central theme of contemporary theology is accommodation to modernity."[15] He wants a new agenda for theology in the final years of this century. That agenda is "to begin to prepare the postmodern Christian

14. Paul M. Van Buren, *Discerning the Way: A Theology of the Jewish-Christian Reality* (New York: Seabury Press, 1980), 54.
15. Thomas C. Oden, *Agenda for Theology: Recovering Christian Roots* (San Francisco: Harper & Row, 1979), 29.

community for its third millennium by returning again to the careful study and respectful following of the central tradition of classical Christianity."[16]

As Oden looks at modern society he sees social processes deteriorating under the impact of "radical autonomous individualism"; he is troubled by "narcissistic hedonism" and "naturalistic reductionism" as symptoms of the decay of Western secular society.[17] This society rejects the wisdom of earlier times, makes scientific empiricism the final court of appeal, and continues to cultivate "an optimistic evolutionary historical progressivism." Comments Oden: "While modernity continues blandly to teach us that we are moving ever upward and onward, the actual history of late modernity is increasingly brutal, barbarian, and malignant."[18]

It is far from Oden's desire to return to a premodern, precritical kind of Christian orthodoxy. Rather, he speaks of a "liberated orthodoxy," freed "by historical perspective and by evangelical faith from the illusions of modernity and for a eucharistic existence."[19] The church and its worship life figure strongly in Oden's agenda for the renewal of classical Christianity. It has happened before: as the rosy claims of secularism prove empty, the Christian community rediscovers the power and importance of its sacramental life. So it was in the nineteenth century when church leaders made the eucharist a focal point of life and unity in the midst of the machine age.

Harvey Cox is another theologian with liberal credentials who is raising questions about the modern secular mind. His book *Religion in the Secular City* reports on resurging American fundamentalism and Latin American liberation theology as two religious movements with conservative roots which are making an impact on the public sphere. The phenomenon is surprising because it is usually assumed that it is the liberal, secularist version of religion which shows the most interest in problems facing the general public.

Both of these movements are highly critical of established religious institutions, of modern theology, and of the modern world itself. The Latin American movement charges that both Protestants and Catholics, in attempting to come to terms with the modern world, eventually accepted "the autonomy of the whole secular sphere."[20] They entered into a

16. Ibid., 31.
17. Ibid., 38.
18. Ibid., 40.
19. Ibid., 86.
20. Harvey Cox, *Religion in the Secular City: Toward a Postmodern Theology* (New York: Simon and Schuster, 1984), 94.

"questionable concordat" with secular ideologies, leaving the churches with little to do but prepare people for the world to come. Politics and science became "neutral areas outside the scope of churchly influence or theological criticism."[21]

The defects in the "concordat," says Cox, were not only that it divided reality between faith and reason, science and religion, the sacred and profane. More, it robbed the churches of most of their functions in the world, and even worse, "it left out most of the people in the church and most of the people in the world."[22] It left out ordinary working people, women, racial minorities, and the majority of people outside Europe and North America.

To the extent that recent theology has caved in to the modern mind, as Cox puts it, one readily sees the need for a Christian humanism whose function precisely is to reclaim the right of the gospel to critique modern secular culture. Wherever the welfare of human beings is concerned, whether in science, politics, economics, or the environment, the church must speak its liberating message unintimidated by secularism's claim that it alone possesses the authority to prescribe what is good for the human family.

When Cox, Oden, and Van Buren voice their criticisms of modern theology, they have in mind especially the kind of liberal theology which in the past had bent too far in the direction of accommodating the gospel to the secular sphere. That modern theology has failed, writes Harvey Cox, "because by accepting the intellectual and political rulers of the modern world as its interlocutors, and by agreeing to the contract that turned the economic and technical spheres over to allegedly autonomous inner dynamics, it forfeited its ability to say anything to the margin."[23] "But it is from the margins," adds Cox, "that the postmodern world is coming to birth." The very people whom modern theology in its concordat with secularism consigned to the edges of the good life are the ones who make up the church and much of the world.

A new concept of the church is arising from the Latin American basic Christian communities. Harvey Cox notes, significantly, "that the single most informative and revealing element of any theology is its ecclesiology," that is, its view of the nature and function of the *church*.[24] In

21. Ibid.
22. Ibid., 96.
23. Ibid.
24. Ibid., 137.

Latin America a church is coming forth from the people. Latin American Christians frequently speak of the church as "the People of God." This term helps correct the older idea of the church as primarily an institution and at the same time depicts the church as a body of living persons in constant dialogue with the contemporary world.[25]

Among marginal, excluded persons the church is also understood as the church of the poor. Pope John XXIII made a statement to this effect in 1962, before the opening of the Vatican Council. He said, "With respect to the underdeveloped countries, the church appears as it is and wants to be: the church of all the people and, in particular, of the poor."[26]

For the radical critics associated with Latin American liberation theology and the Christian basic communities, the church of the poor implies that God cannot be the patron of the privileged, the rich, and the powerful. Rather, God is one who vindicates the powerless. But that does not mean that God simply comforts the poor while urging them to accept their miserable lot. Instead, while suffering with the people, God stands with them against their oppressors and leads them to freedom. The biblical God of the exodus is the model for the God of liberation theology. The life, teachings, and death of Jesus Christ reveal the character of this God. Jesus came to his death by taking his stand against evil and corruption on behalf of the poor and defenseless.

The poor and exploited come to their understanding of God from hearing the Bible and considering its message even as the daily struggles of life go on. Theirs is indeed a theology "from below" rather than one "from above." The experience of meeting God in the midst of social, political, and economic oppression reinforces the biblical claim that divine love is revealed by the coming of God into the human sphere.

Such a fresh apprehension of God can make an impact on the secular order. As long as theology was content to speak of God as majestic and powerful but far removed from the dusty plains of human suffering and hope, the secular mind could remain unmoved and unchallenged in its long-standing assumption that politics, economics, and science were totally autonomous, immune from criticism. But when theologies arise that assert both the power and the active compassion of God on behalf of the poor and powerless, the complacency and potential emptiness of some secular

25. Ibid., 139.
26. Ibid., 110, citing Albero Barreiro, S.J., *Basic Ecclesial Communities: The Evangelization of the Poor* (Maryknoll, N.Y.: Orbis Books, 1982), 4.

attitudes are soon exposed. More important, the possibility is made alive for God's liberating work to be extended into wider circles of human experience.

The idea of Christian humanism means, among other things, the refusal to allow positivistic, secularistic humanism to assume the mantle of the authoritative standard for all human values. It is a sign of hope that theologians and others, past and present, are not willing to leave the imagined citadel of modernity undisturbed, but are expressing severe doubts about its claim to sovereignty. This cause should be taken up by a broader spectrum of believers. Long ago St. Augustine put his finger on the self-defeating nature of human pride which spurns divine reality: "By craving to be more, man becomes less; and by aspiring to be self-sufficing, he fell away from Him who truly suffices him."[27]

Christian humanism, as Harris Kaasa wrote, is a view of human existence and a way of living under the sovereignty of God. The critique of modern secular thought becomes at the same time the occasion for the reaffirmation of the doctrine of God, creator and ruler over all. In the ongoing debate as to what constitutes a sound humanism, it is the privilege and obligation of Christian humanism to take issue with secularism's pretensions to cultural hegemony. It dares to talk about the rule of God in human life, not only in the private but also in the public realm.

God and Public Life

The God whom believers of all times have honored is not, as the modern secularist holds, merely the custodian of private religion, but is a force in the public life of the nation and the world. Christian humanism honors the God of the Bible as a participant in the affairs of the world and humanity, but it recognizes that divine participation in the affairs of the world takes place through the hidden artistry of love and not always according to majority vote.

The classical theology of the church has always held that the living God, who is sovereign power and grace, is profoundly devoted to the human scene and quietly at work to make existence on this earth more human, more humane, for everyone. As noted above, however, theology needs

27. Augustine, *City of God,* bk. 14.

correcting when its "God-talk" flies too high, making God seem remote. God seeks to be present with the human family. Some lively theologies of recent years have stressed this point with new insight and new persuasion. God is not confined to heaven but, because all is *not* right with the world, God is at work to heal and mend creation, invading those very secular arenas where conventional thought, both religious and secular, assumed that God would remain at best a polite observer, hardly a participant.

With respect to the prospect of "God in Public Life," Christian humanism differs from the religious right which clamors for official recognition of God in government and legislation, and from the secularistic left which opposes any suggestion that God can or should be a factor in public affairs. The keen interest of the Christian right in the political sphere is of course a development of the last two decades and a marked departure from Protestant evangelicalism's older reputation of remaining aloof from public issues. Many secularists are baffled by the political aggressiveness shown by the Christian right. They have found much to criticize in the Moral Majority of the 1980s and in attempts in the early 1990s to limit federal funding of the arts, to cite two examples, but they cannot deny the right of religious conservatives to enter the give-and-take of the political arena.

What Christian humanism wants to contribute toward the humanizing of the common life is the testimony that God is moving in today's world to overthrow the forces of oppression and to bestow liberating grace on all people. The conviction that God participates in all aspects of humanity's struggle is not a pious wish nor a radically new idea, but a serious, reasoned position born of known human experience, Holy Scripture, and long tradition. It is a distortion of basic Jewish and Christian belief in God to relegate the living Lord of the universe to a tame, innocuous existence within the limited sphere of private religious feelings.

Two powerful examples of the effort to apply theological insight to public life were the statements issued by the National Conference of Catholic Bishops in 1983 and 1984. In the former statement the bishops condemned nuclear war and gave support to a bilateral, verifiable nuclear freeze. In 1984, the bishops published a pastoral letter calling for economic justice for the poor. The letter had two purposes: first, to provide moral guidance on economic matters to Roman Catholics, and second, "to add our voice to the public debate about U.S. economic policies."[28]

---

28. *New York Times,* November 15, 1984. Two surveys of this theme in American history and in politics today are Martin E. Marty, *Religion and Republic* (Boston: Beacon

The bishops stated very clearly the close relationship between faith in God and human welfare. The fundamental criterion for economic decisions, they wrote, is that they must be "at the service of human beings. The economy was made for people, *all* people, and not the other way around." Economic policy and organization has a significance "that goes beyond purely secular or technical questions to profoundly human, and therefore moral, matters. It touches our very faith in God and what we hope and believe about the destiny of humanity."[29] The letter pointed out the high unemployment rates in the nation, a level of poverty that was then the highest since 1965, and the aggravating of these problems by the investing of human and material resources in the production of weapons of war.

The fact that such a letter was issued as a contribution to the public debate on the economy is a significant and welcome action. For too long the general public has been lulled into accepting the secularistic dictum that religious convictions can claim legitimacy only as long as they are held privately. Richard John Neuhaus attacks the privatization of religion and the secularization of the state in his book *The Naked Public Square*. The public square is "naked" when it is deprived of the contribution of religious thought to the discussion of important public issues. "Once religion is reduced to nothing more than privatized conscience, the public square has only two actors in it — the state and the individual. Religion as a mediating structure — a community that generates and transmits moral values — is no longer available as a countervailing force to the ambitions of the state."[30]

Predictably, the reaction of some journalists reporting the bishops' letter was to tell their readers that the issuing of such a pastoral statement on the economy represented a departure from the "traditional" role of religion as offering solace to individual consciences. Some news analysts, however, rightly called attention to the continuity between the 1984 bishops' letter and Pope Leo XIII's encyclical "Rerum Novarum," issued

---

Press, 1987); and A. James Reichley, *Religion in American Public Life* (Washington: Brookings Institution, 1985).

29. *New York Times,* November 15, 1984. Two important statements representing Roman Catholic opinion on the role of the Church are Mario Cuomo, "Religious Belief and Public Morality," *Origins* (September 27, 1984), 230-37; and J. Bryan Hehir, "The Discipline and Dynamic of a Public Church," *Social Thought* (Winter 1985), 4-8.

30. Richard John Neuhaus, *The Naked Public Square* (Grand Rapids: Wm. B. Eerdmans, 1984), 82.

in 1891 to support labor unions and decent wages for workers. The Roman Catholic Church was hardly departing from past practice when its American bishops presented their views on the economy.

Another significant point regarding reactions to the bishops' letter was made by columnist David S. Broder when he put his finger on the "shaky morality of conservative economics." Broder suggested that the angry criticism of the letter by conservatives reflected their unease at the uncovering of the greed and acquisitiveness which they try to mask by the formula that capitalism can be equated with freedom and individual self-perfection. Greater wealth supposedly brings the individual or nation closer to happiness. But the bishops know better, wrote Broder. Their faith prompts them to assert "that capitalism, like any other human institution, should be judged, not just on the criterion of freedom, but of justice and equality as well."[31] The conservatives' criticism of the pastoral letter on the economy reveals a mind-set that approves when church leaders preach about personal morality but complains loudly when they apply the faith of the church to matters of public concern.

The privatization of religion has indeed had its prominent spokespersons. Both John F. Kennedy in 1960 and Geraldine Ferraro in 1984 assured audiences that while they were Roman Catholics, that fact would not influence their public performance since their faith was "a private matter." Needless to say, when such visible political figures express themselves in this way it is not surprising that the population at large is reinforced in the mistaken opinion that religious values have no place in the discussion of public issues that affect everyone.

Harvey Cox relates that the well-known fundamentalist of an earlier period, William Jennings Bryan, resigned his position as secretary of state because "he could not in good conscience execute what his Christian conscience told him was a warlike and belligerent foreign policy."[32] Bryan too could have said that his faith or conscience was something private, but more relevant was

31. David Broder, "Shaky Morality of Conservative Economics," *Manchester Guardian Weekly,* December 2, 1984.

32. Cox, *Religion in the Secular City,* 64. Three recent treatments of this theme are David Nichols, *Deity and Domination: Images of God and the State in the Nineteenth and Twentieth Centuries* (London: Routledge, 1989); Thomas V. Morris, *Divine and Human Action: Essays in the Metaphysics of Theism* (Ithaca: Cornell University Press, 1989); and Conor Cruise O'Brien, *God Land: Reflections on Religion and Nationalism* (Cambridge, Mass.: Harvard University Press, 1988).

the fact that he could not in conscience separate his Christian conviction from his public responsibility. Another, more recent example of a courageous moral decision by a public figure was the one-day abdication of the king of Belgium in 1990 because he could not sign a bill legalizing abortion.

The Roman Catholic bishops are also seeking to meet a public responsibility in a manner consistent with Christian faith. They want to bring God's sovereign claims into the political and economic realms.

The objections to God in public life are numerous and familiar. The issues are too complex, it is said. Religion and politics don't mix. Religious beliefs are all too diverse. Whose God is being served if one allows God into the public domain?

One does not dismiss these objections lightly. There will be good people on both sides of any given issue. Politics, as everyone says, is the art of compromise. Even so, the fact remains that some policies are dangerous to the health of persons and society while others offer hope for human betterment. Difficult as the political game may be, neither elected officials nor the voting public is excused from looking beyond national and self interest to ask, What policies will be most beneficial for the larger human constituency? What specific issues in the world provide opportunities for an enlightened humanism to provide energy for improving the human lot?

It is taken for granted that any list of problems will soon be outdated, but it is worthwhile to identify a few that society is likely to live with for some time to come and to see how the tradition of Christian humanism relates to each.

Peace

A humanism informed by faith in God will endorse the human longing for a peaceful world as over against a world armed for destruction. The sorry fact is that not everybody wants peace. Taking a stand for peace often means clashing with powerful forces prepared to profit from war and preparations for war. Yet the blessing of God is with the peacemakers. The Gulf War of 1991 reminds us that, whatever the short-term gains of armed conflict, war exacts a stiff cost in the dislocation and suffering of defenseless civilians. Christian faith offers a humanizing environment in which to grapple with the very real problem of balancing the gain and loss when facing the choice of armed conflict.

International Harmony

Christian humanism affirms a world community of interrelated persons, transcending the national state, and therefore it must object to a national chauvinism that maneuvers for every advantage in behalf of selfish national interest at the expense of the welfare of other nations. "The very notion of 'humanity' as a concrete social universal, inclusive of *all* nations, races, tongues, and classes — and both sexes! — owes more to Christianity (traditional Christianity, at that!) than to any other source," writes Albert C. Outler.[33]

National Humility

It is indeed part of humanistic responsibility to love one's country, but to do so may call for criticism instead of endorsement of certain national policies. Even in the wake of America's foreign military successes, there must be a place for national humility as well as national pride. There is no cosmic decree that the United States of America must always be "first." Jesus said that the one who would be first of all should be servant to all. Those who like to picture the United States as God's chosen nation should read their Bibles again and learn that Israel was called to be the *servant* people of God.

Protecting Human Life

The events of history since the defeat of Hitler are grim reminders that the lessons of the Holocaust are not automatically learned. The mission of every humanism to guard human beings from exploitation, destruction, and genocide is obvious in an age of terrorism, kidnapping, abortion, euthanasia, child abuse, and other threats to human life. Granted, some abortions and some instances of ceasing life-supporting measures may have their justification, but the dangerous prospect of a society becoming nonchalant about the value of life requires the counter-influence of a rigorous, caring humanism.

33. Albert C. Outler, *Who Trusts in God* (New York: Oxford University Press, 1968), 113.

Reduction of Violence

To be a humanist places one on the side of measures to reduce violence against persons throughout society and to foster a safer atmosphere of trust and mutual helpfulness in cities, towns, and rural areas. But is anyone against such decent aims? Unfortunately, yes. There are people who grow rich and influential from the sale of guns, drugs, and pornography, and they know how to twist constitutional freedoms to their advantage and against the health and well-being of their fellow citizens. The Bible and theology account for the human propensity toward violence by the doctrine of sin, and offer teachings of love and justice to move humankind toward a less violent world.

Saving the Environment

As Christians look at the environment in the light of God's continuing creative work, they are not persuaded that concern for soil, streams, and forests is simply one political opinion with an equally valid one available on the other side. Bad agricultural policies and shortsighted practices result in tons of rich topsoil being washed away every day; streams, rivers, and oceans are polluted by industrial waste and sewage; fossil fuels are being squandered; global warming is threatening the planet; forests are being destroyed and not replaced; farmers are forced to expand their operations or quit, and the family farm is rapidly disappearing. The still, small voice that can scarcely be heard in the rush to turn irreplaceable natural resources into instant profits is saying that this greedy generation has no right to rob the next generation of food, energy, beauty, and a safe environment.

Lifting the Oppressed

Christian humanism is taught by the Bible to provide for the poor, the hungry, and the outcasts of the world, but at the same time it is hearing a side of the biblical message that conventional charity had forgotten. Poverty, hunger, and racism are evils to be fought against because they dehumanize people. Churches and societies have a clear mandate to feed the hungry, clothe the naked, free the oppressed, and provide economic structures for the elimination of these ills. A further realization is that God is with the poor and deprived ones in the midst of their sufferings. God's gracious power is exerted among the weak and powerless, showing that true humanity does not depend upon worldly riches and power.

Enriching Education

The educational establishment is one of the acknowledged centers of influence in the modern world. Once the guardian of the humanistic tradition in all its rich variety, it has become more and more the apologist for a narrow, technology-serving positivism that reduces human beings to functions and objects of analysis. Without realizing it, the modern university belongs to an age that is passing away. Its impressive laboratories deal minutely and exhaustively with the external data of existence but its students receive little help in grappling with the question of the quality of human life. "A liberal education," writes Theodore M. Hesburgh, "should enable a person to humanize everything that he or she touches in life."[34]

Christian humanism retains the vision of the *universitas,* a place of learning dealing with the whole of reality and hence open to and interested in the light that religion sheds on the nature and destiny of human beings. Public life is impoverished when education on all its levels accedes to the secularistic view that questions of God and faith should be excluded from the process of developing young minds.

To desire a larger place for religion in the university and in the public schools is not the same as the Christian right's determination to "put God back in the classroom" by means of coercive legislation.[35] It is rather an appeal to educators to recognize that the rich story of the religious life of the human family has a legitimate place in humanistic studies, and that to leave it out is to deprive young people of an important ingredient in their education.

In the 1990s the university world seems more open to serious dialog

34. Theodore M. Hesburgh, in *RF Illustrated* (published by Rockefeller Foundation), 1:2 (February 1973).
35. Cf. Oden, *Agenda for Theology,* 35. On the campaign against humanism in books see David Underhill, "Voltaire Arraigned in Alabama: The Textbooks Humanism Case," *The Christian Century* (May 6, 1987), 438-40; and Joseph Conn, "Inquisition in Alabama: Federal Court Lends a Hand to Religious Right's Secular Humanism Crusade," *Church and State* (April 1987), 6-12.

about profound human questions than was once the case. Over 90 percent of the nation's public-supported colleges and universities are now offering courses in religion. Once citadels of secularism, these institutions are discovering that in their zeal to exclude "sectarian" viewpoints they have deprived students of a great body of human experience and learning. As Harold Schilling has written, "Clearly, an institution of higher learning that is without specialists who are conducting research and giving instruction in religion can not be regarded as a real university any more than if it had no productive physicists or philosophers."[36]

Now at the end of the twentieth century, whether through formal courses in religion or through other forums, the colleges and universities are feeling the impact of biblical scholarship, the history of religions, and the work of such great theological minds as Karl Barth, Martin Buber, Abraham Heschel, H. Richard and Reinhold Niebuhr, and Paul Tillich. The walls of positivism and scientific humanism are beginning to erode. Some philosophers now argue that metaphysics cannot be removed from philosophical thought. Humanists are challenging the elevation of science to a philosophy of "scientism." Some social scientists are recoiling from a behavioralism that reduces human beings to responding organisms.

These few indicators hardly presage the "victory" of Christian humanism, but they suggest a new openness to those great and permanent issues — the nature of God, of human personality, and of the universe — which have always been the concern of the classical learning enterprise and specifically of Christian humanism, itself one of the original architects of the university in the Western world.

Despite these encouraging signs, the Christian right is justified to some extent in still maintaining its alarm at the pervasiveness of secular humanism in our education and culture, and it can be credited with calling attention to an element in the intellectual life of society that needed to be questioned. To the extent that only ideologically correct, usually leftist and stridently antitranscendent points of view are allowed a voice in much of academia, a full dialogue with the entire range of the experience of humankind is foreclosed. As mentioned earlier, some erstwhile liberal theologians are expressing their disillusionment with the secular mentality

36. Harold Schilling, "The University and the Church," lecture delivered at the University of Chicago to "The Fellowship of Campus Ministry" of the United Church of Christ, 1955. On the proper Christian challenge to secularism in education see Virgil Blum, "Secularism in Public Schools," *Crisis* (March 1987), 22-24; and Jeffrey L. Pasley, "Not-So-Good Books," *The New Republic* (April 22, 1987), 20-22.

and the chaotic world it has helped produce. When the secularistic interpretation of humanity and the world claims for itself the prestige of science
and reason, and presents itself as the normative view of what makes for a
good society, it has to be exposed as the barren, dying ideology that it is.
The decline of Marxism is the most striking example of the truth of this
assertion, and it is not surprising that it seems the last place this decline
is being acknowledged is on many American university campuses.

There are some dangers even now, however, in the way the Christian
right pursues its protest against secular humanism. First of all, it fails to
understand the history and meaning of the humanistic tradition in the
West even as it continues to issue a blanket condemnation of *all* humanism.
Thus it not only blinds itself to the positive contributions made to culture
by many fine humanistic individuals and movements but also in a curious
fashion accepts unthinkingly the definition of humanism set forth by a
vanishing breed of old-style secular atheists. With even a modest amount
of historical homework the supporters of the Christian right would discover, if they were open to the idea, that there is and long has been such
a thing as "Christian humanism," the appreciation of human concerns
informed by the Christian message.

A second flaw in the Christian right's attack on secular humanism
is that instead of meeting its targeted enemy on the plane of ideas, it girds
itself to rout secular humanism by means of political muscle. It mobilizes
opposition by invoking the myth of the United States as a Christian nation,
declaiming that the teachings of secular humanism are antimoral and
anti-American, and thus aiming to muster the votes to throw the secular
humanists out of office and to replace them with politicians of its own
stripe. It is a strategy of political force rather than persuasion.

One representative of the Christian right reveals a curious combination of theological and secular values when he complains that humanists
"have totally rejected God, creation, morality, the fallen state of man, and
the free-enterprise system." He continues his attack on humanists: "As
such, they are the mortal enemy of all pro-moral Americans, and the most
serious threat to our nation in its entire history."[37]

---

37. Tim LaHaye, *The Battle for the Mind* (Old Tappan, N.J.: Fleming H. Revell, 1980),
18. On the context of the antihumanism crusade see Gabriel Fackre, *The Religious Right and
Christian Faith* (Grand Rapids: Wm. B. Eerdmans, 1982); and Samuel S. Hill and Dennis E.
Owen, *The New Religious Political Right in America* (Nashville: Abingdon, 1982).

Christian Humanism and Public Life

Where Christian humanism differs from the Christian right is not in upholding certain moral goals or in accepting the usual rules of political struggle, but in how the action of God in transforming the world is to be understood. The Christian right advocates direct political action to realize the vision of a Christian nation. Christian humanism by contrast harbors no theocratic yearnings. It respects the mystery and indirect mode of God's humanizing activity. It has learned from Scripture, worship, and theology to be suspicious of schemes that put God on the side of the majority. God moves in strange ways and in unexpected places. A surprise move for peace and justice may occur in some unknown corner of the world; some very unlikely persons may turn out to be agents of truth. In 1989 the world was stunned by a series of such surprises, symbolized by the fall of the Berlin wall. When all human resources seem exhausted, God may do an entirely new thing to bring hope and healing to people and nations.

Christian humanism also differs from the Christian right with respect to the attitude toward secular humanism. While joining in the critique of the secular worldview, Christian humanism acknowledges at the same time that all persons concerned for the well-being of the human family must work together as fully as they can. Christian humanism unapologetically prays for the exercise of God's rule in the public life of the nation, but it does not claim the wisdom to detect at every turn where God's will is being executed and where it is being thwarted. It is not ashamed to use the words "in our opinion." Christians in particular are taught to respect God's freedom, and to remind themselves that divine power may be revealed in weakness. They must also remember that more than once in history the secular realm has been ahead of the church in demanding justice and freedom for the oppressed.

Christians serve their country whenever they express gratitude for the extraordinary blessings God has bestowed on this nation, but it is also part of citizenship to turn a critical eye on their own society. Harvey Cox asks, "Are fundamentalists ready to test the Christian bases of their nearly uncritical support of American foreign policy and the capitalist economic system?"[38] A comparable question might be formu-

---

38. Cox, *Religion in the Secular City*, 63. On the history of the political tactics of the Christian right see Steve Bruce, *The Rise and Fall of the New Christian Right: Conservative Protestant Politics in America 1978-1988* (Oxford: Oxford University Press, 1990); and Robert

lated for the secular apostles of modernity in the universities: Are they ready to test the secularistic bases of their nearly uncritical support of a society controlled by scientific technology and bureaucracy? One may extend the questioning to the mainline churches: Are they ready to recognize the humanizing power of the gospel they preach to the point of committing churchly time, money, energy, and bodies to the struggle against the antihuman forces raging destructively right outside their stained-glass windows?

Christian humanism is a way of looking at human existence, including public life, from the standpoint of classical Christian faith. Unlike the Christian right, Christian humanism has no visible political presence. It is simply a witness, invoking Scripture, worship, and theology, to the great humanistic resources in the Christian tradition and as such a leaven in a society which is newly open to them.

Because Christian humanism has its origins in the Bible and because it makes use of the language of theology, in this chapter specifically the doctrine of God, some might gain the impression that "the case for Christian humanism" is simply church-talk, another sermon for the faithful. Three comments are called for in response to this suggestion.

First, what is at stake primarily is the survival and protection of human beings. The term "humanism" is used repeatedly in these pages as a way of directing attention to the exalted value of human persons. Present conditions in the United States and throughout the world still include serious threats to humans, to individual persons, and to the entire human race. War and the rumors of war have not disappeared with the easing of superpower tensions. Therefore every available resource must be explored in searching for ways to protect human beings, and Christian humanism is among such resources.

Second, Christian humanism consciously uses the language of the church and points to the reality of the church in making its case before the world. The time has come for Christians and all others who cherish human values to realize that the gospel preached in the church is a revolutionary power capable of restoring persons to their full humanity. It is a divine message and at the same time a humanizing message because it announces the entry of God into the human community. Christian humanism also makes its case by showing that in the church the humaniz-

Wuthnow, *The Struggle for America's Soul: Evangelicals, Liberals and Secularism* (Grand Rapids: Wm. B. Eerdmans, 1990).

ing work of God has already begun. God is present in specific human communities where the divine name is praised and believing persons strive to follow the ways of God in their daily lives.

Moreover, to a degree most people fail to recognize, the church remains a bulwark against secular totalitarianism. "The secular wisdom can put up with religion that is private, individualistic, subjective,"[39] notes Richard John Neuhaus, but it is the institutions of religion, that is, the churches, that rouse the ire of Hitler, Stalin, and their imitators because such groups represent a human social dynamic that the tyrant cannot control. Imperfect as it is, the church is a key part of God's strategy in lifting the level of human life in this world, as the next chapter will seek to show.

Third, the meaning of Christian humanism with its God language is not just for the church but also applies to the whole of the secular order. That, in effect, is the point of this entire chapter. Secular powers have been all too effective in spreading the claim that all the important human concerns are managed by government, the economy, the press, the courts, and the military. The community of faith insists, on the contrary, that the God of heaven and earth will not be confined to the secret places of the heart and the quiet sanctuaries of worship. Jews rightly address God as "King of the universe" and Christians know that Jesus centered his entire teaching on the kingly rule of God. "Your kingdom come. Your will be done on earth as it is in heaven," Jesus prayed.

The time has come to set forth the power of God-centered humanism over against what we can now see to be the exhausted pretenses of a discredited secularism. God the creator and redeemer remains free to exert sovereign rule in every sphere of human activity. God is a living power who in freedom and love struggles continually in this world to bring about a greater measure of human fulfillment among all people.

39. Neuhaus, *Naked Public Square*, 190.

Chapter 11

Christ and the Human Fellowship

C hristology is that branch of theology that deals with the significance of Jesus Christ. It seeks to interpret the meaning of Christ for the needs of each generation, and in so doing gives richer understanding to how Christ is now acting in the world. A number of developments point to a rebirth of aspects of Christian humanism in Christology in the last one hundred fifty years. These are often allied to the liturgical emphases we have summarized.[1]

The theological mainstream today has learned, with the ancient church, to speak again of the humanity of Christ without reducing him to old liberalism's merely human Jesus. There had been the danger of making Christ too austere and remote, just as older theologies stressed the forbidding distance of God from the human scene. But as shown in the previous

---

1. This has been a marked feature of Anglican Christology in the last century. Books that survey this development, in chronological order, are: Edward Norman, *The Victorian Christian Socialists* (Cambridge: Cambridge University Press, 1987); Leanne Payne, *Real Presence: The Christian Worldview of C. S. Lewis as Incarnational Reality* (Westchester, Ill.: Crossway, 1988); Geoffrey Wainwright, ed., *Keeping the Faith: Essays to Mark the Centenary of Lux Mundi* (Philadelphia: Fortress Press, 1989); Robert Morgan, *The Religion of the Incarnation: Anglican Essays in Commemoration of Lux Mundi* (Briston: Classical Press, 1989); A. N. Wilson, *C. S. Lewis: A Biography* (London: Collins, 1989); Michael Ramsey, *The Gospel and the Catholic Church* (Cambridge: Cowley Press, 1990).

chapter, Karl Barth himself wrote an essay on "The Humanity of God" reflected in the mirror of the humanity of Jesus Christ. Since Barth's time, christological thought has continued to explore the ramifications of the ancient teaching that Christ is fully human as well as truly divine.

Today, in mission, worship, and ecumenical dialogue, there is a general recapturing of the fact that Christ is not distant but is closely identified with a human community. Modern theologians portray Jesus as one who, as God's servant, draws near to men and women. The effective presence of Christ in the church and in the world enables persons to realize in a deeper way what it means to be human.

Many writers have suggested that the major christological developments of the twentieth century find their common focus in a new doctrine of the church: Jesus Christ is present on earth in a concrete human institution, the church. With its order, eucharist, and mission, the church is a necessary part of the gospel, the Word announcing the crucifixion and resurrection. This alone has been a radical development, for from the end of the Reformation to the nineteenth century there was little effort among theologians to define a doctrine of the church. To a great extent, Christians simply lived within the framework of its given structures.[2]

The church was conceived among Roman Catholics, to the degree that it was discussed at all, primarily in terms of its hierarchical and political structures, not in its relationship to Christ. Liberal Protestants sacrificed most of the essentials of the church, often portraying institutional religion as a perversion of the gospel. Protestant evangelical preaching made Christ seem equally remote from the historic church. The favorite christological formula for almost all evangelicals has been "Jesus Christ as personal Savior." Accepting Jesus as "my personal Savior" has been the

2. For a survey of this theme among Protestants and Roman Catholics see W. R. Matthews, *The Problem of Christ in the Twentieth Century: An Essay on the Incarnation* (Maurice Lectures: 1949, 1950); John Kent, *The Unacceptable Face: The Modern Church in the Eyes of the Historian* (London: SCM, 1987); Gerhard Spiegler, *The Eternal Covenant: Schleiermacher's Experiment in Cultural Theology* (New York: Harper & Row, 1967); Gustave Martelet, "Christology and Anthropology: Toward a Christian Genealogy of the Human," in R. Latourelle and G. O'Collins, eds., *Problems and Perspectives of Fundamental Theology* (New York: Paulist Press, 1982), 151-67; Wolfhart Pannenberg, "The Christological Foundation of Christian Anthropology," in Claude Geffré, ed., *Humanism and Christianity* (New York: Herder and Herder, 1973), 86-100; J. Peter Schineller, "Christ and the Church: A Spectrum of Views," *Theological Studies,* 37 (1976), 545-66; and Kevin McNamara, "The Idea of the Church: Modern Developments in Ecclesiology," *The Irish Theological Quarterly,* 33 (1966), 99-113.

exclusive way in which evangelicals have expressed the human relationship to Christ. This usage served among some Protestants, and certainly this is still true of the Christian right today, to devalue further the humanistic dimensions of faith and confine Christianity to a private, spiritual realm.

And yet in the nineteenth and twentieth centuries, in the midst of pressing human problems of enormous dimensions, a way forward was found among both Protestants and Catholics for reassociating Jesus with human persons in the church. The Catholic theologian Johann Adam Möhler could write in 1832 that the visible church is no less than "the Son of God himself, everlastingly manifesting himself among men in a human form, perpetually renovated, and eternally young."[3] We are astounded when we discover that such theologians could write, over a hundred years ago, that the eternal purposes of God are entrusted to ordinary men and women, for Jesus is identified in their pages not only with the hierarchy but also with the laity.

The theme of Christ in the human fellowship evolved in opposition to the triumphant nationalism of the last century and a half. In the nineteenth century human unity and fellowship were most often linked to nationalism. Loyalty to the nation collided with the universalism of Christianity. For example, the Revolution in France severed the ties of the French church with Rome and subjected religion to the will of the national state. Berlin stood at the center of a German society in which the church was increasingly dominated by the bureaucracy of the state. Some German Christians absolutized the nation as the "highest value to be found in creation."[4]

The high tide of anti-Christian nationalism was reached in the nineteenth century when the Italian national liberation movement of Garibaldi and Cavour deprived the papacy of the Italian Marches and Umbria, then of the Romagna, and finally, in 1870, severed Rome from

3. Johann Adam Möhler, *Symbolism,* trans. James B. Robertson (New York: Scribner, 1844), quoted in *Readings in Christian Humanism,* ed. Joseph M. Shaw, R. W. Franklin, Harris Kaasa, and Charles W. Buzicky (Minneapolis: Augsburg, 1982), 450. A complete bibliography of Möhler is given in R. W. Franklin, *Nineteenth Century Churches: The History of a New Catholicism in Württemberg, England, and France* (New York: Garland Publishing, 1987), 529-40; and a short introduction in English is Hervé Savon, *Johann Adam Möhler: The Father of Modern Theology* (Glen Rock: Paulist Press, 1966).

4. Emil Brunner, *Christianity and Civilization* (New York: Charles Scribner's Sons, 1948), vol. 1, 559-60; on the cult of nationalism in opposition to Christian faith see Jon Halliday, ed., *The Artful Albanian: The Memoirs of Enver Hoxha* (London: Chatto and Windus, 1987).

the papacy itself. The high tide in the twentieth century was perhaps reached in 1967 when the Albanian dictator Hoxha declared Albania to be the first country in history from which all aspects of God had been exiled in the name of the nation. God was banished, "for the religion of Albanians is Albania."[5]

Christian theologians would have to ask: In such a society what protects the human? What prevents the destruction of humanity? They would have to reject such a nationalism, which openly imperils human solidarity, in the name of a worldwide fellowship, "the union of the family of man greatly consolidated and perfected by the unity which Christ establishes among the Sons of God."[6] From Johann Adam Möhler in 1832 to the Second Vatican Council in 1962, from the Protestant "dialectical theologians" of the 1930s to World Council of Churches documents of the 1980s, the rediscovery that the church is "one body of Christ" fired a spiritual vision of the unity of all humankind. Christ in the church, Christ in his people, Christ in the world fellowship: these have been humanistic themes of modern Christology.

Johann Adam Möhler (1796-1838)

German Catholic Christology has been dominated by the work of Johann Adam Möhler. Möhler grew up amid the ruins of the church in southwestern Germany, the result of the secularization of Catholicism in Germany by Napoleon Bonaparte in 1803, acting in the name of revolutionary France. In 1822 the young Catholic seminarian made the unprecedented gesture of traveling north to Berlin to study with the leading continental Protestant theologian, Friedrich Schleiermacher. Möhler returned to the Protestant University of Tübingen in the small state of Württemberg and proceeded to publish two of the most important books of nineteenth-century Catholic theology: *The Unity in the Church* (1825) and *Symbolism* (1832).

Möhler's theology was shaped by his growing fears of the might of the state. In 1835 the young teacher was forced out of Tübingen by the Protestant government of Württemberg. The king of Württemberg was

5. Peter Nichols, *The Pope's Divisions* (London: Penguin Books, 1981), 294.
6. *Gaudium et spes*, quoted in *Readings in Christian Humanism*, 618.

attempting to eliminate the possibility that the Catholic church or Catholic professors might emerge as an independent political influence. From exile in Munich, Möhler closely followed religious developments to the north in Prussia: the imprisonment of a Rhineland archbishop and then a Polish archbishop because both refused to sanction government orders directed at their clergy. Behind these events Möhler saw already dawning upon humankind the monstrous figure of the totalitarian state.

"If there will be no higher power than the state in Europe, then human freedom has come to an end," Möhler wrote in 1837.[7] To offset the divisive tendencies of the new nationalism, he spread abroad the Christian vision of the unity of all in the church. Only in a free, international religious community could the liberties of the individual be guaranteed; only in an institution with a marked transcendent dimension could a full humanism be guaranteed for Europeans.

A fresh descent of the Spirit could break down human walls and build up social cohesion in a revolutionary age of atomization, industry, war, and fragmentation. The church was called to be a new witness to the Spirit because it is the sacramental manifestation of God's saving mercy, and it is identified with Jesus Christ in the closest possible way. Möhler summarized his conviction that the humanizing mission of Jesus is continued by the church: "The Savior manifested Himself in that He walked as a man among men, but still a greater revelation of Him was to be the history of the Christian Church. . . ."[8]

The German Catholic is here at one with the Danish Lutheran Grundtvig in reminding us that if there were no church in which Christ's influence is ultimately felt, even the Bible would be for us but a dead letter, breathing no life. A Catholic of our time put Möhler's message this way: "We do not learn the ultimate truth about Christ at the scholar's desk or in the sobriety of his study. We will learn it only in the sacred spaces, flooded with super-natural life in what we call the 'body of Christ,' in his living Church."

Möhler carried the humanistic implications of this a step further than Grundtvig in that he was the first Catholic theologian for a thousand

---

7. Johann Adam Möhler, "Über die neueste Bekämpfung der Katholischen Kirche," *Gesammelte Schriften und Aufsätze* (Regensburg: G. J. Manz, 1839-40), vol. 2, 229; Möhler also deals with the church as protector of freedom against the totalitarianism of the state in *Life of St. Anselm, Archbishop of Canterbury*, trans. Henry Rymer (London: Jones, 1842).

8. Johann Adam Möhler, *Athanasius der Grosse und die Kirche seiner Zeit* (Mainz: Kupferberg, 1827), 162.

years to argue that the ground of the unity of the church was not the clergy or the state but Christ present in believers. For example, in the seventeenth century the Jesuit theologian Robert Bellarmine had nurtured the ideal of unity in the absolute monarchy of the papacy. To be a member of the church was to be a subject of the sovereignty of the pope. Bellarmine perceived the church as a militant *perfect society* of ordered ranks "like the Kingdom of France or the Republic of Venice."[9]

In contrast, Möhler beheld Christianity not as rules and dogma but as a life lived in common. Möhler's definition of the church as a corporate unity, rather than as a legal entity, is based on his concept of the Incarnation: Jesus continues to dwell on earth in his church. The goal of the Incarnation, the joining of matter and spirit and divinity and humanity in Christ, continues to be carried out in the assembly of Christians. Christ touches the world through the members of the church; they are his agents for forging bonds of unity. Christ the cornerstone in this way "unites with the strongest bands of love . . . and holds [humanity] together in the covenant of eternal unity. . . ."[10] Möhler contended that humans are, in a deeply mysterious way, instruments of the salvation of which they are also the beneficiaries.

Möhler was convinced that his unusual, for a Roman Catholic, vision of the church would one day capture the imagination of Protestants, and he remarks as an aside in his 1832 *Symbolism:*

> This is the point at which Catholics and Protestants will, in great multi-
> tudes, one day meet, and stretch a friendly hand one to the other. Both,
> conscious of guilt, must exclaim, "We all have erred — it is the Church
> only which cannot err; we all have sinned — the Church only is spotless
> on earth."[11]

9. Karl Adam, *The Christ of Faith: The Christology of the Church* (New York: Sheed and Ward, 1957), 16; Bellarmine, in Nichols, *The Pope's Divisions,* 107; an analysis of these views of the church is given in Jaroslav Pelikan, *The Christian Tradition,* vol. 4, *Reformation of Church and Dogma 1300-1700* (Chicago: University of Chicago Press, 1984). On this point see Patrick Granfield, "The Church as *Societas Perfecta* in the Schemata of Vatican I," *Church History,* 48 (1979), 431-46; and Knut Walf, "Die katholische kirche — eine 'Societas Perfecta'?", *Theologische Quartalschrift,* 157 (1977), 107-18.

10. Möhler, *Symbolism,* quoted in *Readings in Christian Humanism,* 453.

11. Ibid., 349.

From Yves Congar to the
Second Vatican Council (1935-1965)

In 1928 in the encyclical *Mortalium animos* Pope Pius XI made it clear in no uncertain terms that Catholics and Protestants were *not* to meet and stretch out a friendly hand, and that the official Roman version of unity was still that all Christians should be subject to the papacy. The first twentieth-century steps beyond this narrow, juridical Catholic view were proposed in the 1930s and the 1940s by a young French Dominican of the Paris Province, Yves Congar, O.P. Two of Congar's works were landmarks of the stature of Möhler's books; they are *The Laity in the Church* and *Christians Divided.*

Möhler was Congar's inspiration and his source. Congar wrote: "Thanks to Pierre Chenu, I was given the first idea, global in its implication, of Möhler. . . . I felt that I had not only found a breach in the bastion of the post-Tridentine church, but an inspiration, a source, a new synthesis."[12] Amid the pressures of world events, as the horrors of the Nazi state spread over Europe and the uniqueness of human beings was being placed in jeopardy by the National Socialist ideology, Congar popularized Möhler's hopeful incarnational theology and his bright universalist perspective. In this way Möhler's phrase "the church as the mystical body of Christ" came to stand behind the thinking of many of our contemporary German and French theologians who fashioned a revised understanding of the relationship of Jesus to the church for the Vatican. All the great theologians who prepared the way for this change of thinking at the Second Vatican Council (1962-1965), from Cardinal Ratzinger to Hans Küng, would admit some debt to Möhler or Congar. Rarely in history has an ecumenical council owed so much to two men. In the documents of Vatican II, such as *Lumen gentium* and *Gaudium et spes,* the great mystery of the church as a royal priestly people pilgrimaging in time can be expressed in no more fitting terminology than Möhler's "the church as the body of Christ":

> By communicating His Spirit to His brothers Christ made them mystically into His own body. In that body, the life of Christ is poured into the

12. Yves Congar, "Johann Adam Möhler," *Theologische Quartalschrift* (1970), 47; see also Yves Congar, "Sur l'évolution et l'interpretation de la pensée de Möhler," *Revue des Sciences Philosophiques et Théologiques,* 27 (1938), 204-12; and Aidan Nichols, *Yves Congar* (London: Cassell, 1989). Möhler's position was also popularized for Roman Catholics in the twentieth century in the influential book, Karl Adam, *The Christ of Faith: The Christology of the Church* (New York: Sheed & Ward, 1957).

believers who are united in a hidden and real way to Christ. This reality is compared to the mystery of the Incarnate Word.[13]

At the same time, Congar went beyond Möhler to propose a concept of human unity in the church which, for the first time, in specific ways included non-Roman Catholics. To Möhler the "unity of the church" is given by Christ. Congar went on to say that the "catholicity" or "universal nature" of Christianity is received from human beings. The goal of the "catholicity of the church" is to join together in one solidarity all persons, as well as every value of humanity. For Congar, all of humanity's religious experiences must be assimilated into the church for their divinely intended fulfillment. Thus the Catholic church must respect the legitimate diversity of non-Roman religious expressions and ought not seek to reduce them to a common denominator.

No other theologian expanded the vision of the Roman church in the matter of understanding unity to the extent and with the depth that Congar's books did; for now a way was open for Rome to make a positive assessment of other Christian churches. The Second Vatican Council for the first time recognized separated Christians as sisters and brother. "We know where the Church is," said the Council; "it is not for us to judge where the Church is not."[14]

The Final Report (1982)

In the 1970s, following the directives of the Vatican Council, the Roman Catholic Church gave resonance to a new ecumenical theological concept,

13. *Ecclesiam Suam,* in Peter Foote, *Vatican II's Dogmatic Constitution on the Church* (New York: Macmillan, 1969), 16, 18; for more on these connections see Alberic Stacpoole, ed., *Vatican II Revisited By Those Who Were There* (Minneapolis: Winston Press, 1986); and Patrick Granfield, "The Mystery of the Church," *The American Ecclesiastical Review,* 160 (1969), 1-20.

14. Christopher Bulter, *The Theology of Vatican II* (London: Darton, Longman, and Todd, 1981), 119; on ecumenism at Vatican II, in addition to essays in the Stacpoole collection noted above see one of the most thorough commentaries in English on the "Decree on Ecumenism" by W. Becker and J. Feiner, "Decree on Ecumenism," *Commentary on the Documents of Vatican II,* ed. H. Vorgrimler (New York: Herder and Herder, 1968), 1-164; the retrospective commentary of W. M. Brown, "Commentary on the Decree on Ecumenism," *The Church Renewed: The Documents of Vatican II,* ed. G. Schner (New York: University Press of America, 1986), 37-54; and James Crumley, "Reflections on 25 Years after the Decree on Ecumenism," *Ecumenical Trends,* 18 (1989), 145-50.

"regional and international bilateral consultations and commissions." This new network of relationships among world families of churches has led to significant christological advancement. The first major example of international ecumenical theology has been the document released in 1982 by the Anglican-Roman Catholic International Commission known as *The Final Report. The Final Report* is a treatise of one hundred pages in which eighteen scholars drawn from the Anglican Communion and the Roman Catholic Church express their unanimous agreement on such formerly divisive issues as the eucharist, the nature of the ordained ministry, and authority in the church. *The Final Report,* a result of twelve years of study, research, and dialogue, leads the churches to a further stage of comprehending oneness in Christ.

The Final Report is a significant essay for Christian humanism because in it two world communions ally Christian unity with the cause of the reconciliation of all humanity: "The Church is the community of those reconciled with God and with each other because it is the community of those who believe in Jesus Christ. It is also the reconciling community, because it has been called to bring to all mankind, through the preaching of the Gospel, God's gracious offer of redemption."[15]

"*Koinonia* for *Diakonia* — Fellowship for Service" is the key phrase of *The Final Report.*[16] Never before had the mystical body of Christ been described as a *koinonia* so as to mean "a fellowship of reconciled world communions."[17] Here is proposed a model of unity in which the particular churches are not blended but reconciled. The *Report* makes the case that true *koinonia* can never be realized only in a local church; *koinonia* must be grasped in communion with Christians around the globe. *The Final Report* defines the purpose of the ordained ministry and even the papacy in terms of building up a worldwide fellowship of believers.

---

15. *The Final Report* (London: CTS/SPCK, 1982), 119; an introduction to the extensive literature on this document can be found in J. Robert Wright, "The ARCIC Final Report: An Annotated Bibliography," *Anglican Theological Review,* 66 (1984), 177-87.

16. *The Final Report,* 6-7; the implications for humanism of the *Report* are discussed in Kenneth Leech, "Artisans of a New Humanity?: Some Anglican and Roman Catholic Approaches to Social and Political Action," in Mark Santer, ed., *Their Lord and Ours* (London: SPCK, 1982), 73-89. See also A. M. Allchin, *Eucharist and Unity* (Oxford: SLG Press, 1972); and Robert Runcie, *Windows onto God* (London: SPCK, 1983).

17. *The Final Report,* 37; for an expansion of these themes see Emmanuel Sullivan, "*Koinonia* as a Meta-Model for Future Church Unity," *Ecumenical Trends,* 18 (1989), 1-6; "Christian Unity: The Gift, The Vision and the Way," *The Emmaus Report* (London: ACC, 1987), 6-37; and The Anglican-Reformed International Commission, *God's Reign and Our Unity* (London: SPCK, 1984).

The *diakonia* of papacy and ministry is not only explained as an inward, ecclesiastical service. The external *diakonia,* the humanistic service of papacy and ministry, is described as joint action to symbolize and strengthen the fundamental unity of the human family. An example of what had been envisioned by *The Final Report* actually took place on May 29, 1982. *The Final Report* had discussed the universal embrace of the church, but on that day in May, in Canterbury cathedral, people saw human reconciliation in the church visibly realized. They beheld not formal ecumenical statements, but rather an actual coming together of Christians from different countries, different cultures, and different histories, and they saw an acting out of a primordial meaning of the word religion — *re-ligare,* to bind back together.

In the midst of the Falklands war between a Protestant and a Catholic state, Britain and Argentina, within a United Kingdom in which a province is still divided by a conflict of Catholics with Protestants which makes of religion a fertile stage for terrorism and degradation, in May 1982 Pope John Paul II and the head of the worldwide Anglican Communion, Archbishop Robert Runcie, met in the ancient English cathedral of Canterbury to give thanks to God for the progress that has been made in the reconciliation of the churches. When the pope and the archbishop rose from prayer and gave each other the sign of peace, and their faces were seen to be streaked with tears of joy, the packed congregation in the cathedral burst into spontaneous applause, drowning the organ in the acclamation.

The service in Canterbury, witnessed by millions on television, drove home to viewers that the commitment of the churches to unity is a journey in which all men and women are inescapably involved. Can we not see in the vivid hope of this moment the radical humanistic consequences of theological change?

The World Council of Churches and Baptism, Eucharist, and Ministry (1948-1982)

There have been other such public occasions, among Protestants, which demonstrate that overcoming formerly divisive issues in Christology can lead to greater human unity. On a sunny morning in August 1983 the same Archbishop Robert Runcie participated in a second act of worship which was a further sign that divisions that threaten life on this planet are being broken down. On that morning 3,500 Christians representing the whole inhabited earth streamed into a huge moveable canvas tent in Vancouver, Canada. They had come to celebrate the eucharist, "the feast of life," using the Lima Liturgy, which represents the first agreement among the churches on a form of the Lord's Supper in which nearly all are willing to participate. The Lima Liturgy is based on a second historic convergence statement of 1982, *Baptism, Eucharist and Ministry.*

The Archbishop of Canterbury, acting as chief celebrant of the eucharist, was joined by six other ministers: a Lutheran woman pastor from Denmark, a Reformed woman pastor from Indonesia, a Methodist from Benin, a Baptist from Hungary, a Moravian from Jamaica, and a minister from the United Church of Canada. All of these Christians witnessing from different national and theological perspectives were now able to join together in the central act of the body of Christ.

The setting of this eucharist was the Sixth Assembly of the World Council of Churches. The origins of the World Council, which held its formative assembly at Amsterdam in 1948, lay in a sharp encounter between Christians and totalitarian nationalism and a strong Protestant recovery of incarnational Christology. During World War II many Protestants who were in the resistance movements in Germany and the occupied countries, in the neutral capitals, and in Britain saw the universalism of the church with new clarity. They became aware of a deep intimacy and a common purpose shared by Christians from many denominations, and when the war was over they aimed at creating an international council that could sustain a lasting movement toward unity.

The generation of leaders who produced and guided the World Council had been profoundly influenced by a Protestant theological revival known as "dialectical theology." Some "dialectical theologians," particularly Karl Barth, Emil Brunner, and Dietrich Bonhoeffer, were determined to recover the importance of Christ in the church for Christian thinking and living in the twentieth century. This school was also called the "theology of crisis" because it pointed to the grave "crisis" or "turning-point" Western civilization had come to in the 1930s and 1940s with the threat of Nazi totalitarianism hanging over Europe. Bonhoeffer (1906-1945), perhaps the most famous Christian martyr to the Nazis, influenced the first two decades of the World Council of Churches perhaps more than any other theologian.

Dietrich Bonhoeffer's position, born in the fire of trial and imprisonment, became like Möhler's a century before strongly christological, and for similar reasons Bonhoeffer made the closest identification of Christ with the church. He argued that Christ exists today as the church or, in his words, the church is "Christ existing as community."[18] For Bonhoeffer, like Möhler, since Christ is not merely Lord of the church but of the world, the church cannot be something apart from the world as an enclave within it, but like its Lord, the church is there in and for the world. Bonhoeffer asserted the strongly humanistic potential of Christology as a basis for dealing creatively and redemptively with an increasingly secular, and dehumanizing, modern existence.

Under the impact of catastrophic external events, the immanental revelation of the Incarnation popular at the beginning of our century in liberal Protestantism was abandoned by Bonhoeffer. He brought back the traditional conception of transcendence in the Incarnation but identified it with the "collective person" of the church active here and now. Here is a passage from his 1930 dissertation *Sanctorum Communio* that contains in germ what he would say with greater force and ethical suggestiveness later:

> The social significance of Christ is decisive. He is only present in the church, that is, where the Christian community is united by preaching and the Lord's Supper for brotherly love. . . . The sole content of the church is in any case the revelation of God in Christ. He is present to the church in his Word, by which the community is constituted ever anew. The church is the presence of Christ, as Christ is the presence of God.[19]

This presence of Christ in the church, even in the darkest times, gave Bonhoeffer a confidence before the dark night of Nazism, which he put in the first stanza of a hymn:

> By gracious powers so wonderfully sheltered,
> and confidently waiting come what may,
> we know that God is with us night and morning,
> and never fails to greet us each new day.[20]

18. Dietrich Bonhoeffer, *Letters and Papers from Prison* (London: SCM Press, 1971), quoted in *Readings in Christian Humanism,* 388; for the context see Eberhard Bethge, *Dietrich Bonhoeffer* (New York: Harper & Row, 1970).

19. Dietrich Bonhoeffer, *Sanctorum Communio — A Dogmatic Inquiry into the Sociology of the Church* (London: Collins, 1963), 84-85; the theme appears especially in these two other works of Bonhoeffer, *Christ the Center,* trans. John Bowden (New York: Harper & Row, 1960); and *The Cost of Discipleship,* trans. R. H. Fuller (New York: Macmillan, 1949).

20. This hymn, translated by F. Pratt Green, is no. 695 in *The Hymnal 1982*; on Bonhoeffer's impact see W. Visser 't Hooft, *The Genesis and Formation of the World Council of Churches* (Geneva: World Council of Churches, 1982); and H. Fey, *The Ecumenical Advance: A History of the Ecumenical Movement 1948-1968* (Philadelphia: Westminster Press, 1970).

Even in its state of corruption, the world of Adam, Bonhoeffer argued, could participate in the world of Christ. The communion of sinners· is linked to the saints through Christ and his grace. The hidden God, after all, has revealed himself in Christ, and when the world went up in flames, and the genius of God's children was perverted into an orgy of brutality, God was found weeping and suffering, not almighty, but weak and powerless in the presence of Christ in the world.

Bonhoeffer's Christian humanism here is very close to that of Karl Barth on the "humanity of God" surveyed in the previous chapter, and from Basle in 1955 Karl Barth paid his "deepest respect" to Bonhoeffer's vision of Christ in the human fellowship in *Sanctorum Communio.* Would he, Barth wrote, ever from his place and in his own language be able to express himself as powerfully as "that young man did then?"

The influence of Bonhoeffer may be seen clearly also in the themes of the assemblies of the World Council of Churches. The work of the last five assemblies has focused on the Christ of redeemed humanity: "Christ the Hope of the World" (Evanston, 1954), "Christ the Light of the World" (New Delhi, 1961), "Christ Makes All Things New" (Uppsala, 1968), "Jesus Christ Frees and Unites" (Nairobi, 1975), and "Jesus Christ the Life of the World" (Vancouver, 1983). In these great gatherings of Christians from over three hundred churches, the World Council has been saying that Jesus, as the messiah for those who follow him, is the source of their life made whole in this world. To the extent that humans are liberated by Jesus, they can help enlarge and deepen life on this planet and perhaps become the decisive implements for peace and for the restoration of the created order.

Baptism, Eucharist and Ministry (BEM), published in 1982 by the Faith and Order Commission of the World Council of Churches, though the work of one hundred theologians representing not only WCC churches — Protestant as well as Orthodox — but the Roman church and some nonmember evangelicals, goes into significant detail about how the churches are called to convey to the world the image of the new humanity grounded in Jesus Christ. *BEM* provides a comprehensive theological defense for understanding the church as a sharing and healing community whose ministry is an extension of the actual power of Christ himself. At the societal level the presence of the "Lord of Life" means that all barriers, whether of sex or race or of politics and economic status, may be transcended.

BEM achieves a rich ecumenical consensus in going beyond old Protestant-Catholic-Orthodox divisions over justification by faith and baptismal regeneration. Baptism is described as the sacramental bond of unity of all Christians and as an ongoing growth process. Maturing in faith is a sign that human beings can be regenerated. Born anew in baptism, Christians experience a gradual transformation into Christ. Tasting liberation in themselves, believers are impelled to bear witness to Christ, a witness that flows out into the world as service.

In *BEM* the implications of baptism, which initiates the reality of the new life given in Christ, are not narrowly religious in content. Baptism has serious humanistic connotations that involve Christians in fostering God's will on earth: the freeing of humanity from everything that harms human life and the bringing to fulfillment all the powers and joys that God intends for human beings as God's children. In this ongoing action all believers are called "to themselves make Christ present on earth."[21]

Christ, the Church, and Humanity

The paragraphs above have pointed to a number of common insights regarding Christ and the church that have appeared in both Catholic and Protestant Christology in the last century and a half, the fruits of which can be seen in significant ecumenical statements of the 1980s. Though theology is not identical to Christian humanism, these developments express very well what Christian humanism is all about. It is a way of looking at and valuing men and women in the light of the definitive reality which is Jesus Christ. It is an enthusiastic expression of the greatness of the human creature which is fully Christian. The admiration of men and women is grounded in devotion to Christ. It is, furthermore, in Christ and through Christ that human creatures find the full meaning and significance of their existence. It is now time to place in systematic order these regnant themes of Christ in relation to humanity that have appeared in recent Christology and in the ecumenical movement.

21. *Baptism, Eucharist, and Ministry* (Geneva: World Council of Churches, 1982), 20; among the recently available theological commentaries on *BEM* are the following: *Ecumenical Perspectives on Baptism, Eucharist and Ministry*, ed. M. Thurian (Geneva: World Council of Churches, 1983); *The Search for Visible Unity: Baptism, Eucharist, Ministry*, ed. J. Gros (New York: Pilgrim Press, 1984); and *Catholic Perspectives on Baptism, Eucharist and Ministry: A Study Commissioned by the Catholic Theological Society of America*, ed. M. Fahey (New York: University Press of America, 1986).

The Body of Christ

A few years before he was accidentally electrocuted in a Bangkok hotel, the great American spiritual pioneer Thomas Merton wrote, "true Christian humanism is the full flowering of the theology of the Incarnation."[22] The Incarnation is the deed in which God has committed the divine self to the good of humankind in the most complete and radical way imaginable: coming fully into the human family in the person of him who is God's own son, Jesus Christ of Nazareth, an authentic human person.

The theologians cited above have broadened the doctrine of the Incarnation to suggest that the totality of Christ's body consists not just of Jesus, but of Jesus and his church. The whole of the church's life is a kind of enlargement and prolongation of what God has done in Christ. This means that the church is not just an institution of this world. It has an inner dynamic drawn from Christ and dependent on his grace. Figures from Möhler to Bonhoeffer have been grateful for the church, even though it can be a wretched company of the sinful, because it is the channel through which Christ has touched them. Faith is awakened through living persons, a friend, a parent, a Christian teacher, even a stranger, someone who speaks a timely word: we meet Christ through believers, through the church.

The Church: A People

Möhler wrote in 1832, "Even the faithful are called 'the body of Christ.'"[23] One hundred years later an Anglican bishop who had been touched by the Catholic theological revival cried out in anguish and shame before a meeting of triumphant ecclesiastics, "You have your Mass, you have your altars. Now go out into the highways and hedges and look for Jesus in the ragged and the naked, in the oppressed and the sweated, in those who have lost hope, and in those who are struggling to make good. Look for Jesus in them; and when you have found him,

22. Thomas Merton, "Virginity and Humanism in the Western Fathers," in *Mystics and Zen Masters* (New York: Farrar, Straus & Giroux, 1967), 114; see also David Cooker, "Thomas Merton's Christian Humanism in a Post-Christian Era," *Living Prayer* (November-December 1988), 9-17. Cooper's *Thomas Merton's Art of Denial: The Evolution of a Radical Humanist* is forthcoming from the University of Georgia Press.
23. Möhler, *Symbolism,* quoted in *Readings in Christian Humanism,* 450.

gird yourself with his towel of fellowship, and wash his feet in the person of his brethren."[24]

An entirely new note is being sounded in these passages. "The people" has become the primary association surrounding the concept of the church. Theology is moving from juridical concepts such as *perfect society* toward defining the church as "one people." Protestants and Catholics are making the bold proclamation that Jesus continues to make his dwelling on earth in *all* his faithful people. There has been a renewed sense that God calls the whole of humanity to become God's sons and daughters. God's purpose is that all should share in the fellowship of the church. Mission is carried out in the context of a "fellowship of believers."[25] The corporate character of witness springs from the wider grasping of the church as the body of Christ. The humanistic implications of this theme are obvious. "Christ advances his kingdom through man," Dr. Pusey proclaimed to adherents of the Oxford Movement.[26]

One People: One Church

The broadening of the doctrine of the Incarnation in the direction of humanity is linked to the contemporary opening of the borders of the churches to embrace all who confess Jesus as Lord. The theologians have taken Galatians 3:28 — "You are all one in Christ Jesus" — to mean that we behold Christ not only in the members of our own church; we recognize him among separated sisters and brothers who share the common seal of faith.

A popular appreciation for how Christ's presence leads to unity appears in a recent hymn:

> As Christ breaks bread for all to share
> Each proud division ends.
> That love that made us makes us one,
> And strangers now are friends.

24. H. Maynard Smith, *Frank Weston, Bishop of Zanzibar* (London: Macmillan, 1926), 302.

25. *Baptism, Eucharist and Ministry,* 20; Teresa Berger, "Unity in and through Doxology? Reflections on Worship Studies in the World Council of Churches," *Studia Liturgica,* 16 (1986-87), 1-11. For a World Council series on humanism see David Jenkins, ed., *The Humanum Studies 1969-1975: A Collection of Documents* (Geneva: World Council of Churches, 1975).

26. E. B. Pusey, *Parochial and Cathedral Sermons* (Oxford: Rivington, 1882), 322.

Together met, together bound,
We'll go our different ways,
And as his people in the world,
We'll live and speak his praise.[27]

One of the significant gains for humanism in the church has been this recognition that Christianity comprises a family of persons from many nations, diverse backgrounds, and all races. The drive for unity has underscored the humanistic insight that God's creative and redemptive work in the world is intended to bring humankind together in one community. How to realize this wider unity of the human family is one of the church's immediate tasks.

One Body: One Humanity

A leading Catholic demographer, Fr. Arthur McCormack, believes that very soon there could be a global ecological disaster if people show the same indifference to the world situation in the first years of the next century that they have shown in the last years of this one. What threatens potential catastrophe, he says, is that the nations are not geared to solving world problems. They are engaged in wars and disputes when they ought to be bending every effort for the survival of the human race.

Fr. McCormack goes on to cite the Club of Rome report of 1980 that demonstrates that the functional unity of world polity continues to be the national state. Nationalism still persists, and it acts as a stubborn block to world solidarity. The partitioning of the globe into one hundred fifty sovereign entities works against human interdependence and kills the spirit of trust betwen peoples. In the absence of trust, nations seeking security are drawn into a frantic arms race spreading from the great powers to scores of other countries, including the poorest. Even with the ending of the Cold War, an arms race fueled by nationalism lifts before humanity the grim prospect of chemical or nuclear destruction. The quality of existence is endangered when an exorbitant proportion of the earth's resources is poured into national defense.

Painful economic restrictions, the spread of terrorism, continuing political violence — all of these disorders take the concept of a worldwide family of brothers and sisters out of the sphere of utopian dreaming

27. Hymn no. 304 in *The Hymnal 1982.*

and give further weight to the need for cooperative planning. But, Fr. McCormack goes on to say, there is not time to build a new international order.

The instruments for survival must largely be those already at hand. One such instrument can be the Christian church. In concentrating on survival, the human race will have to do many of the things suggested by the sort of humanism, the Christian humanism, that has emerged in such recent ecumenical documents as *The Final Report* and *Baptism, Eucharist and Ministry*.

The same point was made by Aldo Moro, the best known of Italy's politicians, in his last letter of March 1978 before he died at the hands of the Red Brigades terrorist group. Moro wrote these words to his friend Pope Paul VI: "what other voice if not that of the Church, can break the crystallization [of violence and terror] which has taken shape; or what humanism is there higher than Christian humanism?"[28]

The reconciled churches can stand before the world as the new machinery of humanism. Because it is spread all over the globe — there are only five countries without Christians, Afghanistan, the two Yemens, Bahrain, and Oman — Christianity is not committed to any one culture or to any one economic system. The international structure and mentality of Christianity grant it the freedom to rise above the political stricture of the ideologies of nations.

Baptism, Eucharist and Ministry proclaims this position boldly: the churches acting together at the grass roots and internationally can press upon decision makers the preservation of basic human values, which are not always taken into account when diplomatic agreements are negotiated. United, the churches can call on those who possess power to use their might to bridge gaps between rich and poor, male and female, young and old, black and white. Joining in international solidarity, Christians can give to the oppressed within single nations the courage to rise up in the struggle for justice and dignity and the creation of a more humane political order. Believers acting as one can turn their governments away from plans to deploy additional nuclear weapons and move statesmen to reduce present nuclear zones.

"As though in preparation for such a time as this," William Temple wrote fifty years ago on his enthronement as Archbishop of Canterbury, "God has been building up a Christian fellowship which now extends into

28. Aldo Moro, quoted in Nichols, *The Pope's Divisions*, 329.

every nation, and binds citizens of them all together in true unity and mutual love. Almost incidentally the great world-fellowship has arisen; it is the new fact of our era."[29]

These words bear a special relevance to the decade of the 1990s when the post-1945 order has crumbled in Europe and fresh hopes, but also dangers, lie ahead. We are witnessing the collapse of the "fragile ecumenism of Marxist-Leninism" that succeeded in holding together the peoples of many cultures only by brute force and tyranny. To offset the potentially divisive setbacks of a new age of nationalism, Pope John Paul II has spread abroad a vision of the unity of the old continent in Jesus. In the utterly surprising configuration of power that was born in 1989, the pope is proposing a pan-European strategy of survival that draws upon the tradition of Christian humanism. To Christian humanism, said the pope in an influential speech before the former Hapsburg palace in Vienna:

> Europe owed its riches and its power, the flowering of the arts and sciences, scholarship and research, philosophy and civilization. . . . Among the elements of Christian faith it is in particular the Christian conception of man that left its mark. The belief that Man is created in the image of God and that he has been redeemed by Jesus Christ, the Son of Man, has founded the respect and dignity of the human being. . . . It is thus only logical that the universal rights of man were first formulated and proclaimed in the Western world.[30]

Drawing upon the themes outlined in this chapter that go back to Möhler and the pre-1945 Germans who shaped his thinking as he was coming of age in Central Europe, the pontiff has urged that the restoration of the continent can not take place in isolation from the re-establishment of full communion of sacramental life among the separated churches. The prerequisite of the rebirth of one culture from Ireland to the Urals is the unity of the European peoples at the level of faith that involves the re-claiming of a common heritage.

29. F. A. Iremonger, *William Temple, Archbishop of Canterbury: His Life and Letters* (New York: Oxford University Press, 1948), 387.

30. English *Osservatore Romano* (September 11, 1983), 1; see also the speech of John Paul II, "Affirm the Values of Christian Humanism in Your Service," English *Osservatore Romano* (March 25, 1985), 3; and on the theme in his background see G. H. Williams, *The Mind of John Paul II* (New York: Seabury Press, 1981), and Maureen Sullivan, "The Christian Humanism of Paul VI: Its Christological Foundations," Ph.D. diss., Fordham, 1985.

We close with a papal excerpt in which John Paul II sums up so much of what has been said in this chapter about the relation of ecumenism to humanism, with special relevance to the current world situation:

> Europe, Eastern Europe as well as Western Europe, cannot understand *itself* — hence, cannot understand the meaning of its history . . . if *it* prescinds from the tragedy of the mutual estrangement between Rome and Constantinople. . . . Could the two sister Churches that have given rise to the spiritual dynamism of Europe, by that fact conditioning *its* destiny, ever abandon it to *its* own devices at such a critical time in *its* history? The Church of the East and of the West knows how to love everything that today, as yesterday, is stirring and fermenting among the peoples of *this continent*. . . . The Church today understands that it is called to give *united witness* to this solidarity, in the conviction that in this way it offers a contribution of primary importance to the development of a peaceful and prosperous society, interwoven with vital exchanges among the European peoples.[31]

An incisive effort to reshape the mind of Europe, to reclaim a Christian basis for social analysis and for cultural plentitude, can not proceed in isolation from greater Christian unity. Where such unity is attained, Christ is present, in the human fellowship.

31. English *Osservatore Romano* (February 27-28, 1984), 1-2; on ecumenism, unity, and humanism see the important statement of Kevin McDonald, "The Ecumenical Ministry of Pope John Paul II," English *Osservatore Romano* (September 29, 1989), 7; and three studies by G. H. Williams: *The Law of Nations and the Book of Nature* (Collegeville, Minn.: St. John's University, 1984); *The Contours of Church and State in the Thought of John Paul II* (Waco: Baylor University, 1983); and "The Ecumenism of John Paul II," *Journal of Ecumenical Studies*, 19 (1982), 681-718. For a similar plea linking ecumenism and human advance from the Archbishop of Canterbury, a university divinity school, and the Christian right see Robert Runcie, "Anglican-Roman Catholic Relations Today," *The Ecumenical Bulletin*, 98 (1990), 8-14; George MacRae, "Ecumenism Inspires Global Christian Approach," *Harvard Gazette* (September 26, 1980), 4; and Harry E. Winter, "Reluctant Ecumenist: Francis A. Schaeffer," *Ecumenical Trends* (May 1985), 71-73.

Chapter 12

The Holy Spirit in Human Living

Just as the doctrines of God and of Christ inform Christian humanism by showing how God comes to be near the human community, so also the doctrine of the Holy Spirit illumines the divine purpose of lifting the human creation to its intended fulfillment. This third basic Christian doctrine is, for the Christian community, the humanistic doctrine *par excellence* because the Holy Spirit is uniquely God in creative interaction with the human spirit. The Spirit *is* God, states theologian John Macquarrie, which also means "that he is God at his closest to us."[1]

The ancient hymn, "Veni, Creator Spiritus," attributed to Rhabanus Maurus (776-856), conveys the Spirit's actions on behalf of humanity in these selected stanzas:

> Creator Spirit, by whose aid
> The world's foundations first were laid,
> Come, visit ev'ry humble mind;
> Come, pour thy joys on humankind;
> From sin and sorrow set us free,
> And make thy temples fit for thee.

1. John Macquarrie, *Principles of Christian Theology,* 2nd ed. (New York: Charles Scribner's Sons, 1977), 333.

Creator Spirit, heav'nly dove,
Descend upon us from above;
With graces manifold restore,
Your creatures as they were before.[2]

These few lines help us appreciate the comprehensive nature of the Spirit's work: creator Spirit, acting to lay the world's foundations; personal Spirit, visiting the humble; universal Spirit, generously bestowing gifts on all of humanity; and renewing Spirit, restoring God's creatures to their intended condition.

Holy Spirit and Human Spirit

The two previous chapters reported that recent theology talks about God in terms of human experience and interprets Christ as present in the human fellowship. A similar development can be observed in the interpretation of the Holy Spirit, as in the title of a book by Arnold B. Come, *Human Spirit and Holy Spirit*.[3] Professor Come points out in his discussion of human spirit that the human person's psychological dimension and capacity to receive the Spirit of God must not be taken to mean that these are "something foreign" to the human being. Such a view dehumanizes persons either by pushing them down toward animality or by pushing them upward to be absorbed into the being of God.[4]

The doctrine of the Holy Spirit performs a special service in the interests of Christian humanism by safeguarding the uniquely human from both of these dangers. Christian thought might seldom be guilty of regarding humans as animals, but it is tempted at times to deify human beings. This may be done in the fashion of Christian mysticism, which sees pure devotion to God as leading to one's absorption into the godhead. Or it may happen through an arrogant humanism that takes the fact that humans are spirit to mean that they intrinsically possess divine status.

2. *Lutheran Book of Worship,* prepared by the churches participating in the Inter-Lutheran Commission on Worship, Lutheran Church in America, The American Lutheran Church, The Evangelical Lutheran Church of Canada, The Lutheran Church — Missouri Synod (Minneapolis: Augsburg, 1978), hymns 164 and 284.
3. Arnold B. Come, *Human Spirit and Holy Spirit* (Philadelphia: Westminster Press, 1959).
4. Ibid., 80.

Recent thinking on the Holy Spirit aims to show that the Spirit's mission in people's lives is not to make little gods out of them but to lead them to understand and experience their true human calling. It is to that end that the divine Spirit supports the human spirit. The Holy Spirit is a humanizing Spirit. As Albert C. Outler writes, "Man as spirit (selfhood) is man in concourse with the Creator Spirit — and with his fellow human spirits. This is the source of our true humanity, the bolster of the truest sort of *humanism.*"[5]

In the past, the doctrine of the Holy Spirit was often so treated as to leave out the dimension of ordinary human experience. Either the discussion led into problems of Trinitarian thought where intellectual complexities abounded, or into the region of charismatic experiences, where speaking in tongues and faith healing dominated the agenda. What needs to be emphasized today is that the Holy Spirit carries forward the process of humanization by sanctifying the ordinary elements of daily life.

The aim in this chapter is to speak of the Holy Spirit as God's power moving persons toward their fuller humanization. The first part of the chapter deals with the biblical witness concerning the Holy Spirit and the power of the Spirit for human renewal in personal life and in the life of the church. The second part presents five examples of Christian communities in which human renewal, the fruit of the Spirit, is being experienced in the context of corporate worship, prayer, study, service to the world, and the quest for Christian unity. The Holy Spirit enables people to find their identity in the fellowship of word and sacrament and to radiate the reconciling love of Christ in the world.

The Holy Spirit in the Bible

At the beginning of the Bible we read that the Holy Spirit, the breath of God, moves over the waters as creative energy; at the end of the Bible the Holy Spirit joins the bride, that is, the church, in the prayer for Jesus Christ to come and bring human history to its intended fulfillment. From creation to restoration, the Holy Spirit gives human beings the power they need in order to accept and employ God's gifts to the human race. Human beings need the Spirit to understand and participate in what God is doing

5. Albert C. Outler, *Who Trusts in God* (New York: Oxford University Press, 1968), 36.

in the world, for the creative, redemptive, and sanctifying work of God is never self-evident to unaided human vision.

In the earlier of the two biblical creation stories the ancient writer makes the very existence of the distinctively human being depend on the "breath" or "spirit" of God. Because of divine inbreathing, "man became a living being" (Genesis 2:7), that is, a fully human person, something more than simply a physical creature of dust. Writes Arnold Come, "man's *psyche* (or *nephesh*) [Greek and Hebrew words for "soul"] is never merely natural or animal but consists of the unique form of life created by God."[6]

In the Hebrew Bible generally, the characteristic mode of the Spirit's movement among humans is that of endowing some key individual with extraordinary power, as in Samson's great physical feats or Saul's astonishing gift of prophecy (1 Samuel 10:6, 10). But a future ideal is set forth by Moses when he hears of two men, not among the seventy elders, who also received the spirit and were prophesying: "Would that all the LORD's people were prophets, and that the LORD would put his spirit on them!" (Numbers 11:29).

In the Second Isaiah texts dealing with the servant of the Lord it is said that the Lord has put his Spirit upon this servant who, at times, is identified as Israel (Isaiah 42:1; 49:3). The opening words of Isaiah 61, "The Spirit of the Lord is upon me," are cited by Jesus when he begins his public ministry in his home town of Nazareth (Luke 4:18-19). That endowment by the Spirit empowered Jesus for such humanizing deeds as preaching good news to the poor, proclaiming release to captives, giving sight to the blind, and setting at liberty the oppressed.

The birth stories in both Matthew and Luke pointedly relate the action of the Spirit to the birth of Jesus. "The Holy Spirit will come upon you," the angel tells Mary (Luke 1:35), and Joseph too learns that what is conceived in Mary "is from the Holy Spirit" (Matthew 1:20). The Spirit comes upon Jesus at his baptism (Matthew 3:16), and Jesus conducts his public ministry in the consciousness that the Spirit is the effective power in his work. "But if it is by the Spirit of God that I cast out demons, then the kingdom of God has come to you" (Matthew 12:28).

A particularly instructive passage in John's Gospel makes clear that it is the mission of the Holy Spirit in the world to direct human attention to Jesus Christ and to enable humans to experience all that Christ offers. The Fourth Gospel has Jesus explaining, "He [the Holy Spirit] will glorify

6. Come, *Human Spirit and Holy Spirit*, 80.

me, for he will take what is mine and declare it to you" (John 16:14). The apostle Paul presents a similar thought. It is the Holy Spirit who enables a person to believe in Jesus. He writes, "No one can say 'Jesus is Lord' except by the Holy Spirit" (1 Corinthians 12:3).

The early Christian community believed that the prophet Joel's prophecy that the Spirit would be poured out on all flesh in the last days was fulfilled on the day of Pentecost when the followers of Jesus assembled in Jerusalem "were filled with the Holy Spirit" (Acts 2:4). This dramatic experience can be read as God's reversal of the confusion of tongues at the tower of Babel (Genesis 11:1-9). The unity of humankind originally intended by the creator but thwarted at Babel is now about to be realized. This coming of the Spirit marked the beginning of the life of the church, which in turn prefigures a new humanity. The Spirit's descent upon the whole community of faith was a sign that the new age had arrived.

The bestowal of the Spirit upon the entire community of faith is consonant with the Pauline teaching that the church is the body of Christ. Although the Spirit was certainly present in the life of ancient Israel, New Testament thought emphasizes more strongly the closeness of the Spirit to the community of faith. Since the church is organically related to Christ, the same Spirit who came upon the earthly Jesus now animates the body which is the church. "There is one body and one Spirit, just as you were called to the one hope of your calling, one Lord, one faith, one baptism, one God and Father of all, who is above all and through all and in all" (Ephesians 4:4-7).

At the same time, and without any lessening of the corporate wholeness of the church, the New Testament teaching on the Holy Spirit is unequivocal regarding the believing individual's beneficial interaction with the Spirit of God. Each Christian is under a mandate to "live by the Spirit" (Galatians 5:16, 25), to take care not "to quench the Spirit" (1 Thessalonians 5:19), and to "be ardent in Spirit" (Romans 12:11).

We see the humanizing efficacy of the Holy Spirit in connection with the idea of the gifts of the Spirit. The pertinent passages are Romans 12:3-8, 1 Corinthians 12:4-31, and Ephesians 4:1-16. The invaluable contribution to humanism of these teachings is that as the divine power of the Spirit raises the level of individual selfhood by the bestowal of gifts (*charismata,* or *pneumatika*), so also at the same time it builds up and enriches the life of the community, the church. In the words of the apostle Paul, "To each is given the manifestation of the Spirit for the common good" (1 Corinthians 12:7).

In summary, the important biblical teachings relating the Holy Spirit to human concerns are the following: (1) throughout the Bible, *the Holy Spirit is a humanizing power,* from the creation of the first humans, through the life of Israel and the church, to the Christian prayer for the return of Christ; (2) in the New Testament, *the activity of the Holy Spirit centers on Jesus,* his birth, his ministry, and his continuing meaning; (3) the Holy Spirit through Christ *creates the fellowship of the Spirit,* the body of Christ, and bestows gifts upon individuals which simultaneously enrich the humanity of the individual believer and strengthen the corporate fellowship.

The Holy Spirit and Humanization

That the work of the Holy Spirit can help people realize their intended humanity has not occurred to many Christians because they have tended to draw a sharp distinction between "the human" and "the spiritual." Some activities, such as praying, reading the Bible, and attending certain kinds of religious meetings, are regarded as "spiritual" activities, while the daily routines of eating, sleeping, working, and playing are not understood to be related to the life of the Spirit.

Modern theological thought and pastoral practice have worked hard to correct such a limitation of spiritually significant matters by insisting that God is creator of all things, that Christ claims the whole person, and that the Spirit can bring divine power into every phase of human conduct. When the Spirit's work is associated only with unusual events, such as flames of fire and speaking in tongues, insufficient attention is given to the Spirit's association with familiar, ordinary affairs. For example, if one were to speak of such activities as serving, teaching, exhorting, contributing, giving aid, and performing acts of mercy, how many people would realize that they were hearing Paul's list of charismatic gifts *(charismata)* in Romans 12:6-8? They all sound so *ordinary,* many would think.

Yet it was the achievement of Paul and other early Christians precisely to interpret the Holy Spirit's work in terms of the day-to-day responsible actions of Christian people rather than to confine the Spirit either to explicit devotional practices or to dramatic instances of faith healing, speaking in tongues, and the like. The Spirit is there to help those who are not extraordinary in their skill and power. Paul himself wrote that "the Spirit helps us in our weakness; for we do not know how to pray as we ought, but that very Spirit intercedes with sighs too deep for words" (Romans 8:26).

In order to speak adequately of the Holy Spirit and humanization one must honor the freedom of the Spirit to influence human beings in various ways, times, and places. In a book on the Holy Spirit called *The Final Act*, author Peter Kjeseth writes, "The Spirit is free and produces freedom. The Spirit is free to work through the church, but the entire universe is also the sphere of his free activity."[7] The scriptural text to support such statements might well be John 3:8, "The wind blows where it chooses, and you hear the sound of it, but you do not know where it comes from or where it goes. So it is with every one who is born of the Spirit."

It is important to know that the Bible's teaching on the Spirit focuses on Israel and the prophets, on Jesus and the church which confesses him to be the Christ, and on the growth in faith, hope, and love of believing persons. At the same time, one cannot set limits on the Spirit's work. The Bible recognizes that the Spirit is God, and God is not bound to any one community, person, time, or place. The creator Spirit who moved over the face of the primordial waters has the freedom to roam the whole world to touch people with the renewing power of God's love.

Christian humanism takes into account both the inclusive, universal aspect of the Spirit's sphere of operation and the Christian witness to Christ as the definitive human being toward whom all human aspirations are moving. Jesus said of the Spirit, "He will glorify me." Therefore, wherever the wind of the Spirit blows the refreshing, renewing breath of God into the human family, there the humanizing power of Christ will be felt.

Technology can be dehumanizing, but people with fresh ideas are able to make technological advances beneficial to the human community. Groups and nations live in estrangement, but separating walls fall down and the time comes when former enemies find themselves saying of one another, "We found that they're human too." As the nations of the world go about their business in fresh circumstances one thinks of the peacemakers whom Jesus declared blessed (Matthew 5:9).

Some peacemakers belong to the Christian community but many do not. Yet one has to believe that wherever men and women and children are praying and working for peace, there the Spirit of God is creating a fuller measure of humanness in the world.

7. Peter L. Kjeseth, *The Final Act: The Role of the Holy Spirit in the Life of God's People* (Minneapolis: Augsburg, 1967), 109.

The Holy Spirit in Personal Life

Theologian John Macquarrie comments on the new conception of the Spirit that came to view through the revelation in Christ. He states that the New Testament idea of the Holy Spirit moves away from placing chief emphasis on interpreting dreams, predicting the future, and speaking with tongues "and looks for that work instead in the highest qualities of personal being."[8] Macquarrie continues by observing that St. Paul certainly recognizes the place of the ecstatic spiritual gifts, "but the 'higher gifts' are personal, and the most excellent is love."[9]

The Spirit's work in furthering the highest quality of personal life is the appropriate extension of the Spirit's primary task in human history, to direct attention to Jesus Christ and to enable persons to commit their lives to him. Just as the Spirit makes possible the appearance on earth of Jesus Christ, the man chosen by God to show the world what a truly human being is meant to be and makes that presence possible again and again in the eucharist, so the Spirit endows people with those particular gifts that will make their personal lives more and more like that of Christ.

Admittedly, such theological talk all too easily drifts off into platitudes about a mode of life that seems totally unattainable. But the language of Paul is not vague and idealistic. When he writes about walking by the Spirit or cultivating the fruit of the Spirit he concentrates on what Macquarrie calls "the entirely personal qualities of love, joy, peace, patience, kindness, generosity, faithfulness, gentleness, self-control,"[10] the qualities listed in Galatians 5:22-23.

Heading the list, one notes, is love, the "still more excellent way" with which Paul concludes his discussion of spiritual gifts in 1 Corinthians 12. As one looks carefully at Paul's great "love" chapter, one is struck by the concrete, attainable, and communal nature of this *agape* love. While agape is uniquely the love that has its ultimate source in God, it is at the same time a love that can be experienced in practical life among the members of the community. It is patient, kind, not envious or boastful, a love that avoids arrogance and rudeness, irritability and resentment. This love, fashioned in human beings through the power of the Holy Spirit, rejoices in the right, not the wrong. It never ends, enduring when prophe-

8. Macquarrie, *Principles of Christian Theology*, 334.
9. Ibid.
10. Ibid.

cies, tongues, and knowledge have come and gone. This love, made real within the community of faith, moves a person from childish ways toward maturity. With faith and hope it constitutes the most enduring of all human realities and remains the greatest of all.

Significantly, it is in defining love that the congregation becomes important. Time and again in this book we return to the community of believers as the fundamental setting for Christian humanism. Earlier, in 1 Corinthians 12, Paul's discussion of spiritual gifts had dealt with certain gifts that pertained to leaders in the church, apostles, prophets, teachers, and others, though he never lost sight of "the common good" and the "one body." At the end of that chapter Paul said, in effect, that not all could be apostles, prophets, teachers, miracle workers, and the like, but that all should desire "the higher gifts," and then he launched into the way of love. The clear meaning of this arrangement of material is to open the sphere of love to all. As John Macquarrie states the point, "These higher gifts . . . are not restricted to exceptional individuals, but are characteristic of the whole community of faith."[11]

The Holy Spirit in the Life of the Christian Community

A twentieth-century Pentecost hymn offers a concise reading of the relationship between Spirit and church:

> Filled with the Spirit's power, with one accord
> The infant Church confessed its risen Lord.
> O Holy Spirit, in the Church today
> No less your pow'r of fellowship display.[12]

The hymn effectively expresses a basic Christian view that accords well with New Testament teaching and with centuries of experience. The church is the body of Christ; it is also the fellowship of the Spirit (2 Corinthians 13:14; Philippians 2:1). The Greek word *koinonia* can mean "participation" or "sharing in" as well as "fellowship." It has the same stem as the Greek adjective *koinos,* which means "communal, common." Those who believe in Christ participate in a common venture together.

11. Ibid.
12. *Lutheran Book of Worship,* hymn 160, text by John R. Peacey.

Theologian Macquarrie writes, "So the community of faith is also a community of the Spirit, who works in and through it and gives to it its unity. The community becomes the agency by which the Spirit works in the world and by which it continues the work of reconciliation begun by Christ, or rather, raised to a new level in Christ."[13] Everyone would agree that *unity* and *reconciliation* are among humanity's deepest needs. Recalling again the biblical story of the tower of Babel, when human arrogance and anxiety led to confusion of language and the dispersing of peoples across the face of the earth, one sees more clearly the task of the Spirit to restore human unity and reconcile alienated human families. In this process the Spirit is free to work in various ways, but Scripture and experience attest that the search for human unity is always going on in and through the church.

But there is more at stake than finding a respectable theological interpretation of the Spirit's activity toward unity and reconciliation in the life of the church. There is a need to demonstrate to Christians and secularists alike that the Christian tradition offers not only theological statements but living resources for addressing such human problems as separation, alienation, and dehumanization.

The case for Christian humanism is that the Christian tradition contains both intellectual and practical resources for addressing the problem of making and keeping human life human.[14] The intellectual resources of Bible, creeds, and theology may assume practical dress in actual, living Christian communities where ordinary men and women discover the Holy Spirit at work to counteract dehumanizing influences and to guide their feet into the way of peace.

The concluding section of this chapter sets forth five vivid examples of such living communities of faith. These five represent countless others in which the humanizing power of the Spirit is being experienced in the midst of daily problems and the new opportunities of our era. They indicate in unique ways, here and abroad, how a revival of Christian humanism in the church, in theology, and in liturgy can illuminate the problems that press on men and women at the level of ordinary daily life.

The five stories that follow reveal a hopeful picture: that the positive affirmation of human life and culture which constitutes Christian

13. Macquarrie, *Principles of Christian Theology*, 336.
14. Paul L. Lehmann, *Ethics in a Christian Context* (New York: Harper & Row, 1963), 14.

humanism is now guiding churches and people into forms of more effective ministry. As noted above, the Spirit is not active only in unusual, exceptional, or miraculous events, such as speaking in tongues and prophesying. In the communities described below we believe we can see the work of the Spirit clearly in the continuing order, harmony of life, steadfastness, patience, and endurance of institutions where the name of Christ is confessed.

Western Civilization — Rome — St. Egidio

Rome has always symbolized an important and an enduring legacy for Christian humanism. When the church came into being with its base in Western civilization, Rome inspired and enriched that civilization in such a way as to be able to claim a unique responsibility toward it. Christian humanism was first formulated and proclaimed to the Western world from Rome, and the city provided a kind of heredity and environment crucial for its growth.

Today the abandoned convent church of St. Egidio, close to the Vatican in the Trastevere quarter of the city, has become the center of a flourishing movement of Christian renewal. Taking its identity from this venerable name, St. Egidio seeks to circulate new life into the tissues of old Rome, knowing that a renewed Christian humanism must now take upon itself the task of changing the textures of daily existence in the city as well as altering its religious culture. The community of St. Egidio was begun by six high school youths in the climate of student revolts taking place all over Europe in the spring of 1968. The original aims of the founders were, first, to live radically the gospel in their own lives and, second, to become aware of the dehumanizing reality of the secular culture around them and to develop a critical attitude regarding this culture. The community sought to find "a human and at the same time a religious way of believing which can be lived by all and in all situations."[15]

St. Egidio first came to public notice when a group of Roman toughs threw gas over a sleeping African near the Piazza Navona in the city and set him afire. The community held an all-night vigil at the spot where this Somali was killed, and they quickly attracted members — 2,500

15. *The Community of St. Egidio* (Rome: Community of St. Egidio, 1982), 16. The community issues regular *Letters from Saint Egidio* (Rome: Communitá Egidio, Piazza S. Egidio).

The Holy Spirit in Human Living

people in the matter of a few years. Today St. Egidio is divided into a university group of 400 students, high school cells, a young workers' community, and a community of elderly persons. Some members are married, others are celibate. Financing is by self-taxation. Each person in the community has a secular occupation that guarantees a means of livelihood. In addition to this, everyone has a second occupation for the gospel, and evenings are devoted to prayer in common until the end of the day.

From the beginning, St. Egidio has maintained a close tie with the Diocese of Rome. To the founders it is not accidental that the community was born in Rome: "The Church of Rome generated us to faith. From this realization we matured a grateful sense of love towards its life and history."[16] The ideals of the community are rooted in the Second Vatican Council and in the renewal that the council wrought inside the Catholic church. Members have spent a number of evenings with Pope John Paul II; they with him at Castelgandolfo and he with them at St. Egidio. The pope sees the community as a practical realization of his hopes for a revival of Christian humanism at the end of the twentieth century.

St. Egidio exists primarily to give glory to God through the prayer and praise of the holy eucharist. Each satellite community of the movement revolves around the eucharist as a "feast of faith refound or never known."[17] The style of the St. Egidio eucharist is contemplative in atmosphere, with the homily almost always delivered by a lay person. There is a distinctive, thoroughly relaxed music, almost like a modern version of Gregorian chant, which accompanies the psalms, hymns, and prayers. Yet there is no feeling of "looking back to the good old days" in this worship. In the packed Church of St. Egidio one has the impression of people with a remarkable sense of the presence of the risen Christ in their midst.

Quickly St. Egidio learned "a taste for humanity" from prayer and worship.[18] During the period that the community was being formed Rome was attracting hundreds of thousands of immigrants from southern Italy who had traveled north expecting to find a job. But there is no industry in Rome, and the result was the formation of a nonworking class responsible for much of the violence and crime that came to the city in the aftermath of shattered hopes.

16. *The Community of St. Egidio*, 16.
17. Ibid., 7.
18. Peter Nichols, *The Pope's Divisions* (London: Penguin Books, 1981), 140.

St. Egidio saw in the uncontrolled expansion of the city a microcosm of the crisis of humanity in the modern world. The enormous Roman dormitory quarters of the poor were to the community a desert where the southern immigrants were deprived of every ideal except the consumerism offered by Italian television, a technological culture that works on the whole to degrade human and intellectual standards. In the shantytowns that ringed the periphery of Rome, people were plunged into depersonalized anonymity and despair.

St. Egidio began to found little cells on the edge of the city to be signs that God cares about human welfare and acts to restore broken lives. The cells were based upon the biblical model of the servant of the Lord who carries sorrows, establishes justice, teaches, and sustains the weary with a word. These cells have operated nursery schools, which are managed by immigrant parents themselves as an expression of Christian solidarity. They teach 1,500 children abandoned by the Italian state institutions, and they retrain marginalized young people and drug addicts as apprentices. In addition, the cells run twenty-five area day centers where old people are provided with an opportunity to meet others, read newspapers, perform theatricals, and go on trips to the sea.

"What does what we are doing mean to us?" one of the St. Egidio founders asked recently. "It means how to be Christian in a big city. To affront solitude we try to be a community of lay persons, normal people, who live the life of the city like everyone else, including the traffic. But we try to show that it is not essential to live just for one's self."[19] By 1990 cells of St. Egidio had spread to five other Italian cities and embraced over five thousand Italians.

Worship and the Sacraments — New York City — Saint Peter's Church

In 1968, the same year that the community of St. Egidio was formed in Rome, the congregation of Saint Peter's Lutheran Church in New York City adopted a statement of mission strikingly similar to that of the Roman high school students. It is entitled "Life at the Intersection" and says, in part, "We must actively serve New York City. Saint Peter's sees the city as part of redeemed creation. To us, the landscape of the

19. Ibid., 141.

so-called 'urban confusion' is transformed and consecrated as an arena for God's will."[20]

Saint Peter's is located at the opposite end of the social spectrum from St. Egidio, amid elegant apartment complexes and soaring commercial towers at Lexington Avenue and Fifty-fourth Street on the east side of Manhattan. Its "intersection" is the strongest retail area in North America, with such institutions as Bloomingdale's and Alexander's five blocks away and within the sound of the great Fifth Avenue stores.

Saint Peter's had been founded in 1862 to serve an immigrant German Lutheran community, and the language of the liturgy there continued to be German until the 1930s. In the late 1960s it seemed to some that the parish might be driven out of the city into the safer suburbs or from its neo-Gothic edifice into the apartments of its members. City congregations were dwindling and there was pessimism about urban life and church institutions.

In the face of this prevailing negativism, members of Saint Peter's formed groups to discuss the situation; they decided to remain in place and relate themselves purposefully to the city. Rather than retreat to the catacombs, the people of Saint Peter's were determined to affirm human life from a Christian perspective among the skyscrapers. In a time of transition Saint Peter's sought to preserve and witness from the best forms of its tradition.

These were not people in search of a new identity. The center of Saint Peter's "life as a community is the life, death, and resurrection of Jesus Christ" as experienced in the eucharist.[21] "Life at the Intersection" meant first of all a commitment to the recovery of the eucharist as the source of renewal and teaching for the whole congregation. What it means to be human, what the appropriate setting for human existence might be — all focused on worship. From 1968 the congregation instituted a Sunday and daily eucharist as the principal form of service, joining the celebration of God's presence in word and deed to solid dedication to neighborhood ministry. Gail Ramshaw-Schmidt, who often goes to Saint Peter's, has written that the community gained a new freedom to embark on a radical venture through the corporate recital of the images of faith in sacramental worship. This new venture was the construction of a new church building that would announce these liturgical images powerfully to a largely secular urban milieu:

20. Ralph E. Peterson, "Social Values and Religious Architecture," *Journal of the Guild for Religious Architecture* (Fall 1976), 2.
21. Ibid.

the shepherds hear the heralds, the demoniac screams "Holy One!" and we chant the Gloria; Isaiah's angels sing "Holy," the crowd yells "Hosanna," and I reverence the body; the bath kills, the death feeds, the sacrifice nurtures; the Lamb, slain for my festival, reigns forever; the maid of Nazareth is Mother of the Church and Queen of Heaven; and we, grubby lot, are kings and queens and priests.[22]

In 1977 the Cambridge architect Hugh Stubbins completed this building in such a way as to attract the eye of the urban dweller. Stubbins's Saint Peter's suggests a huge shaped rock that stands out in sharp contrast to its environment. It maintains a distinct identity against the aluminum and glass of the surrounding commercial structures through the use of bold stone sheathing that silhouettes St. Peter's against the sky. This is a church in, but not of, its world.

The building opens up on the inside to reveal a resplendent seven-story sanctuary that rises full of light to display the firmament through an opening in the ceiling. Stubbins built the interior in this exuberant manner to suggest that God has created humans for celebration and jubilation "and that we can serve our society by having a place for feasts in the midst of the city," a space where the arts can contribute to the feast, where the eucharist can be danced, where jazz and poetry and chorale and fugue can share in the enrichment of the feast.[23] Clear windows reveal the organ pipes on Lexington Avenue and remind us of Grundtvig's wish that churches be built to lift up joy in life and Pusey's assertion that an urban population is best "assaulted" by the holy influence of an imposing church and its rich liturgy.

There are other areas of Saint Peter's that illustrate themes of Christian humanism. Stubbins built rooms "in which we can rediscover our humanity, places where we can be human among the skyscrapers, spaces in which we can be at home."[24] There are floors where people learn from one another, corners set aside for quiet, intimate meetings, reading, and resting; there are kitchens and dining rooms and areas that minister to the human mind with lectures, films, live theatre at noon, and forums for adult education. There is a garden flowing with water and flowers offering refreshment in the marketplace — another Grundtvig-like emphasis translated into a late twentieth-century setting.

Saint Peter's became one of New York's notable institutions as it

22. Gail Ramshaw-Schmidt, "The Language of Eucharistic Praying," *Worship*, 57 (1983), 430; see also her *Worship: Searching for Language* (Washington, D.C.: Pastoral Press, 1989).

23. Peterson, "Social Values and Religious Architecture," 2.

24. Ibid., 2-3.

strove to be a center of what is good, true, and beautiful. In a city where only 0.65 percent of the population is Lutheran, the community has attracted 560 confirmed adults, with an average of 330 people at its Sunday eucharist. Saint Peter's, an old immigrant church, found in Christian humanism a new mission: "This time we were serving religious and cultural immigrants who were facing a situation quite unlike any they had known before. . . . We have found [here] a deep need for a place in which we can rediscover our humanity."[25]

The Quest for Wisdom — Minnesota — The Colonial Church

The Colonial Church, until recently known as the Colonial Church of Edina, founded in the western suburbs of Minneapolis in 1947, had grown by the 1980s to be the home of 3,000 Christians in the American congregationalist tradition, drawn from the whole Minneapolis area and from all social classes. In the eighties Colonial completed its move into a "village" designed by Richard Hammel that has made the congregation more visible for its citywide and statewide mission. Hammel's "Colonial Village" has won several international awards for new buildings of all kinds.

Richard Hammel and the Colonial congregation believed that a contemporary design for a functional church could be conceived out of the simple, stark lines of the late Puritan architecture of eighteenth-century New England. Above all, they sought to revive the concept of the "meetinghouse" as a place for God to meet God's people and also for the secular town to come together. The Colonial Church Meetinghouse thus serves the suburban town of Edina, as well as the church, as a center for musicians and creative artists. The St. Paul Chamber Orchestra's baroque series and the Palm Festival of the Arts are only two of many such activities.

The architecture of Colonial brings back the theological idea of a "people of the Word and Sacrament" gathered around its reading and preaching and celebration on three sides. The meetinghouse is built to express the nature of a company of love "looking at and caring about each other — a company in whose loving presence the Risen Christ is seen to be."[26]

25. Ibid., 1-2.
26. Arthur A. Rouner, Jr., "Senior Minister's Report," *Colonial Church of Edina*

For Christian humanism, even more significant than this bold architecture has been Colonial's attempt to revive the Calvinist and Puritan
concept of the parish as a learning community. The Reformation in Switzerland under John Calvin established a minister of the local church as a
teaching elder. His function was to equip members of the congregation
biblically and theologically so that they could share in the total ministry
of the church. It was in the educated laity that Calvin ultimately put his
trust. He concluded that to interpret the Bible rightly, the laity needed to
acquire a classical humanist education similar to the one he himself had
received. Calvin perceived that the proper foundation for the Christian life
was to be found in the Bible, and to establish that foundation it was
necessary to be able to read biblical texts accurately and interpret them
intelligently, skills achieved through humanistic study.

Drawing on Calvin's understanding of education, the American
Puritans perpetuated the tradition that in the parish under the tutelage of
Christ and through the operation of the Holy Spirit, the covenantal community of learning might licitly pursue the knowledge of good and evil.
The American Puritan love of learning is reflected in the 1702 statement
of the theologian and historian Cotton Mather that wisdom is a river of
grace that will irrigate the desert of the New World, "a river, without the
streams whereof, these regions would have been mere unwatered places for
the devil."[27]

Colonial Church has restored the position of a teaching elder who
carries on in this venerable Reformed tradition. The teaching elder is a
resident theologian and biblical scholar who assists the Colonial company
through learning "to grow into a mature body of Christ."[28] His ministry
is to establish the church as a "House of Learning" for all members of the
congregation: "God has *spoken* and we can listen and respond. We *listen* in
the quiet of our studies. This is why we study."[29]

Just as it was for Calvin and the Puritans, the pursuit of ancient
languages is the foundation of the Colonial program. "Language at Colonial

---

Annual Report (1979-1980), 1; on the building see "Colonial Church of Edina," *Architecture
Minnesota,* 7:6 (1981-82), 42-44.

27. George Huntston Williams, "Translatio Studii: The Puritan's Conception of
Their First University in New England, 1936," *Archiv für Reformationsgeschichte,* 57 (1966),
160.

28. Robert S. MacLennan, "The Teaching Ministry" (Colonial Church of Edina,
1979), 1.

29. Robert S. MacLennan, "Teaching Minister," *Colonial Church Reports,* 6.

is a necessary contribution to becoming a 'people of the Book.' Language opens doors to hear what the biblical author is saying in his or her own language. It is a valuable tool, a way to listen more carefully to what is being said."[30] The parish therefore offers courses in the biblical languages, three sections of New Testament Greek and one of Hebrew. Each Monday morning the teaching elder leads a two-hour Bible study, and Monday evenings are devoted to intensive study of a single book of the Old or New Testaments. There are four other "Learning Communities" on Sunday morning, and Wednesday evening is a study night for the whole church family. These classes read Christian classics from Augustine to Bonhoeffer and Christian novelists like Dorothy Sayers, Walker Percy, and J. F. Powers. They have explored such contemporary problems as world hunger and the food crisis from the perspective of what Minnesota corporations can do to solve them. In addition, Colonial's Theological Roundtable meets each Thursday at noon in downtown Minneapolis to look at the origins of the basic doctrines of the church.

The aim of all this education has been simple: practical and worthy living and the development of skills for survival in today's world as an effective Christian. An average of 1,500 people a year have been attracted to these programs, 300 to the Monday morning Bible study alone, and 500 high school students come to the learning communities for young people. The importance of peer ministry has been stressed, and 32 lay Bible teachers have emerged from the congregation to offer their own courses to others. In this way one parish church has become a theological resource for an entire city.

Space for Human Values and Social Justice — Rural Minnesota — ARC Ecumenical Retreat Community

The next example of a fresh style of Christian community takes us from the urban parish to a quiet rural setting. The ARC community described below is reminiscent of the ideals of Virgil Michel: his love of worship, simplicity of life-style, and "surroundings becoming to human beings."

30. Ibid., 5; see also on other models and examples William A. Koppe, *How Persons Grow in Christian Community* (Philadelphia: Fortress Press, 1973); W. Kent Gilbert, "The Parish as a Learning/Teaching Community," *The Lutheran World*, 2 (1976), 127-31; and Thomas H. Groome, "The Parish as an Educating Community," *St. Luke's Journal*, 21 (1978), 113-23.

An hour's drive north from the Colonial Church is a beautiful spot among what local inhabitants call the Grandy Pines. Following signposts reading "ARC Ecumenical Retreat Community," the visitor arrives at a large, handsome lodge constructed of western red cedar logs and is quickly welcomed into the extended family life of a unique and thriving retreat community. Carved into the cornerstone next to the main entrance are the words, "Joyful, Simple, Merciful."

The quiet hospitality of ARC soon provides the guest with warm evidence of these human qualities. Individuals, families, and small groups come to this Ecumenical Retreat Community, founded by Loren and Ruth Halvorson and their five children, "not to escape, but to gain new perspectives on who we are and where we are going," as Ruth has written.[31] Since ARC was first put into operation in 1978, more than 10,000 guests have found their way to the retreat community in order to renew their inner lives and to absorb a fresh vision of how men and women, old and young, can combine prayer and social concern.

The purposes of ARC are set forth in a mission statement: "The ARC Retreat Community is a Christian residential community and retreat center ministering to guests seeking rest and spiritual renewal in order to carry out their vocations in the world."[32] How that mission is carried forward is indicated by a series of statements describing the covenant the community seeks to uphold:

1. root its life in Christian tradition through daily worship and regular eucharistic celebration;
2. seek the guidance of the Holy Spirit through listening and discernment in prayer and contemplation;
3. encourage the gifts and resources of all in an inclusive and participatory sharing of work and community life;
4. provide a safe, quiet space and a gentle hospitality inviting guests to pursue their own spiritual journeys;
5. pray and work for local and global justice, peace, and ecumenism;
6. offer a learning environment that fosters engagement with major life issues;
7. emphasize a spirituality that is rooted in and interconnected with all creation and embodied in a simplified and compassionate life;

31. Ruth Halvorson, ARC brochure.
32. *ARC Mission Statement.*

8. be open to the pioneer creative expression of community, ministry, and life-style;
9. live joyfully, simply, mercifully;
10. be a sign of hope![33]

The acronym ARC stands for Action, Reflection, Celebration. Those three words intentionally link the Ecumenical Retreat Community in rural Minnesota with two significant European centers of spiritual renewal. The Halvorsons borrowed the concepts of Action, Reflection, and Celebration from the Laurentius Konvent near Bonn, Germany. They were also strongly influenced by the Communité de Grandchamp near Neuchatel, Switzerland, which Ruth Halvorson had first visited during an international prayer group retreat with five other women in 1972. Grandchamp is the sister institution to the Taizé monastic community located in southeastern France. During a two-year stay in Geneva the Halvorsons made several visits to Grandchamp and Taizé.

When they returned to Minnesota, Loren and Ruth knew that they had found a model for an ecumenical retreat community, Ruth's quiet dream for some years. The life of prayer, social concern, meditation, and holistic simplicity at Grandchamp inspired their decision to sell their home and invest their resources, time, and energies in establishing ARC on a beautiful 57-acre parcel of woodland donated to their nonprofit corporation by Ken and Corrine Skogen in 1976.

At the present time the ongoing life at ARC embodies two aims, a residential community and a retreat ministry. The semipermanent, intentional community consists of Loren and Ruth Halvorson and a small number of volunteer members committed to a simple life of worship, study, and mutual service. This extended family is one version of a "Basic Community" described by Loren Halvorson in "From Hidden Roots: A Study of Basic Communities."[34] The similarity of concept with Latin American Christian base communities is very deliberate. Dr. Halvorson has had considerable firsthand experience with such groups in Brazil, Chile, and Argentina, and Ruth Halvorson has visited Central America to gain further knowledge of this form of Christian expression. Guests at ARC discover both the international flavor of the place and the community's passion for justice in local, national, and global contexts.

33. Ibid.
34. Loren Halvorson, "From Hidden Roots: A Study of Basic Communities," unpublished typescript.

The second key aspect of ARC is its retreat ministry. Living and worshipping side by side with the intentional community is a succession of guests, individuals, families, and groups, whose stay will vary from a day or two to a few weeks. Since the beginning retreats have been used by college and seminary personnel, national committees of church bodies, businessmen and -women, women's groups, staffs of large city churches, and individuals of many faiths and no faith. The philosophy at ARC is not to convert or change anyone, but to provide a quiet setting for personal reflection and growth. An ARC brochure quotes Henri Nouwen on hospitality:

> Hospitality means primarily the creation of free space where the stranger can enter in and become a friend instead of an enemy. Hospitality, therefore, is not to change people, but to offer space where a change can take place.[35]

Loren Halvorson continues to teach at Luther Northwestern Theological Seminary in St. Paul three days a week as professor of church and society. Ruth is the full-time director of ARC. She has been concerned for many years with the need to relate Christianity and feminism, which she sees as part of the retreat ministry offered by ARC. Ruth organized and led ecumenical retreats prior to the founding of ARC through an organization she initiated called "Women Concerned for Wholeness." Her unwavering dedication to feminism, the inward journey, and social justice has coalesced opportunely with Loren's varied career in which the theme has always been the use of new forms to penetrate society with the gospel of Christ. The Halvorsons and their associates agree that social change will not come through directives issued from above but through persons at the base whose actions are grounded in personal integrity and shared human values. "God is hidden in those closest to you."[36]

Through their travel in many parts of the world the Halvorsons have established personal ties with a large network of priests, monks, nuns, theologians, pastors, business leaders, local and national churches, colleges, seminaries, and retreat centers and religious communities of every description. For example, on a small mountain in the New Territories, Hong Kong, Loren and Ruth found a tiny community led by an Anglican couple, Mary and Murray Rogers, who had been forced to leave Jerusalem for having hosted Jews and Arabs together. In Hong Kong, together with a

35. Henri Nouwen, cited in ARC brochure.
36. Conversation with Loren Halvorson, November 9, 1984.

woman from Scotland and a woman from Switzerland, this couple was converting a garage into a place of hospitality and retreat. The Ecumenical Retreat Community in the Grandy Pines in rural Minnesota draws strength and purpose from the knowledge that it belongs to a global fellowship of such basic ecumenical communities far and near.

When the visitor to ARC is ready to leave, he or she is sent off with a moving gesture of the community's friendship and the words of what is believed to be an old Indian blessing:

> May the long time sun shine upon you
> All love surround you
> And the pure light within you
> Guide you on the way home.

At the ARC Ecumenical Retreat Community what is being realized may be described as a new form of monasticism, an opportunity for silence, reflection, worship, and renewal in the presence of God and other persons. As with the old monasticism, the spiritual energy generated in such small, hidden communities as ARC is transmitted to the wider world through men and women in the form of human transformation, love, and justice.

Monasticism — France — The Taizé Community

Taizé is the name of a tiny village hidden away in the hills of Burgundy in southeastern France. Burgundy calls to mind the influence of a monastic humanism which reached all over Europe in the Middle Ages, for this region was the home of the monastery of Cluny (910) and the powerful monastic reformer Bernard of Clairvaux (1091-1153). The history of monasticism has shown many deviations from the norm of Christianity, but it has also presented vivid examples of how Christian faith can engender sound living. Today a thriving new religious community at Taizé shows that Western monasticism is not only a thing of the past; it is still a current phenomenon that can inspire Christian humanism.

When Roger Schutz, a young theologian active in the Swiss Student Christian Movement, first came to Taizé in 1940 he dreamed of starting a community "on account of Christ and the Gospel."[37] By 1949 Schutz

---

37. Roger Schutz, *Parable of Community* (London: Mowbray, 1984), 85. For biog-

DOING THEOLOGY IN CHRISTIAN HUMANISM

had been joined by six other "brothers" from Protestant denominations who committed themselves to celibacy and to religious life together. After World War II many drifters came to Taizé because it was known as a safe spot where they could rest and be welcome, where they could be listened to and not just taught.

Since 1967 young people between the ages of 18 and 30 have been coming to Taizé in ever-increasing numbers. In 1974 a "Council of Youth" was opened with 40,000 in attendance, and the council has continued to involve representatives from all over the globe each summer for the last ten years. Taizé provides young people with space for prayer, for reflection, for rest, and for contemplation. They come to southeastern France in order to gather around someone who can teach them and provide direction in life. The community acts as a place of silence and freedom, for drawing apart to reexamine lives.

There is a reluctance to talk about monasticism or being monks in Taizé. Today the brothers emphasize community and the renewal of the human family rather than monasticism. Yet the 1952 *Sources of Taizé* continues the traditions of earlier monasticism: the importance attached to liturgical prayer three times a day, the necessity of meaningful labor, the carefully calculated moderation of the way of life, all as part of the community service of Christ. Undergirding the *Sources* is a strong desire to take the gospel out of the monastery into the world and let it speak to men and women living in the midst of secular life. In the 1990s more than half of the eighty religious brothers, who themselves come from all over the world, are not at Taizé but are away on mission in over twenty countries doing humble, difficult, and unrewarding types of work and sharing solidarity with others engaged in such tasks.

The brothers see their activity in industry and in the Third World as the presence of Christ himself through the members of his mystical body. This "presence is based firmly on the knowledge that Jesus Christ in his incarnation did not exclude any part of the world, or any man, or any kind of society, that the life of Christians is the life of Jesus Christ within them. A simple 'presence' in the world cannot be without effect."[38]

---

raphies of the founder see Kathryn Spink, *A Universal Heart: The Life and Vision of Brother Roger of Taizé* (San Francisco: Harper & Row, 1986); and Rex Brico, *Taizé: Brother Roger and His Community* (London: SPCK, 1978).

38. Malcolm Boyd, "The Taizé Community," *Theology Today*, 15 (1959), 498; on the history of the community see J. L. G. Balado, *The Story of Taizé* (New York: Seabury Press, 1981).

The appearance of the brothers in the workplace speaks the message that there is an outcome to human existence, that workers and students and immigrants are not caught on a meaningless treadmill, but that there is a future for humankind and for the universe.

From time to time the brothers take representatives of the "Council of Youth" with them on mission, and the young people and the Taizé brothers write letters to allow others to reflect on topics that are crucial to them. The letters have become a lively contemporary source of Christian humanism. *The Acts of the Council of Youth* were written in 1978 in one of the worst slums of Africa, Kenya's Mathare Valley. Roger Schutz and another group wrote a *Letter to all Communities* in 1979 while sharing the life of the poor district of Temuco, in the south of Chile, and *A Second Letter to the People of God* was issued from Calcutta during a stay of several weeks there among the poorest of the poor. The December 1985 Worldwide Pilgrimage of Trust in Madras, India, produced additional writings.

The original dream of Roger Schutz was the reunification of the churches; ecumenism as a starting point for reawakening the church continues to be an underlying conviction. Many of the recent writings and activities of the brothers cry out to Christians by asking them to forget their differences and enter into a global fellowship. The brothers see youth as the motivators toward this goal. Brother Roger is convinced that young people, raised in the nuclear age, can often see the gospel vision more clearly, and he cites Jesus' teachings on children and the kingdom as the basis of this.

Today European youngsters come to Taizé not only for prayer and reflection but also for dialogue and fellowship. In fact, fellowship has become quite central to Taizé recently, because of the base communities of youth that have grown out of the "Taizé experience." The youth movement in Europe in the 1990s has powerful dimensions and an even greater role now in a continent moving toward unity, and Taizé has been a springboard for much of it. The idea of Taizé appeals to a generation in search of deeper roots than can be nourished in the thin soil of secularism, but it appeals also to those who sense that Europe is not yet done with Christianity — new spiritual ore can still be mined from the old workings.

The *Letters* and *Acts* are addressed to "parishes and congregations — those large communities at the *base* of the Church."[39] Though they announce a new "springtime" for the church, the letters recognize the importance of traditional ecclesiastical institutions already in place. They urge

39. Schutz, *Parable of Community,* 88.

Christians to take an active part in the local parish church and not become "a movement apart."[40] Taizé holds that through a process of forgiveness and reconciliation renewal can come in every congregation, however routinized into hardened forms it may be. The local church is a hearth, and all these rekindled hearths, Catholic, Protestant, and Orthodox, can gradually make a Christian home on earth again. The parishes can enter into a "common creation of a new humanity. . . . The People of God can build up a parable of sharing in the human family."[41]

The Holy Spirit and the Ties that Bind

In the end it is the parishes, congregations, and other intentional institutions — monasteries, retreat communities, colleges, universities — that will make the case for Christian humanism in this new era and into the next millennium. In them are found the elements that have held Christians together through all the centuries and in every circumstance, and will do so again. Those perennial elements provide a fitting conclusion to a chapter exploring how the Holy Spirit works in human lives.

The Bible

Christian humanism is anchored solidly in the Bible. It takes its starting point not within the human situation as such but with the fact of divine activity extended toward the human race in the good news of the gospel of Christ. The authority of the Bible is not expressed in the inerrant perfection of a book but in the fact that God addresses humans through the Word as delivered to the community of believers. The genius of the Bible is found in its power to convince, convict, and persuade hearers of the gracious fact that God expresses love and purpose for humanity in and through human beings and their circumstances.

40. Ibid. On worship see Horton Davies, "Worship at Taizé: A Protestant Monastic Servant Community," *Worship,* 49 (1975), 23-34; Thomas O'Meara, "The Liturgy of Taizé," *Worship,* 36 (1962), 638-45.
41. Schutz, p. 87; on ecumenism see James Hammond, "Taizé's Spirit of Ecumenism," *America,* 149 (1983), 372-73; and Charles Boyer, "Taizé, a Center of Ecumenism," *Unitas,* 13 (1961), 239-46.

Because of a remarkable era of productive biblical scholarship and the dissemination of its results to the general public, comprehensive and detailed knowledge of the Bible is at hand for all who choose to make use of it. This readily available biblical criticism traces the various human factors — personal, social, and historical — that have influenced the form and content of the Bible, not for the purpose of denying the Bible's credibility as the Word of God, but for a fuller understanding its message.

The Church

The humanism to which the Christian tradition points finds embodiment as a specific fellowship of men and women in the church. If God in touching humanity creates the church, human beings may respond by taking part in its life, there to discover more fully their destiny. As Christ's body in the world, the church lives under the obligation to work and pray for the humanizing of all persons. The reconciliation of people is essential in the life of the church. Ultimately, such reconciliation is based on God's reconciling work in Christ and is illustrated by the universal nature of the people of God.

Sacraments and Worship

The richness of sacramental life is of particular interest to Christian humanism. The divine and the human are brought together in the water, the bread, and the wine of worship. Humanity can be enhanced through believing participation in sacramental worship. Transcendental beauty in celebration is not a luxury but a necessity in modern society:

> A party, a festivity, a celebration, a liturgy has, for people who live daily with the aching pain of want, a psychological and social function whose healing power those who do not so live can scarcely imagine. . . . You must not deny the body — the eye, the touch, the ear, the scent, the taste . . . as well as the stomach.[42]

42. Robert W. Hovda, "The Amen Corner," *Worship,* 57 (1983), 262-63.

The Quest for Wisdom and Culture

As Harris Kaasa wrote, Christian humanism is not ashamed "to love God with the mind."[43] Intellectual statements of faith offer a deeper understanding of how Jesus Christ is now acting in the world. Early humanism took reading and learning beyond the universities out to a wider public. Christians have repeatedly discovered, over hundreds of years, that without knowledge of literature, philosophy, languages, and history a strong faith can not long endure. Humanistic study as an ally of the gospel has fitted countless believers for handling the biblical record skillfully and with depth of understanding. Christian humanism includes the view that church people should seek, present, and enjoy the treasures of human culture, for "the God who is at work in creation and redemption alike is named Beauty no less than Truth and Goodness. Man's life for its healing and fulfillment needs the touch of all that is gratuitous and inexplicable, evanescent and lovely."[44]

A Leaven for Humanizing the World

Christian humanism acts as a humanizing leaven with the potential to permeate many different spheres of the common life. As it informs and inspires persons from all walks of life, it is carried into those corners of society where public institutions do not readily find entrance. The nature of leaven is to be largely unseen, quiet, but powerful in its effects. Christian humanism does not aspire to become another structured movement, building a complex organization and raising funds, but it works in, through, alongside of, and beyond existing institutions. It is this quiet approach to Christian witness which now offers an alternative to the discredited ag-

43. Harris Kaasa, unpublished essay on Christian humanism, 167; a classic text on this point is Jacques Maritain, *Integral Humanism,* trans. J. W. Evans (Notre Dame: University of Notre Dame Press, 1973).

44. A. M. Allchin, "Grundtvig's Catholicity," *N. F. S. Grundtvig: Theolog og Kirkelaer* (Copenhagen: Konvent for Kirke og Theologie), 11. Four articles which deal with the indispensable contribution of Christian humanism to academic life are Paul Oskar Kristeller, "The Humanities and Humanism," *Humanities Report* (January 1982), 17-18; Martin E. Marty, "Simul: A Lutheran Reclamation Project in the Humanities," *The Cresset* (December 1981), 7-14; Martin E. Marty, "Christian Humanism Among the Humanisms," *Humanities Report* (February 1982), 15-16; and Parker Palmer, "Truth is Personal: A Deeply Christian Education," *The Christian Century* (October 21, 1981), 1051-55.

gressive schemes of the past two decades. The themes of renewal at work in the past as well as in the modern era that we have labeled Christian humanism must now be re-evaluated as resources for fresh ministry and teaching.

The examples given above of unique Christian communities rediscovering the humanistic dimensions of the gospel demonstrate how the Holy Spirit is creating forms of Christian witness at the end of this century. The Spirit is God in living contact with the human family. In parishes, in colleges and universities, in seminaries and monasteries old and new throughout the world, the Spirit is summoning the church now to face up to its mission of protecting and nurturing human beings. In these settings themes that had disappeared from the headlines and were dismissed as shopworn — the study of Scripture, the renewal of worship, ecumenism, social justice — are lively growth points that still point the way to the future of Christianity.

Central to the ministry of the Holy Spirit in the world and the key to the Spirit's humanizing work is the constant witness to Jesus Christ, the incarnate Son of God. Jesus himself taught that acts of kindness toward needy human beings are, in fact, loving actions toward the Son (Matthew 25:40). Awakening that sense of mutual human responsibility among persons of all races and regions is indeed the Holy Spirit's continuing task in the world. When genuine community is realized among people we can be sure that Christ the incarnate one is at work extending his saving health to the people.

An earlier chapter spoke of "God in Public Life," insisting that the sovereign God of the universe is at work on the central stage of human history to make and keep the common life more human. Christians are not necessarily wiser than others in practical politics, but they do have an obligation to fight against the deadly dehumanizing forces at large in the world and, on the positive side, to devote their energies to supporting measures that allow human life to flourish on this planet.

That the image of leaven immediately suggests bread is an entirely appropriate way to conclude this book that has looked to Scripture as the bread of life and to the bread of the eucharist as a symbol of human unity. What Christian humanism and its advocates are ultimately concerned about is that the world should receive the bread that it needs, both material and spiritual. It is no accident that at the heart of the Lord's Prayer is the petition, "Give us this day our daily bread." One does not have to be a Christian to recognize the critical importance of bread for all, but especially for the starving and the poor. Neither can anyone fail to grasp what Jesus meant when he quoted from the Hebrew Bible, "A person does not live by bread alone, but . . . by everything that proceeds out of the mouth of the LORD" (Deuteronomy 8:3). Human beings need bread, indeed, but more than bread!

Christian humanism is a concern for the well-being of humans that has its source in the central message of Christianity, the good news that in Jesus Christ God comes to befriend and fulfill the entire human race. Conservatives and liberals alike, non-Christians as well as Christians, have nothing to fear in opening themselves to this humanism based on Christ and the gospel. The church needs to articulate for this new age its humanizing mission and the world needs to see that the Christian view of reality strongly and graciously affirms human beings in ways that are particularly suited for our era, for the sake of God and for the benefit of humankind.

Bibliographical Essay

The purpose of this book has been to bring into plain view the enduring strength and amplitude of the humanism found in historic Christianity. This particular way of looking at human existence is not merely a page from a Christian catechism; it is the source of much of the substance and energy of Western civilization. While pointing to clear lines of development in the text, we have wished also to introduce in the notes the rich and varied literature that supports our claims. The notes serve as a guide to further reading.

This concluding essay does not repeat in detail what is found in the notes. Rather, its purpose is to summarize in conclusion the main features of the case for Christian humanism by calling attention to the principal books and articles that challenge the tradition and those that support it in a variety of fields.

Detailed studies of the origins and the connotations of the word "humanism" can be found in Augusto Campana, "The Origin of the Word Humanist," *Journal of the Warburg and Courtauld Institutes,* 9 (1946), 60-73; Vito Giustiniani, "Homo, Humanus, and the Meanings of 'Humanism,'" *Journal of the History of Ideas,* 46 (1985), 167-95; and two books by Paul Kristeller, *Renaissance Thought: The Classic, Scholastic, and Humanist Strains* (New York: Harper & Row, 1961), and *Renaissance Thought II: Papers on Humanism and the Arts* (New York: Harper & Row, 1965).

The antihumanism arguments of the Christian Right are summarized best in Francis Hill, *What Is Humanism and How You Can Help Your Child* (Minneapolis: Osterhus, 1979); Tim LaHaye, *The Battle for the Mind* (Old Tappan, N.J.: Fleming H. Revell, 1980); R. J. Rushdoony, "The World's Second Oldest Religion: Humanism Has Been an Adversary of God's Plan from Earliest History," *New Wine*, 11:2 (1979), 4-7; Francis A. Schaeffer, *How Should We Then Live?: The Rise and Decline of Western Thought and Culture* (Old Tappan, N.J.: Fleming H. Revell, 1976); and by the same author, "The Decline of Twentieth-Century Man: The Inherent Death Wish of Secular Humanism," *New Wine*, 11:2 (1979), 25-29.

This campaign has been analyzed in a number of articles from the 1980s: John Hallwas, "Fundamentalist War on Humanism," *Free Mind* (January-February 1985), 2-3; Charles Krauthammer, "The Humanist Phantom," *The New Republic* (July 25, 1981), 20-25; and Corliss Lamont, "The Battle for Humanism," *The Humanist* (September-October 1982), 21-58.

The rise of the Christian Right and the current political and cultural influence of its antihumanism are assessed in: Steve Bruce, *The Rise and Fall of the New Christian Right: Conservative Protestant Politics in America 1978-1988* (Oxford: Oxford University Press, 1990); Robert Clouse, "The New Christian Right, America, and the Kingdom of God," *Christian Scholar's Review*, 12 (1983), 3-16; Frances Fitzgerald, "A Disciplined, Charging Army," *The New Yorker* (May 18, 1981), 53-141; Gabriel Fackre, *The Religious Right and Christian Faith* (Grand Rapids: Wm. B. Eerdmans, 1982); David E. Harrell, "The Roots of the Moral Majority: Fundamentalism Revisited," *Occasional Papers of the Institute for Ecumencial and Cultural Research*, 15 (1981), 1-12; Samuel S. Hill and Dennis E. Owen, *The New Religious Right in America* (Nashville: Abingdon, 1982); Martin E. Marty, "Morality, Ethics, and the New Christian Right," *The Hastings Center Report* (August 1981), 14-17; McCandlish Phillips, "Francis Schaeffer: The Man Behind the Manifesto," *Moody Monthly* (January 1982), 10-15; and Robert Wuthnow, *The Struggle for America's Soul: Evangelicals, Liberals, and Secularism* (Grand Rapids: Wm. B. Eerdmans, 1990).

Two conservative, evangelical defenses of Christian humanism are "A Christian Humanist Manifesto," *Eternity*, 33:1 (1982), 15-19; and J. I. Packer and Thomas Howard, *Christianity: The True Humanism* (Waco: Word Books, 1985).

The arguments of secular humanism against Christianity are summarized best in *Humanist Manifestos I and II* (Buffalo: Prometheus Books, 1973); "A Secular Humanist Declaration," *Free Inquiry*, 1:1 (1980-81), 3-7;

and two books by Paul Kurtz, *Forbidden Fruits: The Ethics of Humanism* (Buffalo: Prometheus Books, 1988), and *The Humanist Alternative: Some Definitions of Humanism* (Buffalo: Prometheus Books, 1973).

Critical analyses of the arguments of secular humanism against Christianity appear in N. V. Baneyee, *Buddhism and Marxism: A Study in Humanism* (New Delhi: Orient Longman, 1978); David Bollier, "The Witch Hunt Against Secular Humanism," *The Humanist* (September 1984), 11-19; Owen Chadwick, *The Secularization of the European Mind in the Nineteenth Century* (Cambridge: Cambridge University Press, 1965); Henri de Lubac, *The Drama of Atheist Humanism*, trans. E. M. Riley (New York: Sheed and Ward, 1950); and Martin E. Marty, "Secular Humanism: The Religion of," *The University of Chicago Magazine*, 79:4 (1987), 2-6.

The campaign of the right has prompted a number of contemporary defenses of Christian humanism. Three of these appeared in the *Humanities Report* in early 1982: Paul Oskar Kristeller, "The Humanities and Humanism" (January), 17-18; Martin E. Marty, "Christian Humanism among the Humanisms" (February), 15-16; and George M. Marsden, "The Evangelical as Humanist" (May), 9-10. See also by Martin Marty, "Simul — A Lutheran Reclamation Project in the Humanities," *The Cresset* (December 1981), 7-14; and Virgil Nemoianu, "Voice of Christian Humanism: The Achievement of Hans Urs von Balthasar," *Crisis* (September 1988), 36-40; Frederick A. Olafson, *The Dialectic of Action: A Philosophical Interpretation of History and the Humanities* (Chicago: University of Chicago Press, 1979); and Ralph Wood, "Walker Percy as Satirist: Christian and Humanist Still in Conflict," *The Christian Century* (November 19, 1980), 1122-27.

Some more venerable testimonies to the Christian humanist tradition are D. J. Forbes, "Christian Humanism," *New Catholic Encyclopedia*, vol. 12 (Washington: The Catholic University of America, 1967), 224-25; Rudolf Bultmann, "Humanism and Christianity," *The Journal of Religion*, 77 (1952), 32; Werner Jaeger, *Humanism and Theology* (Milwaukee: Marquette University Press, 1943); Walter Kasper, "Christian Humanism," *Proceedings of the Catholic Theological Society of America*, 17 (1972), 1-17; and Jacques Maritain, *Integral Humanism*, trans. J. W. Evans (Notre Dame: University of Notre Dame Press, 1973).

Other books deal with the humanism of specific periods of Christianity. For the first five centuries see Geddes MacGregor, *The Hemlock and the Cross: Humanism, Socrates and Christ* (Philadelphia: J. B. Lippincott and Co., 1963); Thomas Merton, "Virginity and Humanism in the Western

Fathers," in *Mystics and Zen Masters* (New York: Farrar, Straus & Giroux, 1967); and Charles L. Stinger, *Humanism and the Church Fathers* (Albany: State University of New York Press, 1977).

Two books that will serve to introduce the humanism in Western monasticism are Jean LeClercq, *The Love of Learning and the Desire for God: A Study of Monastic Culture* (New York: Fordham University Press, 1961); and Esther de Waal, *Seeking God: The Way of St. Benedict* (Collegeville, Minn.: The Liturgical Press, 1984). For humanism in the Middle Ages generally, see Ruth M. Ames, *Chaucer's Christian Humanism* (Chicago: Loyola University Press, 1984); Etienne Gilson, *The Christian Philosophy of St. Thomas Aquinas* (Austin: Octagon, 1956); R. W. Southern, *The Making of the Middle Ages* (New Haven: Yale University Press, 1953); Rowan Williams, *The Wound of Knowledge: Christian Spirituality from the New Testament to St. John of the Cross* (London: SPCK, 1979).

The literature of humanism in the Renaissance is vast, but seven key studies that deal with our themes are W. J. Bouwsma, *The Interpretation of Renaissance Humanism* (New York: Macmillan, 1959); Ernst Cassirer et al., *The Renaissance Philosophy of Man* (Chicago: University of Chicago Press, 1971); Anthony Grafton and Lisa Jardine, *From Humanism to the Humanities: Education and the Liberal Arts in Fifteenth- and Sixteenth-Century Europe* (London: Duckworth, 1987); Myron P. Gilmore, *The World of Humanism 1453-1517* (New York: Harper & Row, 1962); Richard De Molen, *The Spirituality of Erasmus of Rotterdam* (Nieuwkoop: De Graaf, 1988); Eugene F. Rice, *The Renaissance Idea of Wisdom* (Cambridge: Harvard University Press, 1958); and the classic treatment by J. A. Symonds, *The Renaissance in Italy* (New York: G. P. Putnams, 1970).

For the humanism of the Protestant Reformation see André Biéler, *The Social Humanism of Calvin,* trans. Paul T. Fuhrmann (Richmond: John Knox Press, 1964); William J. Bouwsma, *John Calvin: A Sixteenth-Century Portrait* (Oxford: Oxford University Press, 1988); A. Fox and J. Guy, *Reassessing the Henrician Age: Humanism, Politics and Reform 1500-1550* (Oxford: Basil Blackwell, 1986); Guy F. Lytle, "Prelude to the Condemnation of Latimer, Ridley, and Cranmer: Heresy, Humanism, Controversy, and Conscience in Early Reformation Oxford," in D. S. Armentrout, ed., *This Sacred History* (Cambridge: Cowley Publications, 1990), 222-42; J. K. McConica, *English Humanists and Reformation Politics* (Oxford: Clarendon Press, 1963); Heiko O. Oberman, *Luther: Man Between God and the Devil* (New Haven: Yale University Press, 1990); Jaroslav Pelikan, "From Reformation Theology to Christian Humanism," *Luther Magazine* (May 1982),

1-3; and Charles Trinkaus, "The Religious Foundations of Luther's Social Views," *The Scope of Renaissance Humanism* (Ann Arbor: University of Michigan Press, 1983), 302-16.

For humanism in the era of the scientific revolution and the seventeenth and eighteenth centuries, these books will serve as a beginning: J. Bronowski, *Science and Human Values* (New York: Harper & Row, 1975); Julien-Eymard, *L'humanisme chrétien au XVIIe siècle* (The Netherlands: Martinus Nijhoff, 1970); Peter Gay, *The Enlightenment: An Interpretation* (New York: Vintage Books, 1960); Paul Cardinal Poupard, *Galileo Galilei: Toward A Resolution of 350 Years of Debate, 1633-1983* (Pittsburgh: Duquesne University Press, 1988); Pietro Redondi, *Galileo: Heretic,* trans. Raymond Rosenthal (Princeton: Princeton University Press, 1988); and Amos Funkenstein, *Theology and the Scientific Imagination from the Middle Ages to the Seventeenth Century* (Princeton: Princeton University Press, 1986).

For the modern period of the nineteenth and twentieth centuries see these studies which treat the topic broadly: Emil Brunner, *Christianity and Civilization,* vol. 1 (New York: Charles Scribner's Sons, 1948); David Cooper, *Thomas Merton's Art of Denial: The Evolution of a Radical Humanist* (Athens: University of Georgia Press, forthcoming); David Jenkins, ed., *The Humanum Studies 1969-1975* (Geneva: World Council of Churches, 1975); David Nichols, *Deity and Domination: Images of God and the State in the Nineteenth and Twentieth Centuries* (London: Routledge, 1989); Kathryn Spink, *A Universal Heart: The Life and Vision of Brother Roger of Taizé* (San Francisco: Harper & Row, 1986); Robert Woodfield, *Catholicism: Humanist and Democratic* (London: Theology for Modern Man, 1954).

The focus in this volume has been almost exclusively on Christian humanism as it has been manifested in the Western churches. Books that will serve as an introduction to the riches of the Orthodox tradition on this topic include two books by Nicholas Berdyaev: *The Divine and the Human* (London: G. Bles, 1949), and *The Fate of Man in the Modern World* (New York: Charles Scribner's Sons, 1935). Three books by Sergius Bulgakov are *Social Teaching in Modern Russian Orthodox Theology* (Evanston: Seabury-Western Theological Seminary, 1934); *The Orthodox Church* (Crestwood, N.Y.: St. Vladimir's Seminary Press, 1988); and *The Wisdom of God* (New York: The Paisley Press, 1937). See also James Pain and Nicholas Zernov, *A Bulgakov Anthology* (London: SPCK, 1976), and two books by Timothy (Kallistos) Ware, *The Orthodox Church* (Baltimore: Penguin, 1963), and *The Orthodox Way* (Crestwood, N.Y.: St. Vladimir's Seminary Press, 1979).

For an Orthodox perspective on ecumenism, the eucharist, and

Christian humanism, see John Meyendorff, *Living Tradition: Orthodox Witness in the Contemporary World* (Crestwood, N.Y.: St. Vladimir's Seminary Press, 1978), and three books by Alexander Schmemann: *The Eucharist — Sacraments of the Kingdom* (Crestwood, N.Y.: St. Vladimir's Seminary Press, 1987); *For the Life of the World: Sacraments and Orthodoxy* (Crestwood, N.Y.: St. Vladimir's Seminary Press, 1973); and *Introduction to Liturgical Theology* (London: Faith Press, 1966). See also Archbishop Paul of Finland, *Feast of Faith* (Crestwood, N.Y.: St. Vladimir's Seminary Press, 1988), and Vladimir Lossky and Leonid Ouspensky, *The Meaning of Icons* (Crestwood, N.Y.: St. Vladimir's Seminary Press, 1982).

For the Russian tradition, see two works by Nicholas Zernov: *Three Russian Prophets: Khomiakov, Dostoevsky, Soloviev* (London: SCM, 1944), and *The Russian Religious Renaissance of the Twentieth Century* (London: Darton, Longman, and Todd, 1963). See also the important recent work by Anthony Ugolnik, *The Illuminating Icon* (Grand Rapids: Wm. B. Eerdmans, 1988). Two commentaries on Orthodoxy and Christian humanism are Carnegie Calian, *Berdyaev's Philosophy of Hope: A Contribution to Marxist-Christian Dialogue* (Minneapolis: Augsburg, 1969), and Allen Leonard, *Freedom in God: A Guide to the Thought of Nicholas Berdyaev* (London: Hodder & Stoughton, 1950). See also John Meyendorff, *Byzantine Theology: Historical Trends and Doctrinal Themes* (New York: Fordham University Press, 1974), and Vladimir Lossky, *The Mystical Theology of the Eastern Church* (London: J. Clarke, 1968).

As an introduction to our specific topic of humanism in the Bible see Karl Barth, *The Word of God and the Word of Man* (New York: Harper & Row, 1957); J. Christiaan Beker, *Paul the Apostle: The Triumph of God in Life and Thought* (Philadelphia: Fortress Press, 1977); Raymond E. Brown, *The Birth of the Messiah* (Garden City, N.Y.: Doubleday, 1977); Walter Brueggemann, *The Bible Makes Sense* (Winona, Minn.: St. Mary's Press, 1983); Paul D. Hanson, *The People Called: The Growth of Community in the Bible* (San Francisco: Harper & Row, 1987); Jaroslav Pelikan, *Jesus through the Centuries* (New Haven: Yale University Press, 1985); John Reumann, *Jesus in the Church's Gospels* (Philadelphia: Fortress Press, 1973); and Robin Scroggs, *Paul for a New Day* (Philadelphia: Fortress Press, 1977).

On worship and humanism in the first five centuries of the church see: Tissa Balasuriya, *The Eucharist and Human Liberation* (Maryknoll, N.Y.: Orbis Books, 1979); Werner Elert, *Eucharist and Church Fellowship in the First Four Centuries* (St. Louis: Concordia, 1966); David N. Power, *Unsearchable Riches: The Symbolic Nature of Liturgy* (New York: Pueblo, 1984); R. Kevin Seasoltz, ed., *Living Bread, Saving Cup* (Collegeville, Minn.: The

Liturgical Press, 1982). For the Middle Ages see George H. Williams, *Anselm: Communion and Atonement* (St. Louis: Concordia, 1960).

On worship and humanism in the Reformation era: J. E. Booty, "Communion and Commonwealth: The Book of Common Prayer," *The Godly Kingdom of Tudor England* (Wilton, Conn.: Morehouse-Barlow, 1981), 139-216; Harvey D. Hoover, *Living the Liturgy* (Gettysburg: The Lutheran Theological Seminary, 1946); two studies by Kilian McDonnell, "Calvin's Conception of Liturgy," *Concilium*, 42 (New York: Paulist Press, 1969), and *John Calvin, the Church and the Eucharist* (Princeton: Princeton University Press, 1967); A. L. Mayer, "Renaissance, Humanismus und Liturgie," *Jahrbuch für Liturgiewissenschaft*, 14 (1934), 123-70; James Hastings Nichols, "Intent of Calvinistic Liturgy," in John H. Bratt, ed., *Heritage of John Calvin* (Grand Rapids: Wm. B. Eerdmans, 1973); Niels A. Rasmussen, "Liturgy and Liturgical Arts," in John O'Malley, ed., *Catholicism in Early Modern History: A Guide to Research* (St. Louis: Center for Reformation Research, 1988); Frederic Hastings Smyth, *Manhood into God* (New York: Round Table Press, 1940); Hermann Sasse, *This Is My Body* (Adelaide: Lutheran Publishing House, 1977); and Vilmos Vajta, *Luther on Worship* (Philadelphia: Muhlenberg Press, 1958).

On Christian humanism and worship in the seventeenth and eighteenth centuries: Friedrich Kalb, *Theology of Worship in Seventeenth-Century Lutheranism* (St. Louis: Concordia, 1965); A. L. Mayer, "Liturgie und Barock," *Jahrbuch für Liturgiewissenschaft*, 15 (1935), 67-154; Ph. Sellier, *Pascal et la liturgie* (Paris: Presse universitaires de France, 1966); and two studies by F. Ellen Weaver, "Liturgy for the Laity: The Jansenist Case for Popular Participation in Worship," *Studia Liturgica*, 19 (1989), 47-59, and "Jansenist Bishops and Liturgical-Social Reform," in R. Golden, ed., *Church, State and Society under the Bourbon Kings of France* (Lawrence: Kansas University Press, 1982), 27-82.

For liturgy and Christian humanism in the modern period of the nineteenth and twentieth centuries see three studies by A. M. Allchin, "Grundtvig: An English Appreciation," *Worship*, 58 (1984), 420-33; "Grundtvig's Catholicity," *N. F. S. Grundtvig* (Copenhagen: The Danish Institute, 1983), 11-21; and *Participation in God: A Forgotten Strand in Anglican Tradition* (Wilton, Conn.: Morehouse-Barlow, 1988); John Carmody, "Eucharistic Worship, Radical Contemplation, and Radical Politics," *Occasional Papers of the Institute for Ecumenical and Cultural Research*, 20 (1983), 1-8; Donald Gray, *Earth and Altar: The Evolution of the Parish Communion in the Church of England to 1945* (Norwick: Alcuin Club, 1986); Llewellyn Jones,

"Grundtvig as a Scandinavian Precursor of Humanism," *The Humanist,* 1 (1953), 34-36; Aidan Kavanagh, "Liturgical and Credal Studies," in Henry W. Bowden, ed., *A Century of Church History* (Carbondale: Southern Illinois University Press, 1988), 216-44; Kenneth Leech and Rowan Williams, *Essays Catholic and Radical* (Milton Keynes: Bowerdean Press, 1983); two studies by George F. MacLeod, *We Shall Re-Build: The Work of the Iona Community on Mainland and on Island* (Glasgow: The Iona Community, 1944), and *The New Humanity Now* (London: The Fellowship of Reconciliation, 1965); Sonya A. Quitslund, *Beauduin: A Prophet Vindicated* (New York: Newman Press, 1973); Robert L. Spaeth, ed., *The Social Question: Essays on Capitalism and Christianity by Virgil Michel* (Collegeville, Minn.: St. John's University, 1987); Robert Webber, "Ecumenical Influences on Evangelical Worship," *Ecumenical Trends,* 5 (1990), 73-76; and John Baldovin, *Worship: City, Church, and Renewal* (Washington, D.C.: Pastoral Press, 1991).

Humanism in recent theological discussion of the doctrine of God is dealt with in Karl Barth, "The Humanity of God," trans. John Newton Thomas, in *The Humanity of God* (Richmond: John Knox Press, 1960); John B. Cobb, Jr., *God and the World* (Philadelphia: Westminster Press, 1983); Gordon Kaufman, *The Theological Imagination* (Philadelphia: The Westminster Press, 1981); and Thomas C. Oden, *Agenda for Theology: Recovering Christian Roots* (San Francisco: Harper & Row, 1979).

On the humanistic implications of the Christology of the modern period see two books by Dietrich Bonhoeffer, *Christ the Center,* trans. John Bowden (New York: Harper & Row, 1960), and *Sanctorum Communio: A Dogmatic Inquiry into the Sociology of the Church* (London: Collins, 1963); Gustave Martelet, "Christology and Anthropology: Toward a Christian Genealogy of the Human," in R. Latourelle and G. O'Collins, eds., *Problems and Perspectives of Fundamental Theology* (New York: Paulist Press, 1982), 151-67; W. R. Matthews, *The Problem of Christ in the Twentieth Century: An Essay on the Incarnation,* Maurice Lectures, 1949, 1950 (Oxford: Oxford University Press, 1950); Robert Morgan, *The Religion of the Incarnation: Anglican Essays in Commemoration of Lux Mundi* (Briston: Classical Press, 1989); and Wolfhart Pannenberg, "The Christological Foundation of Christian Anthropology," in Claude Geffré, ed., *Humanism and Christianity* (New York: Herder and Herder, 1973), 86-100.

Humanism in the recent theology of the Holy Spirit is dealt with in Arnold B. Come, *Human Spirit and Holy Spirit* (Philadelphia: Westminster Press, 1959); Peter L. Kjeseth, *The Final Act: The Role of the Holy Spirit in the Life of God's People* (Minneapolis: Augsburg, 1967); and John Macquarrie, *Principles of Christian Theology*, 2nd ed. (New York: Charles Scribner's Sons, 1977).

As an introduction to the humanistic possibilities of the ecumenical movement see A. M. Allchin, *Eucharist and Unity* (Oxford: SLG Press, 1972); *Baptism, Eucharist and Ministry*, Faith and Order Paper No. 111 (Geneva: World Council of Churches, 1982); Charles Boyer, "Taizé, a Center of Ecumenism," *Unitas*, 13 (1961), 239-46; "Christian Unity: The Gift, the Vision and the Way," *The Emmaus Report* (London: ACC, 1987), 6-37; *Ecumenical Perspectives on Baptism, Eucharist and Ministry*, ed. Max Thurian (Geneva: World Council of Churches, 1983); *The Final Report* (London: CTS/SPCK, 1982); James Hammond, "Taizé's Spirit of Ecumenism," *America*, 149 (1983), 372-73; Kenneth Leach, "Artisans of a New Humanity?: Some Anglican and Roman Catholic Approaches to Social and Political Action," in Mark Santer, ed., *Their Lord and Ours* (London: SPCK, 1982); Kevin McDonald, "The Ecumenical Ministry of Pope John Paul II," English *Osservatore Romano* (September 29, 1989), 7; and George H. Williams, "The Ecumenism of John Paul II," *Journal of Ecumenical Studies*, 19 (1982), 693-96.

And finally, the papacy and Christian humanism is discussed by Pope John Paul II in "Affirm Values of Christian Humanism in Your Service," English *Osservatore Romano* (March 25, 1988), 12; and "Christian Humanism: A Fruitful Seed," English *Osservatore Romano* (March 25, 1985), 3; as well as in Paolo Miccoli, "Elementi di un Umanesimo Christiano Integrale nei Documenti Conciliari del Vaticano II," *Aquinas*, 14 (1971), 414-24; John O'Malley, *Praise and Blame in Renaissance Rome, ca. 1450-1521* (Durham: Duke University Press, 1979); Maureen Sullivan, "The Christian Humanism of Paul VI: Its Christological Foundations," Ph.D. diss., Fordham, 1985; George H. Williams, *The Law of Nations and the Book of Nature* (Collegeville, Minn.: St. John's University, 1984).

Index

Abraham, 186
Acts of the Council of Youth, 249
Adam, 91, 149
Addams, Jane, 167
Agenda for Theology, 189
Amos, 56
Anglicanism, 130-35, 141-42, 145-55, 213-15
Anglican-Roman Catholic International Commission, 214-15
Anselm, 17
Anthony, Susan B., 13
Apocrypha, 59
Aquinas, Saint Thomas: definitions of humanism, 16-17; free will, 18; science in, 18
ARC Community (Minnesota), 243-47
Aristides, 105
Aristotle, 16
Atheism, 27
Attack upon Christendom, 158
Augustine, Saint: and Christian humanism, 108; *City of God,* 109; *Confessions,* 15; on the eucharist, 107-10; on faith and reason, 15-16; on the family, 109; on the human as image of God, 109; on the international order, 110; on Jesus, 62, 109; his later influence, vii, 19, 108, 116, 119, 121, 122, 128, 129, 149, 185, 193, 243; on the parish, 110; on society, 110

Bach, J. S., xiii, 13
Bacon, Francis, 25
Baptism, Eucharist and Ministry, 42, 215-19, 223
Barth, Karl, xi, xii, 48, 49, 185-87, 201, 207, 216, 218
Beauduin, Lambert, 144, 164-65
Beker, J. Christiaan, 86, 90
Bellarmine, Robert, 211
Benedict, Saint: on the eucharist, 111-13; his later influence, vii, 13; his *Rule,* 111
Benedictines, 35, 111-13, 134, 144, 161-70
Berger, Peter, 183
Bernard of Clairvaux, Saint, 247
Bernini, 138
Betz, Otto, 72
Beuron, Abbey of, 163-66
Bible: Christian humanism in, 34; community in, 49, 54-55, 159; creation in, 51-52; Hebrew, 47-61; historical-critical study of, 34, 37; and the Holy Spirit, 228-34; and humanism, 48; human nature in, 47; human participation in the writing of, 34, 50; Incarnation in, 34; and the laity, 242-43; and liberation, 53; and liturgy, 100; and Paul, 79-93; sacraments in, 158; servanthood in, 59
Black theology, 184
"Body of Christ," the, 36, 86, 87, 210, 212, 220

INDEX

INDEX

McCormick, Arthur, 222-23
McHugh, Antonia, 168
MacLeod, George F., 144, 170-74
Macquarrie, John, 233, 235
Marburg Colloquy, 124
Marcion, 63-64
Maria Laach, Abbey of, 164
Mary, Saint, 13, 65, 229
Marx, Karl, 28-29, 128, 224
Mass Book of the Holy Church, 163, 166
Mather, Cotton, 242
Maurus, Rhabanus, 226
Merton, Thomas, 4, 220
Messiahship, 74-76
Michel, Virgil, 165-70, 243
Migliore, Daniel, 183
Modernization, 140-76
Möhler, Johann Adam, 36, 208-13, 216, 220, 224
Monasticism: Anglican, 149; and Christian humanism, 17, 111-13, 247-50; destruction of, 124; and eucharist, 111-13, 118, 161-70; and liturgy, 111-13, and new forms of, 243-50; and society 113; and work, 111-13, 118; and worship, 111-13, 124
Mont-César, Abbey of, 164, 165
Moral Majority, 43-44, 194
Mortalium animos, 212

Naked Public Square, The, 195
Nation, 196; and church, 129; needs and concerns of, 134
"National Apostasy," 146
Nationalism, 209, 216, 222, 224; destructive of human society, 129
National Conference of Catholic Bishops, 194
Nature, 16, 17, 18, 26, 29, 40, 52, 76, 86; human, 21, 22, 28, 29, 37, 38, 40, 51, 70, 71
Naturalistic humanism, 7
Nazi: times, 12; Nazis, 216; Nazism, 217
Neander, Johann Augustus, 148-49
Neuhaus, Richard John, 195, 205
New covenant: prophesied by Jeremiah, 58
New Revised Standard Version, 90, 91
New Testament, 20, 21, 41, 80, 83, 86, 174, 180, 231; language of vine and branches, 108; transforms sacredness to whole community, 114
New Territories: small Anglican community, 246
Newman, John Henry, 13, 146
Newton, Sir Isaac, 26
Niebuhr, H. Richard, 201; Book: *Christ and Culture,* 87
Niebuhr, Reinhold, 37, 38, 201

Nietzsche, Friedrich, 28, 29
Nineteenth century, 35, 36, 40, 143, 153, 154, 163, 190, 207, 208; materialism in, 163
North America, 191, 239; churches of, 174
Northern humanists, 20, 139
Nouwen, Henri, 246

Oberman, Heiko O., 32n.1
Old Testament, 49, 50, 54, 60, 61, 86
On the Eucharist, 135
On Monastic Vows, 124
"One new man," 109
Orante: posture of the people at worship, 102
Oration on the Dignity of Man, 20
Oratre Fratres: journal later renamed *Worship,* 166, 168
Orthodox, 34, 137, 181; churches, 218; participation of laity in, 155; and Lord's Supper, 115
Oxford Movement, 35, 145-46, 155, 221

Pannenberg, Wolfhart, 39; *Jesus — God and Man,* 39n.7
Parables: of the vineyard, 71; of Jesus, 93; of the kingdom, 187
Participation: meaning of *koinonia,* 90, 234; in eucharist, 118
Pascal, Blaise, 138, 139; and Augustine, 108
Paul, Saint: apostle, 50, 79; and Augustine, 108; and Calvin, 129; and Christian humanism, 80; on justification, 82-84; on love, 233; and people of God, 87
Paul VI, 223
Peace, 6, 11, 197; kiss of, 104
Peacemakers, 232
Pedersen, Johannes, 54
Pelikan, Jaroslav, 62
Pentecost, 230; hymn, 234
People of God, the, 49, 87, 159, 169, 172, 192, 250, 251; in specific parish, 159
"People of the Word and Sacrament," 241
Percy, Walker, 7, 243
Personhood, 10, 11, 55
Persuasio, 133
Petrarch, Francesco, 19, 20
Philosophia perennis, 43
Philosophy, 7, 8, 26, 28, 252; Greek, 15
Pico della Mirandola, 20
Pietas, 20, 21, 85; and Calvin, 128; in Christian humanism, 123
Piety of the Church, The, 164
Pilgrim People of God, The, 49n.2
Pius XI, 212
Poor, the, 6, 199, 200, 254
"Popish rags," 151
Positivism, 28, 200, 201

INDEX

emergence of, 24-30; and individualism, 40; in popular thought, 14
Secular mind, 189, 190, 192
Secularism, 13, 22, 191, 201, 205, 249
Secularization, 175, 209
Selfhood, 11, 55, 84
Self-fulfillment, 8, 9
Septuagint (Greek translation of Old Testament), 47, 100
Sermon: in Calvinism and Lutheranism, 140; in Anglicanism, 141
Sermon on the Mount, 63, 70
Servant, 58, 59; image for biblical humanist, 12
Service, 11, 12, 22, 30, 55, 74, 180; to God and neighbor, 32; lives of, 85; to the world, 228
Shape of the Liturgy, The, 113
Short Breviary for Religious and Laity, A, 166
Sin, 53, 56, 92, 110, 120, 181; in Augustine, 16; forgiveness of, 38, 120; as social condition, 37
Skeptics, 34
Skogen, Ken and Corrine, 245
Small Catechism, by Martin Luther, 185
Social justice, 243, 253
Society of the Sacred Mission, 154
Society of St. John the Evangelist, 154
Solesmes, Abbey of, 162, 165
Song-Book of the Danish Church, 160
Sources of Taizé, 248
Spinoza, 26
Spirit, 5, 11, 12, 30, 50, 58, 210, 229-33, 253; fellowship of, 98; fruit of, 85, 233; gifts of, 87, 88; and matter, 99, 128
Spirit, human, 44, 53, 227, 228
Starr, Ellen Gates, 167
Stones of Venice, The, 143
Stubbins, Hugh, 240
Supernaturalism, 7, 8, 9, 24
Swiss Student Christian Movement, 247

Taizé, 245, 247-50; "Taizé experience," 249
Temple, William, 223
Temptation: Gospel accounts of, 66; of Jesus, 66, 67, 68
Teresa of Avila, Saint, 138, 139
Tertullian, 63, 64
Thanksgiving, 100, 132, 173
Theologia Platonica, 19
Theology, 18, 34, 36, 39, 42, 73, 173, 182, 188, 203-4, 219, 332; "from below," 192; and Christian humanism, 179; classical, 193; definition of, 180

Theresa, Mother, 13
Town Labourer, The, 143
Tracts for the Times, 146
Tradition, 23, 31, 190, 194, 244; of the church, 90; definition of, 181; of the Lord's Supper, 89
Transubstantiation, 136-37
Twentieth century, 38, 40-42, 86, 97, 142, 154, 165, 171, 201, 207, 208, 216

Umbria, 208
United Church of Canada, 216
Unity, 170, 208, 212, 214, 224, 235; in body of Christ, 104; of all Christians, 219; of humans, 209, 215, 222
University, 17, 200, 202
University humanists, 116

van Buren, Paul, 189, 191
Vartov, 155, 158
Vatican II, 169, 209, 212-13, 237
"Veni, Creator Spiritus," 226
Virgil, 19, 136
Vocation, 51, 74; of Jesus, 76, 77; prayer and, 125

Wantage, 153
Wesley: Charles, 13; John, 13
Westminster Abbey, 117
Westminster Shorter Catechism, The, 184
Wine, 11, 87, 90, 98, 100, 102, 103, 104-6, 135-37, 173, 251
Wisdom, 16, 60, 61; of God, 81; of Jesus, 73-74; literature, 59, 60
"Women Concerned for Wholeness," 246
Word, the, 12, 50, 149, 207, 241, 250, 251; of God, 22, 35, 44, 49, 51, 75, 186, 251
World Council of Churches, 42, 209, 215, 216, 218
World War I, 189
World War II, 189, 248
Worship, 11, 31, 35, 97, 142, 159, 161, 167, 203-4, 207, 228, 244, 251; as community activity, 94, 98, 104, 107, 113, 121, 127, 129, 162, 169, 171, 172; history of, 97, 109, 119, 134, 141, 142, 175; and humanism, 40, 98, 122, 127, 164; practice of, 23, 97, 102, 106, 107, 111, 122, 124, 133, 173, 174, 175, 237; theology of, 23, 36, 112; traditions of, 119, 131, 133, 140, 148
Wren, Christopher, 141

Zwingli, Ulrich, 123, 124, 126